MINDFULNESS IN THE MARKETPLACE

Mindfulness in the Marketplace

COMPASSIONATE RESPONSES
TO CONSUMERISM

edited by

Allan Hunt Badiner

Parallax Press
Berkeley, California

Parallax Press
P.O. Box 7355
Berkeley, California 94707
www.parallax.org

Parallax Press is the publishing division of
Unified Buddhist Church, Inc.

Edited by Allan Hunt Badiner.
Cover and text design by Gopa & Ted2.

The paper in this book is made entirely from
post-consumer waste and tree-free fibers provided
by Livingtree Paper Company (www.livingtreepaper.com).

Library of Congress Cataloging-in-Publication
Mindfulness in the marketplace : compassionate responses
to consumerism / edited by Allan Hunt Badiner.
    p. cm.
  ISBN 1-888375-24-8
  1. Consumption (Economics)—Religious aspects—Buddhism.
2. Consumer behavior—History—20th century. 3. Consumption
(Economics)—Moral and ethical aspects. 4. Human ecology—
Religious aspects—Buddhism. 5. Sustainable development—
Moral and ethical aspects. 6. Spiritual life—Buddhism.
I. Badiner, Allan Hunt.
  BQ4570.E25 M56 2002
  294.3'568—dc21
2002011914

1 2 3 4 5 6 7 8 9 10 / 07 06 05 04 03 02

Contents

Acknowledgments

THIS BOOK IS THE RESULT of the generosity of its contributors who gave freely and willingly of themselves and their work. They cannot be thanked enough. Deepest thanks must go to the Venerable Thich Nhat Hanh who has inspired a lifelong commitment within me to devote my time and energy to exploring the application of Buddhist Dharma to contemporary life. I am grateful for the patience, support, understanding, and valuable assistance of my wife, Marion, and the heartwarming and sustaining smiles of my daughter, India.

I am very appreciative of all the direction and hard work provided by the entire staff at Parallax Press, particularly Maria Hirano, Natalie Fisk, Travis Masch, and Larry Ward.

Many people contributed to making this book possible and they have my gratitude: Harvey Alperin, Stephen and Martine Batchelor, Jim Ciment, Guy Claxton, Gary Gach, Alisa Gravitz, Peter Harvey, Alissa Hauser, Rick Ingrasci M.D., Ken Jones, Anuradha Mittal, Bhikkhu Nirodho, Jeremy Russell, John Steiner, and Helen Tworkov.

I am also grateful to organizations such as the Threshold Foundation and the Social Venture Network for the opportunity to explore and discuss the ideas represented in this book, and to be in community with like-minded people who share the belief that commerce and conscience can coexist.

Foreword

by Julia Butterfly Hill

IN THE PAST, human beings understood, acknowledged, and lived according to their sacred, interdependent place in the circle of life.

Today, much of humanity is treating our Earthly home—a priceless treasure beyond compare—like a trash can, or a toxic dumping site, or as something we can dispose of (as if there is such a thing as throwing something away).

In the industrialized economies, the most basic principle of investment seems to have been overlooked in our dealings with the Earth: we have neglected to plan for the long term. As consumers in the global marketplace, the collective power of our seemingly small actions is staggeringly large. Most of us, directly or indirectly, consume our own body weight in the natural resources of the Earth every day. We are literally stealing from the future to pay for our lifestyles today. What kind of planetary portfolio are we leaving behind for those who come after us?

When we walk into a store filled with products wrapped in plastic, paper, and metal, let us choose to look deeply. As we stand in the brightly lit aisles bulging with stuff, may we behold the trees that were cut to produce wasteful packaging; behold the indigenous cultures pushed to the edge of extinction so that raw materials could be extracted from their land; behold the overwhelming amounts of energy, soil, and water wasted in the process; and behold the less privileged citizens of the world who, as a result, are unable to enjoy quality food or clean water. Reopening to this awareness of our oneness, we will see through the myth of consumption that claims we can fill the void in our hearts and spirits with things.

Instead, let us celebrate filling our lives with the company of loved ones, involving ourselves with our communities, nourishing our bodies with living food made locally, walking the land, embracing all forms of life and practicing the mindful art of breathing deeply.

Compassionate consumption is not about sacrificing or giving up things we need. It is about reawakening to the sacred within and around us and celebrating this awareness in every action—and in every transaction. Our conscious choices change the world. You, dear reader, are a powerful being, a bodhisattva for the Earth, and your actions *are* the difference.

Introduction

by Allan Hunt Badiner

CONSUMPTION has become one of the most urgent topics in our lives. The increasing magnitude of this problem has huge implications not only in economics and the environment, but also in the very nature of what it means to be human. As Jonathan Watts and David Loy write in *The Religion of Consumption,* "In the past, it was religion, community, or class that gave us identity. Now, we are what we consume." But this new religion of consumerism is not necessarily bringing comfort or solace to its unwilling adherents. To the contrary, we see it more often leading to personal despair and disempowerment, with certain ecological decline.

Buddhism may have a relatively unique and valuable role to play in our effort to create solutions. Revisiting our moral and spiritual values is an important part of our response to the fundamentally alienating ethic inherent in a consumer culture. The Buddhist perspective offers not only a critique, but also practical ways to empower people to resist the prison of consumerism.

"The ownership and the consumption of goods," wrote E.F. Schumacher in *Small Is Beautiful,* "is a means to an end, and Buddhist economics is the systematic study of how to attain given ends with the minimum means." And the minimum of damage, no doubt. Recognizing the Buddhist truth of interdependence, for example, might help us to anticipate and prevent problems like global warming, which demonstrates how human behavior in one region dramatically affects the ecological and economic well-being of the entire planetary community.

Global forces beyond our control have increasingly penetrated our national and local communities. The power and wealth of some transnational corporations now exceed that of many nation-states. About one third of all economic activity worldwide is generated by only two hundred corporations, which are linked to each other by strategic alliances and interlocking boards. Their models of development presuppose the continuous expansion of production on a planet of limited resources.

For the consuming public, the social and environmental costs of technological progress and global corporatism are high. We have already crossed the threshold into unsustainability, and seem acquiescent in the face of disappearing old-growth forests and the pollution of our atmosphere and oceans. Most urgently, climatic instability threatens food production and human and animal life around the globe. The Center for the New American Dream, an organization that advocates a more moderate lifestyle, estimates that four additional planets would be needed to provide the American lifestyle to every person on Earth.

Future generations are clearly at peril. As the hole in the Earth's ozone layer continues to widen—the result of our toxic emissions—it is they who will likely suffer the most in terms of rising skin cancer rates and other unforeseen effects. Radioactive emissions from nuclear weapons testing, production, and stockpiling have already entered the air, soil, and water, the human gene pool, and our DNA. All of this is tantamount to stealing from our children and grandchildren—compromising their very ability to be born and live a normal life. As educator Patricia Mische has put it, "The right to a healthy environment may become the ultimate right-to-life issue."

There appears to be wide acceptance of the idea that "global corporatization" is inevitable, and a towering logic assures its destiny. Inherent in this view is the notion that people who object to this development and its consequences are misinformed and out of sync with the direction of history. From within the logic of financial transactions, global corporatization does seem inevitable. But there are greater logics and accounting systems. Money is a tool that human beings created in order to serve us in the achievement of human needs and aspirations. But our needs and aspirations do not have to be sacrificed just so large multinational corporations can accumulate greater wealth.

We live in a world where all living systems are inextricably bound together in one interdependent community. There can be no economic security without ecological sustainability. The path to ecological integrity is linked to solving the economic and social problem of gross inequity in the distribution of the Earth's resources. Can we expect governments and corporations to take the lead in moving our economies toward sustainability? Better we cultivate a deep awareness of the consequences of consumerism, and learn to vote collectively with our pocketbooks. The consumer choices we make have immediate impact and the potential to lead our society to a better quality of life for all beings.

There is good news. Examples of ethical industries are numerous: the recent emergence of Ben Cohen's worker-owned SweatX (sweatshop-free) brand of clothing, and the rise of homegrown organic food brands such as Horizon and Earthbound Farms, and outlets such as Whole Foods are notable examples. Socially responsible investments are on the rise, as is shareholder activism. "Consuming in the 21st century," declares Gary Hirshberg of Stonyfield Farm, "is a new form of activism."

The essential question is: Will human society reorganize itself in time to become sustainable, or will the rats, cockroaches, pigeons, feral dogs, sparrows, and crows inherit the Earth? Can we learn to engage the world as mindful, responsible, creative members of the community of life? With this personal realization comes a transformation of the marketplace.

The ongoing assault against the living systems of the Earth might still be abated through a change in consciousness and human choices of behavior. The contributors to this book do not agree on all aspects of the problem, but Buddhism is all about changing consciousness in order to affect changes in behavior. May we be wise enough to use the tools of transformation that the Buddha offered to help us on the path toward salvation and an end to the needless suffering resulting from corporate greed, government indifference, and our own ignorance and delusion.

Allan Hunt Badiner

Big Sur, California

June 2002

PART ONE

The All-Consuming Problem

There is enough for everybody's need,
but not enough for anybody's greed.
— *Mahatma Gandhi*

The Crisis of Consumerism

by Judith Simmer-Brown

WESTERN BUDDHISM must serve the world, not itself. It must become, as the seventh century Indian master Shantideva wrote, the doctor and the nurse for all sick beings in the world until everyone is healed; a rain of food and drink, an inexhaustible treasure for those who are poor and destitute. We can only imagine the kinds of suffering our children will encounter. Even now, we see the poor with not enough food and no access to clean drinking water; we see ethnic and religious prejudice that would extinguish those who are different; we see the sick and infirm who have no medicine or care; we see rampant exploitation of the many for the pleasure and comfort of the few; we see the demonization of those who would challenge the reign of wealth, power, and privilege. And we know the twenty-first century will yield burgeoning populations with an ever-decreasing store of resources to nourish them.

Fueling this suffering is the relentless consumerism which pervades our society and the world. Greed drives so many of the damaging systems of our planet. The socially engaged biologist Stephanie Kaza said that in America each of us consumes our body weight each day in materials extracted and processed from farms, mines, rangelands, and forests — 120 pounds on the average. Since 1950, consumption of energy, meat, and lumber has doubled; use of plastic has increased five-fold; use of aluminum has increased seven-fold; and airplane mileage has increased thirty-three-fold per person. We now own twice as many cars as in 1950. And with every bite, every press of the accelerator, every swipe of the credit card in our shopping malls, we leave a larger ecological footprint on the face of the world. We have squeezed our wealth out of the bodies of plantation workers in Thailand, farmers in Ecuador, and factory workers in Malaysia.

The crisis of consumerism is infecting every culture of the world, most of which are now emulating the American lifestyle. David Loy, in *The Religion of the Market,* suggests that consumption may have actually become the new world religion. This religion of consumerism is based on two unexamined tenets or beliefs:

1) growth and enhanced world trade will benefit everyone, and
2) growth will not be constrained by the inherent limits of a finite planet.

The ground of consumerism is ego gratification, its path is an ever-increasing array of wants, and its fruition is expressed in the Cartesian perversion—"I shop, therefore I am." While it recruits new converts through the flood of mass media, it dulls the consumer, making us oblivious to the suffering in which we participate. Shopping is a core activity in sustaining a culture of denial.

With the collapse of communist countries throughout the world, the growth of consumerism is all but unchallenged. As traditional societies modernize, consumerism is the most alluring path. Religious peoples and communities have the power to bring the only remaining challenge to consumerism. And Buddhism has unique insights which can stem the tide of consumptive intoxication.

How do we respond to all the suffering created by consumerism? How will our children respond? It is easy to join the delusion, forgetting whatever Buddhist training we may have had. But when we return to it, we remember—the origin of suffering is our constant craving. We want, therefore we consume; we want, therefore we suffer. As practitioners, we feel this relentless rhythm in our bones. We must, in this generation, wake up to the threat of consumerism, and join with other religious peoples to find a way to break its grip. We must all find a way to become activists in the movement which explores alternatives to consumerism.

As Western Buddhists, we must recognize the threats of consumerism within our practice, and within our embryonic communities and institutions. From a Tibetan Buddhist point of view, consumerism is just the tip of the iceberg. It represents only the outer manifestation of craving and acquisitiveness. Twenty-five years ago, my guru, the Vidyadhara Chogyam Trungpa Rinpoche, wrote one of the first popular Dharma books in America, *Cutting Through Spiritual Materialism.* Its relevance only increases each year. He spoke of three levels of materialism—physical, psychological, spiritual—that rule our existence as expressions of ego-centered activity. Unchallenged, materialism will co-opt our physical lives, our communities, and our very practice.

Physical materialism refers to the neurotic pursuit of pleasure, comfort, and security. This is the outer expression of consumerism. Under this influence, we try to shield ourselves from the daily pain of embodied existence, while accentuating the pleasurable moments. We are driven to create the illusion of a pain-free life, full of choices that make us feel in control. We need 107 choices of yogurt in a supermarket so that we feel like queens of our universe. We go to 24-Plex movie theaters so that we can see whatever film we want, whenever we want. We need faster pain relievers, appliances to take away all inconvenience, and communication devices to foster immediate exchange. All of these create the illusion of complete pleasure at our fingertips, with none of the hassle of pain. When we are ruled by this kind of physical materialism, we identify ourselves by what we have.

But this is just the beginning. On the next level, psychological materialism seeks to control the world through theory, ideology, and intellect. Not only are we trying to physically manipulate the world so that we don't have to experience pain, we do so psychologically as well. We create a theoretical construct that keeps us from having to be threatened, to be wrong, or to be confused. We always put ourselves in control in this way: "As an American I have rights. As a woman, I deserve to be independent from expectations of men in my society. I earn my own salary, I can choose how I want to spend it. As a Buddhist, I understand interdependence."

Psychological materialism interprets whatever is threatening or irritating as an enemy. Then, we control the threat by creating an ideology or religion in which we are victorious, correct, or righteous; we never directly experience the fear and confusion that could arise from facing a genuine threat. This is particularly perilous for the Western Buddhist. In these times, Buddhism has become popular, a commodity which is used by corporations and the media. Being Buddhist has become a status symbol, connoting power, prestige, and money. His Holiness's picture appears on the sets of Hollywood movies and in Apple Computer ads; Hollywood stars are pursued as acquisitions in a kind of Dharmic competition. Everyone wants to add something Buddhist to her résumé. Buddhist Studies enrollments at Naropa have doubled in two years, and reporters haunt our hallways and classrooms. Buddhist conferences attract a veritable parade of characters like myself, hawking the "tools" of our trade.

Our consumer society is turning Buddhism into a commodity like everything else. The seductions for the Western Buddhist are clear. We are being seduced to use Buddhism to promote our own egos, communities, and agendas in the marketplace.

This still is not the heart of the matter. On the most subtle level, spiritual materialism carries this power struggle into the realm of our own minds, into our own meditation practice. Our consciousness is attempting to remain in control, to maintain a centralized awareness. Through this, ego uses even spirituality to shield itself from fear and insecurity. Our meditation practice can be used to retreat from the ambiguity and intensity of daily encounters; our compassion practices can be used to manipulate the sheer agony of things falling apart. We develop an investment in ourselves as Buddhist practitioners, and in so doing protect ourselves from the directness and intimacy of our own realization. It is important for us to be willing to cultivate the "edge" of our practice, the edge where panic arises, where threat is our friend, and where our depths are turned inside out.

What happens when we are ruled by the "three levels of materialism"? The Vidyadhara taught that when we are so preoccupied with issues of ego, control, and power we become "afraid of external phenomena, which are our own projections." What this means is that when we take ourselves to be real, existent beings, then we mistake the world around us to be independent and real. And when we do this we invite paranoia, fear, and panic. We are afraid of not being able to control the situation. As Patrul Rinpoche (1808–1887) taught:

> Don't prolong the past,
> Don't invite the future,
> Don't alter your innate wakefulness,
> Don't fear appearances.

We must give up the fear of appearances. How can we do this? The only way to cut this pattern of acquisitiveness and control is to guard the naked integrity of our meditation practice. We must have somewhere where manipulation is exposed for what it is. We must be willing to truly "let go" in our practice. When we see our racing minds, our churning emotions and constant plots, we touch the face of the suffering world and we have no choice but to be changed. We must allow our hearts to break with the pain of constant struggle that we experience in ourselves and in the world around us. Then we can become engaged in the world, and dedicate ourselves to a genuine enlightened society in which consumerism has no sway. Craving comes from the speed of our minds, wishing so intensely for what we do not have that we cannot experience what is there, right before us.

How can we, right now, address materialism in our practice and our lives? I would like to suggest a socially engaged practice which could transform our immediate lifestyles and change our relationship with suffering. It is the practice of generosity. No practice flies more directly in the face of American acquisitiveness and individualism. Any of us who have spent time in Asia or with our Asian teachers see the centrality of generosity in Buddhist practice.

According to traditional formulation, our giving begins with material gifts and extends to gifts of fearlessness and Dharma. Generosity is the virtue that produces peace, as the sutras say. Generosity is a practice which overcomes our acquisitiveness and self-absorption, and which benefits others. Committing to this practice may produce our greatest legacy for the twenty-first century.

Patriarchal Roots of Overconsumption

by Fritjof Capra

THE GREAT CHALLENGE of our time is to build and nurture sustainable communities—social, cultural, and physical environments in which we can satisfy our needs and aspirations without diminishing the chances of future generations. A sustainable community is designed in such a way that its ways of life, businesses, economy, physical structures, and technologies do not interfere with nature's inherent ability to sustain life.

The first step in this endeavor must be to become "ecoliterate," i.e., to understand the principles of organization, common to all living systems, that ecosystems have evolved to sustain the web of life. The second step is to move toward ecodesign. We need to apply our ecological knowledge to the fundamental redesign of our technologies and social institutions, so as to bridge the current gap between human design and the ecologically sustainable systems of nature.

Fortunately, this is already taking place. In recent years, there has been a burst of optimism about the dramatic rise of ecologically-oriented design practices, all of which are now well documented.[1] They include a worldwide renaissance in organic farming; the organization of different industries into ecological clusters, in which the waste of any one organization is a resource for another; the shift from a product-oriented economy to a "service-and-flow" economy, in which industrial raw materials and technical components cycle continually between manufacturers and users; the production of ultralight hybrid-electric cars with fuel efficiencies of eighty miles per gallon; and the development of efficient hydrogen fuel cells that promises to inaugurate a new era in energy production—the "hydrogen economy."

Today, the obstacles that stand in the way of ecological sustainability are no longer conceptual, nor technical. They lie in the dominant values of our society. One of the greatest obstacles on the road toward sustainability is the continuing increase in material consumption. In spite of all the emphasis in the "new economy" on information processing, knowledge generation, and other intangibles, the main goal of these innovations is to increase productivity, which ultimately increases the flow of material goods. Biologist and environmentalist David Suzuki notes that in the last forty years, the size of Canadian families has shrunk by 50 percent, but their living spaces have doubled. "Each person uses four times as much space," Suzuki explains, "because we are all buying so much stuff."[2]

In contemporary capitalist society, the central value of moneymaking goes hand in hand with the glorification of material consumption. A never-ending stream of advertising messages reinforces people's delusion that the accumulation of material goods is the royal road to happiness, the very purpose of our lives. The United States projects its tremendous power around the world to maintain optimal conditions for the perpetuation and expansion of production. The central goal of its vast empire—its overwhelming military might, impressive range of intelligence agencies, and dominant positions in science, technology, media, and entertainment—is not to expand its territory, nor to promote freedom and democracy, but to make sure that it has global access to natural resources and that markets around the world remain open to its products.[3] Accordingly, political rhetoric in America moves swiftly from "freedom" to "free trade" and "free markets." The free flow of capital and goods is equated with the lofty ideal of human freedom, and material acquisition is portrayed as a basic human right, increasingly even as an obligation.

This glorification of material consumption has deep ideological roots that go far beyond economics and politics. Its origins seem to lie in the universal association of manhood with material possessions in patriarchal cultures. Anthropologist David Gilmore studied images of manhood around the world — "male ideologies," as he puts it—and found striking cross-cultural similarities.[4] There is a recurring notion that "real manhood" is different from simple biological maleness, that it is something that has to be won. In most cultures, Gilmore shows, boys "must earn the right" to be called men. Although women, too, are judged by gender standards that are often stringent, Gilmore notes that their very status as women is rarely questioned.

In addition to well-known images of manliness like physical strength, toughness, and aggression, Gilmore found that in culture after culture, "real" men have traditionally been those who produce more than they consume. The author emphasizes that the ancient association of manhood with material production meant production on behalf of the community: "Again and again we find that 'real' men are those who give more than they take; they serve others. Real men are generous, even to a fault."[5]

Over time, there was a shift in this image, from production for the sake of others to material possession for the sake of oneself. Manhood was now measured in terms of ownership of valuable goods — land, cattle, or cash — and in terms of power over others, especially women and children. This image was reinforced by the universal association of virility with "bigness" — as measured in muscle strength, accomplishments, or number of possessions. In modern society, Gilmore points out, male "bigness" is measured increasingly by material wealth: "The Big Man in any industrial society is also the richest guy on the block, the most successful, the most competent. . . . He has the most of what society needs or wants."[6]

The association of manhood with the accumulation of possessions fits well with other values that are favored and rewarded in patriarchal culture — expansion, competition, and an "object-centered" consciousness. In traditional Chinese culture, these were called yang values and were associated with the masculine side of human nature.[7] They were not seen as being intrinsically good or bad. However, according to Chinese wisdom, the yang values need to be balanced by their yin, or feminine, counterparts — expansion by conservation, competition by cooperation, and the focus on objects by a focus on relationships. I have long argued that the movement toward such a balance is very consistent with the shift from mechanistic to systemic and ecological thinking that is characteristic of our time.[8]

Among the many grassroots movements working for social change today, the feminist movement and the ecology movement advocate the most profound value shifts, the former through a redefinition of gender relationships, the latter through a redefinition of the relationship between humans and nature. Both can contribute significantly to overcoming our obsession with material consumption.

By challenging the patriarchal order and value system, the women's movement has introduced a new understanding of masculinity and personhood that does not need to associate manhood with material possessions. At the deepest level, feminist awareness is based on women's experiential knowledge that all life is connected, that our existence is always embedded in the cyclical processes of nature.[9] Feminist consciousness, accordingly, focuses on finding fulfillment in nurturing relationships rather than in the accumulation of material goods.

The ecology movement arrives at the same position from a different approach. Ecoliteracy requires systemic thinking—thinking in terms of relationships, context, patterns, and processes—and ecodesigners today advocate the transition from an economy of goods to an economy of service and flow. In such an economy, matter cycles continually, so that the net consumption of raw materials is drastically reduced.

A service-and-flow or "zero-emissions" economy is also excellent for business. As wastes turn into resources, new revenue streams are generated, new products are created, and productivity increases. Whereas the extraction of resources and the accumulation of waste are bound to reach their ecological limits, the evolution of life has demonstrated for more than three billion years that in a sustainable Earth household, there are no limits to development, diversification, innovation, and creativity.

In addition to increasing resource productivity and reducing pollution, the zero-emissions economy increases employment opportunities and revitalizes local communities. Thus the rise of feminist awareness and the movement toward ecological sustainability will combine to bring about a profound change of thinking and values—from linear systems of resource extraction and accumulation of products and waste to cyclical flows of matter and energy; from the focus on objects and natural resources to a focus on services and human resources; from seeking happiness in material possessions to finding it in nurturing relationships. In the eloquent words of David Suzuki:

> Family, friends, community—these are the sources of the greatest love and joy we experience as humans. We visit family members, keep in touch with favourite teachers, share and exchange pleasantries with friends. We undertake difficult projects to help others, save frogs or protect a wilderness, and in the process discover extreme satisfaction. We find spiritual fulfillment in nature or by helping others. None of these pleasures requires us to consume things from the Earth, yet each is deeply fulfilling. These are complex pleasures, and they bring us much closer to real happiness than the simple ones, like a bottle of Coke or a new minivan.[10]

This change of values is fully consistent with Buddhist teachings. In his celebrated doctrine of the Four Noble Truths, the Buddha taught that human suffering and frustration arise from a futile clinging to fixed forms—material objects, people, and categories of thought. In the words of the great contemporary Buddhist teacher, the Dalai Lama:

> Material fulfillment—money, material goods, etc.—gives us satisfaction at the sensory level. But at the mental level, at the level of our imagination and desires, we need another kind of satisfaction which the physical level cannot provide. . . . I have met many people who live in great material comfort and yet are full of anxiety; and they tell me about their many problems. The counter force to this mental disturbance is loving kindness. Human affection, caring, a sense of responsibility, and a sense of community—that is spirituality.[11]

Buddhism in the Global Economy

by Helena Norberg-Hodge

O VER THE PAST TWO DECADES I have had continuous contact with
Buddhist communities, in both traditional cultures and the industrialized West. These experiences have made me keenly aware that
industrial development affects not only our way of living, but our worldview
as well. I have also learned that if we are to avoid a misinterpretation of Buddhist teachings, we need to look closely at the fundamental differences between
societies that are part of the industrialized global economy and those that are
dependent on more localized economies.

In the Buddha's day, societies were more deeply rooted to their place in the
natural world. Economies were more localized—in other words, of a scale
that made explicit the human interdependence with other sentient beings and
the rest of creation. Relations between people and between culture and nature
were relatively unmediated. Direct observations and experiences of the natural world provided the basis for ethical decisions in individual lives.

The Buddha's teachings and precepts were formulated within the context
of societies shaped by these direct connections to community and to the living world. Buddhism is, in fact, about life. It is about the constantly changing
cycles of the natural world: birth and death, joy and sorrow, the opening of a
flower, the waxing and waning of the moon; it is about the impermanence and
interdependence that characterize all that lives.

In the modern industrial world, on the other hand, complex technologies
and large-scale social institutions have led to a fundamental separation between
people, as well as between humans and the living world. Since our daily lives
seem to depend largely on a man-made world—the economy, electric power,
cars and highways, the medical system—it's easy to believe that we depend
more on the technosphere than on life, or the biosphere. As the scale of the

economy grows, it also becomes increasingly difficult for us to know the effects of our actions on nature or on other people. These forms of separation stem from and reflect a fragmented worldview that is essentially antithetical to the Buddha's teachings. In fact, modern society is based on the assumption that we are separate from and able to control the natural world. Thus the structures and institutions on which we depend are reifications of ignorance and greed—a denial of interdependence and impermanence.

The significance of these differences may not be immediately apparent to Western Buddhists—most of whom have grown up within the industrial system and have known no other way of life. It can therefore be easy to confuse rapid technological and economic change with impermanence or the cycles of nature, or to believe that the current attempt to amalgamate diverse economies into a so-called "unified" global economy reflects the Buddha's notion of interdependence. The result is sometimes passive acceptance in the face of changes that are not only counter to Buddhist values, but are fundamentally anti-life.

Engaged Buddhists have a responsibility to examine current economic trends carefully, in the light of Buddhist teachings. I am convinced that such an examination will engender in us a desire to actively oppose the trend toward a global economy, and to help promote ways of life consistent with more Buddhist economics.

Globalization—the eradication of the diversity of life through "free trade" treaties—is a single economic system threatening to encompass the entire planet. At its core this system is based on a very narrow view of human needs and motivations: it is concerned almost exclusively with monetary transactions, and largely ignores such non-material aspects of life as family and community, meaningful work, or spiritual values. The focus on monetized social relations is echoed in the belief that people are motivated primarily by self-interest and endless material desires. Significantly, the Western economic system does not set about trying to temper our supposedly self-centered, acquisitive nature, but rather to exploit it: it is believed that an "invisible hand" will transform the selfish actions of individuals into benefits for society as a whole.

What does the globalized economy really mean? The president of Nabisco once defined it as "a world of homogeneous consumption"—a world in which people everywhere eat the same food, wear the same clothing, and live in houses built from the same materials. It is a world in which every society employs the same technologies, depends on the same centrally managed economy, offers the same Western education for its children, speaks the same language, consumes the same media images, holds the same values, and even thinks the same thoughts. In effect, globalization means the destruction of cultural diversity. It means monoculture.

Cultural diversity is a reflection of people's connection to their local environment, to the living world. Centuries of conquest, colonialism, and "development" have already eroded much of the world's cultural diversity, but economic globalization is rapidly accelerating the process. Along with multilane highways and concrete cities, globalization is bringing to every corner of the planet a cultural landscape dominated by fast food restaurants, Hollywood films, cellular phones, designer jeans, the Marlboro Man, Barbie.

If globalization is bringing monoculture, then its most profound impact will be on the Third World, where much of the world's remaining cultural diversity is to be found. In the Southern Hemisphere the majority still live in villages, partly connected through a diversified, local economy to diverse, local resources: still connected more to the biosphere than the technosphere. Because of pressures from globalization, locally-adapted forms of production are being replaced by systems of industrial production that are ever more divorced from natural cycles. In agriculture—the mainstay for rural populations throughout the South—this means a centrally managed, chemical-dependent system designed to deliver a narrow range of transportable foods to the world market. In the process, farmers are replaced by energy- and capital-intensive machinery, and diversified food production for local communities is replaced by an export monoculture. As the vitality of rural life declines, villagers are rapidly being pulled into squalor in shantytowns. The Chinese government, for example, is planning for the urban population to increase by 440 million people in the next twenty years—an explosion that is several times the rate of overall population growth.

Development not only pushes farmers off the land, it also centralizes job opportunities and political power in cities, intensifying the economic pull of urban centers. Advertising and media images, meanwhile, exert powerful psychological pressure to seek a better, more "civilized" life, one based on increased consumption. But since jobs are scarce, only a fraction succeed. The majority end up dispossessed and angry, living in slums in the shadow of advertisements for the American Dream. Despite the disastrous consequences, it is the effective policy of every government to promote these trends through their support for globalization.

What happens when rural life collapses and people who once relied on nearby resources become tied to the global economy? Consider traditional architecture, in which structures were built from local resources: stone in France, clay in West Africa, sun-dried bricks in Tibet, bamboo and thatch in the Philippines, felt in Mongolia, and so on. When these building traditions give way to "modern" methods, those plentiful local materials are left unused— while competition skyrockets for the monoculture's narrow range of structural materials, such as concrete, steel, and sawn lumber. The same thing happens when everyone begins eating identical staple foods, wearing clothes made from the same fibers, and relying on the same finite energy sources. Because it makes everyone dependent on the same resources, globalization creates efficiency for corporations, but it also creates artificial scarcity for consumers, thus heightening competitive pressures.

In this situation those on the bottom rungs of the economic ladder are at a great disadvantage. The gap between rich and poor widens, and anger, resentment, and conflict increase. This is particularly true in the South, where people from many differing ethnic backgrounds are being pulled into cities where they are cut off from their communities and cultural moorings, and where they face ruthless competition for jobs and the basic necessities of life. Individual and cultural self-esteem are eroded by the pressure to live up to media and advertising stereotypes, images that are invariably based on an urban, Western consumer model: blonde, blue-eyed, and clean. If you are a farmer or are dark-skinned, you are made to feel primitive, backward, inferior. As a consequence, women around the world use dangerous chemicals to lighten their skin and hair, and the market for blue contact lenses is growing in cities from Bangkok to Nairobi and Mexico City. Many Asian women even undergo surgery to make their eyes look more Western.

Contrary to the claims of its promoters, a centrally planned global economy does not bring harmony and understanding to the world by erasing the differences between us. Uprooting people from rural communities by selling them an unattainable urban white dream is instead responsible for a dramatic increase in anger and hostility—particularly among young men. In the intensely demoralizing and competitive situation they face, differences of any kind become increasingly significant, and ethnic and racial violence are the all but inevitable results.

My experiences in Ladakh and in the Kingdom of Bhutan have made me painfully aware of this connection between the global economy and ethnic conflict. In Ladakh, a Buddhist majority and a Muslim minority lived together for 600 years without a single recorded instance of group conflict. In Bhutan, a Hindu minority had coexisted peacefully with a slightly larger number of Buddhists for an equally long period. In both cultures, just fifteen years' exposure to outside economic pressures resulted in ethnic violence that left many people dead. In these cases it was clearly not the differences between people that led to conflict, but the erosion of their economic power and identity. If globalization continues, the escalation of conflict and violence will be unimaginable; after all, globalization means the undermining of the livelihoods and cultural identities of the majority of the world's people.

The Response of Engaged Buddhists

In the difficult situation globalization is creating, Buddhism's philosophical foundation and emphasis on compassion put the followers of these profound teachings in a unique position to lead the way out. Not only can Buddhism provide the intellectual tools needed to oppose further globalization but, more importantly, it can help to illuminate a path towards a localization based on human-scale structures—a prerequisite for action rooted in wisdom and compassion. For how can we make wise judgments if the scale of the economy is so great that we cannot perceive the impact of our actions? How can we act out of compassion when the scale is so large that the chains of cause and effect are hidden, leading us to unwittingly contribute to the suffering of other sentient beings?

Despite the answers Buddhism offers, many Western Buddhists have been slow to address the disturbing social and economic impact of globalization. In part this is clearly because Westerners in general have received very little accurate information about the impact of the global economy, particularly on the so-called Third World. Another reason may be a lack of clarity about the fact that Buddhist teachings refer to the state of the world as it is, in and of itself, unaffected by human intervention. In other words, it refers to the natural world, not an artificially constructed "technosphere" and its corrupt economic system. In fact, the teachings warn against "ignorant" human interpretations of reality—that is, seeing the world as made up of static, separate particles. We need to see many of today's institutions and suprastructures as nothing more than reified ignorance.

The challenge for Western Buddhists is to apply the Buddhist principles

taught many centuries ago—in an age of localized social and economic interactions—to the highly complex and increasingly globalized world in which
we now live. In order to do so it is vital that we avoid the mental traps of conceptual thought and abstraction. Otherwise it is easy, for example, to confound
the ideals of the "global village" and the borderless world of free trade with
the Buddhist principle of interdependence—the unity of all life, the inextri-
cable web in which nothing can claim completely separate or static existence.
The buzzwords—"harmonization," "integration," "union," etc.—sound as
though globalization is leaving us more interdependent with one another and
with the natural world. In fact, it is instead furthering our dependence on large-
scale economic structures and technologies, and on a shrinking number of
ever-larger corporate monopolies. It would be a tragic mistake, indeed, to confuse this process with the cosmic interdependence described by the Buddha.

The Buddhist notion of impermanence can also be distorted unless we are
clear about the fundamental differences between life processes and the global
economic system. The Buddha's teachings are about change and impermanence in the natural world. We are taught to accept the ever-changing flow of
life in the biosphere, the cycles of life and death, the impermanence of all
beings. The changes precipitated by globalization, however, are based on a
denial of the impermanence in nature observed by the Buddha. Megaprojects
such as nuclear powerplants, dams, and superhighways are not a part of the
flow of life that the Buddha taught us to accept, nor is the manipulation of
genetic material through biotechnology. Instead, these are manifestations of a
worldview that seeks to dominate nature, and which pretends that life can be
held static, split into fragments and manipulated to satisfy the needs of a tech-
nologically-dependent consumer culture.

Two final and interconnecting Buddhist concepts can sometimes be mis-
construed to support social apathy: karma, and the three poisons of greed,
hatred, and delusion. The Law of Karma is one way to explain the growing gap
between rich and poor: if one is rich, one must have performed good deeds in
the past. However, an honest examination reveals, of course, that the more
immediate cause of much social inequality is a global economic system which
allows a few to prosper at the expense of the many. Rather than attributing
differences in wealth to karma from the deeds of past lifetimes, we need in
particular to acknowledge the implications of the urbanized Western lifestyle.
The lack of wisdom and compassion inherent in this lifestyle is quite evident:
we in the industrialized parts of the world consume roughly ten times our

share of the world's resources, often oblivious to the incalculable cost to all life on this planet. Without taking the entire responsibility personally for a global system that has been built up over centuries, we nonetheless need to muster the courage to scrutinize our collective contribution to a system which encourages exploitation and social atomization, and which exacerbates inequalities and destruction—often out of sight, on the other side of the world.

The three poisons of greed, hatred, and delusion are to some extent present in every human being, but cultural systems either encourage or discourage these traits. Today's global consumer culture nurtures the three poisons on both an individual and societal level. At the moment, $450 billion is spent annually on advertising worldwide, with the aim of convincing three-year-old children that they need things they never knew existed—like Coca-Cola and plastic Rambos with machine guns. Before the rise of consumerism, cultures existed in which this type of greed was virtually nonexistent. Thus we cannot conclude that the acquisitiveness and materialism of people trapped in the global economic system are an inevitable product of human nature. Instead we need to recognize the near impossibility of uncovering our Buddha natures in a global culture of consumerism and social atomization.

Buddhism can help us in this difficult situation by encouraging us to be compassionate and nonviolent with ourselves as well as others. Many of us avoid an honest examination of our lives for fear of exposing our contribution to global problems. However, once we realize that it is the complex global economy that is creating a disconnected society, psychological deprivation, and environmental breakdown, Buddhism can help us to focus on the system and its structural violence, instead of condemning ourselves or other individuals within that system. The teachings can encourage an understanding of the many complex ways we affect others and our environment, and encourage empathy and a profound affirmation of life. Only by recognizing how we are all part of this system can we actively work together to disengage from these life-denying structures.

Buddhism, in its holistic approach, can help us to see how various symptoms are interrelated; how the crises facing us are systemic and rooted in economic imperatives. Understanding the myriad connections between the problems can prevent us from wasting our efforts on the symptoms of the crises, rather than focusing on their fundamental causes. Under the surface, even such seemingly unconnected problems as ethnic violence, pollution of the air and water, broken families, and cultural disintegration are closely interlinked. Psychologically, such a shift in our perception of the nature of the problems is deeply empowering: being faced with a never-ending string of seemingly unrelated problems can be overwhelming, but finding the points at which they converge can make our strategy to solve them more focused and effective. It is then just a question of pulling the right threads to affect the entire fabric, rather than having to deal with each problem individually.

Stepping Back from Global Economy

At a structural level, the fundamental problem is scale. The ever-expanding scope and scale of the global economy obscures the consequences of our actions: in effect, our arms have been so lengthened that we no longer see what our hands are doing. Our situation thus exacerbates and furthers our ignorance, preventing us from acting out of compassion and wisdom.

In smaller communities, people can see the effects of their actions and take responsibility for them. Smaller scale structures also limit the amount of power vested in one individual. What a difference between the leader of a large nation-state and that of a small town: one has power over millions of faceless people with whom there will never be any real contact; the other coordinates the affairs of a few thousand people, and is an active part of the community. The scale of the modern nation-state has become so large that leaders would be unable to act according to the principles of interdependence, even if they wished to. Decisions are instead made according to abstract economic principles—in the name of "progress"—often disregarding the implications for individual members of society and for the rest of the living world.

In more decentralized economies and political structures it is difficult to ignore the laws of impermanence and interdependence. Being personally accountable to the community means being constantly in tune with its changing social and environmental dynamics. Since the consequences of any action are evident in a smaller community, decisions are more likely to be guided by wisdom and compassion. As difficult as it may sound, our choice as Buddhists seems clear: we need to help move society towards rebuilding smaller-scale social and economic structures which make possible a life based on Buddhist notions of interdependence and impermanence. It is helpful to remember that continuing the competitive race towards increased globalization and larger scale is far more difficult. In fact the global economy represents an impossible dream, since it is eradicating the diversity on which life depends.

An important aspect of moving toward smaller-scale human institutions is reaffirming a sense of place. Each community is unique in its environment, its people, its culture. Human scale minimizes the need for rigid legislation and allows for more flexible decision-making; it gives rise to action in harmony with the laws of nature, based on the needs of the particular context. When individuals are at the mercy of faraway, inflexible bureaucracies and fluctuating markets, they feel passive and disempowered; more decentralized structures provide individuals with the power to respond to each unique situation.

Despite the many environmental, social, and even ethical benefits that decentralized economic activity could provide, governments are blindly promoting exactly the opposite: massive centralization on a global scale. Since economic centralization is promoted in the name of "oneness" and "interdependence," among the first steps we need to take is to educate ourselves and others about the mental confusion these terms engender. By promoting discussion and sharing information we can remove the layers of ignorance that lead us to unwittingly support a system of greed and violence while we are striving in our individual lives to do just the opposite. Once we are more awake, we can join with others to pressure government for changes in policy.

Since the global economy is fueled by transnational institutions that can overpower any single government, the policy changes most urgently needed are at the international level. In theory, what is required is quite simple: the governments that ratified "free trade" treaties like the Uruguay Round of GATT need to sit down around the same table again. This time instead of operating in secret—with transnational corporations at their side—they should be made to represent the interests of the majority. This can only happen if there is far more awareness at the grassroots, awareness that leads to real pressure on policy-makers.

Pressuring for policy change can seem a daunting task. Many today have abandoned any hope of meaningful political change, thinking that we no longer have any leverage over our political leaders. But it is important to remember that in the long term, blind adherence to the outdated dogma of free trade benefits no one, not even the political leaders and corporate CEOs that are promoting it today. Among its other effects, globalization is eroding the tax base and power of nation-states—and that means the budgets and influence of elected officials. It is also threatening the job security of individuals, even at the highest levels of the corporate world.

It is heartening to realize that even the tiniest change in policy towards curtailing the movement of capital and diversifying economic activity at the local and national level would reap enormous systemic rewards. The ability to shift profits, operating costs, and investment capital between far-flung operations has played a key role in the growth of ever more powerful transnational corporations. Today the capital controlled by these businesses, and the ease with which it can be transferred around the world, allows corporations to hold sovereign nations hostage—simply by threatening to leave and take their jobs with them if governments attempt to regulate or restrict their activities. Rules that limited the free flow of capital would therefore help to reduce the advantage that huge corporations have over smaller, more local enterprises, and would make corporations more accountable to the places where they operate.

Steps to decentralize energy development would also be immensely beneficial. All around the world, large-scale power installations are heavily subsidized. Phasing out these multi-billion dollar investments while offering real support for locally available renewable energy supplies would result in lower pollution levels, reduced pressure on wilderness areas and oceans, and less dependence on dwindling petroleum supplies and dangerous nuclear technologies. It would also help to keep money from "leaking" out of local economies.

In less-industrialized countries in particular, large dams, fossil-fuel plants, and other large-scale energy infrastructures are geared towards the needs of urban areas and export-oriented production. Shifting support instead towards a decentralized renewable energy infrastructure would help to stem the urban tide by strengthening villages and small towns. Since the energy infrastructure in the South is not yet very developed, there is a realistic possibility that this could be implemented in the near future if there were sufficient pressure from activists lobbying Northern banks and funding agencies.

A parallel change in regulatory laws could also provide significant systemic benefits. In almost every country, for example, tax regulations currently discriminate against small businesses. Small-scale production is usually more labor-intensive, and heavy taxes are levied on labor through income taxes, social welfare taxes, value-added taxes, payroll taxes, etc. Meanwhile, tax breaks (accelerated depreciation, investment allowances and tax credits, etc.) are afforded the capital- and energy-intensive technologies used by large corporate producers. Financial policies that aim at reversing this bias in the tax system would not only help local economies, but would create more jobs by favoring people instead of machines.

Until now, governments of every stripe have embraced free trade policies in the belief that liberalization and an opening up to economic globalization will cure their ailing economies. However, since these policies are, in fact, eroding the tax base, destroying countless businesses, and leading to widespread unemployment, policy makers will soon be forced to wake up to the real impact of globalization, and reassess the free-trade dogma. Policy changes such as those outlined above would virtually overnight shift the economy towards fuller employment and truly free markets, in which stronger small- and medium-sized businesses have the opportunity to compete. It would also enable local and national governments to generate the taxes they require to fulfill their obligations to society.

Localization: Towards a Buddhist Economics

Even now, without the help from government and industry that a new direction in policy would provide, people are starting to change the economy from the bottom up towards more human-scale structures that are more consistent with a Buddhist viewpoint. This process of localization has begun spontaneously, in countless communities all around the world. Because economic localization means an adaptation to cultural and biological diversity, no single "blueprint" would be appropriate everywhere. The range of possibilities for local grassroots efforts is therefore as diverse as the locales in which they take place.

In many towns, for example, community banks and loan funds have been set up, thereby increasing the capital available to local residents and businesses and allowing people to invest in their neighbors and their community, rather than in a faceless global economy.

In other communities, "buy-local" campaigns are helping locally-owned businesses survive even when pitted against heavily subsidized corporate competitors. These campaigns not only help to keep money from leaking out of the local economy, but also help educate people about the hidden costs — to their own jobs, to the community, and the environment — in purchasing cheaper but distantly produced products.

In some communities, Local Exchange and Trading Systems (LETS) have been established as an organized, large-scale bartering system. Thus, even people with little or no "real" money can participate in and benefit from the local economy. LETS systems have been particularly beneficial in areas with high unemployment. The city government of Birmingham, England—where unemployment hovers at 20 percent—has been a cosponsor of a highly successful LETS scheme. These initiatives have psychological benefits that are just as important as the economic benefits: a large number of people who were once merely "unemployed"—and therefore "useless"—are becoming valued for their skills and knowledge.

One of the most exciting grassroots efforts is the Community Supported Agriculture (CSA) movement, in which consumers in towns and cities link up directly with a nearby farmer. In some cases, consumers purchase an entire season's produce in advance, sharing the risk with the farmer. In others, shares of the harvest are purchased in monthly or quarterly installments. Consumers usually have a chance to visit the farm where their food is grown, and in some cases their help on the farm is welcomed. While small farmers linked to the industrial system continue to fail every year at an alarming rate, CSAs are allowing small-scale diversified farms to thrive in growing numbers. CSAs have spread rapidly throughout Europe, North America, Australia, and Japan. In the United States, the number of CSAs has climbed from only 2 in 1986 to 200 in 1992, and is closer to 1,000 today.

These and countless other initiatives around the world are a reflection of a growing awareness, a realization that it is far more sensible to depend on our neighbors and the living world around us than to depend on a global economic system built of technology and corporate institutions. As Buddhists faced with this same reality, we have little choice but to become engaged. Buddhism provides us with both the imperative and the tools to challenge the economic structures that are creating and perpetuating suffering the world over. We cannot claim to be Buddhist and simultaneously support structures that are so clearly contrary to Buddha's teachings, antithetical to life itself.

The economic and structural changes needed will inevitably require shifts at the personal level as well. In part, these involve rediscovering the deep psychological benefits—the joy—of being embedded in community. Another fundamental shift involves reintroducing a sense of connection with the place where we live. The globalization of culture and information has led to a way of life in which the nearby is treated with contempt. We get news from China but not next door, and at the touch of a TV button we have access to all the wildlife of Africa. As a consequence, our immediate surroundings seem dull and uninteresting by comparison. A sense of place means helping ourselves and our children to see the living environment around us: reconnecting with the sources of our food—perhaps even growing some of our own—learning to recognize the cycles of the seasons, the characteristics of flora and fauna.

As the Buddha taught, our spiritual awakening comes from making a connection to others and to nature. This requires us to see the world within us, to experience more consciously the great interdependent web of life—of which we ourselves are among the strands. In this way we "experience" the teachings of impermanence and interdependence, principles that exhort us to interact with others and with nature in a wise, compassionate, and sustainable way.

Illuminating Darkness: Western Buddhism

by L.D. Ness

A T THE BEGINNING of the new millennium, some of us in the West are in the fortunate position of having encountered the ancient wisdom of Buddhism. My contact with the teachings of the Buddha came through the Gelugpa tradition of Tibetan Buddhism. But as I struggled to understand its meaning and concepts, I was also bombarded with many additional theories (and demands) as to how best to live my life, in particular my spiritual life. A lot of these theories were rooted in the social conditioning we receive via social, economic, and political means, living as members of the largest and (arguably) most successful communities the world has ever seen (my use of the word "arguably" revolves around the definition of what one might call success) — the Western capitalist consumer societies that so dominate the world's affairs.

So you can imagine my dismay when we were told that we must strive to "become more Western" in our approach to Buddhism, a new "sound bite" that began flying around meditation centers, eliciting many changes. To be fair, this is a totally valid proposition that deserves serious consideration, but as is all too often the case, our interpretation of how to attain this is severely compromised by a very efficient system of propaganda and denial in the West today.

What exactly does it mean to "become more Western," and to introduce this into our spiritual practice? And what could the implications of such an approach be for us, for our practice, for the Buddhist community, and for the world at large? While I do not seek to deny my "Westernness," I do wonder if others truly understand the implications of what our culture entails for the rest of the planet, let alone our own spiritual practices.

The Consumerist Utopia

In the West, we live in a so-called "free democracy" that embraces corporate capitalist consumerism as the fundamental organizing principle of life. Our governments, and the political parties that constitute them, though divided by nominal differences, have all, without exception, embraced the goal of maximizing endless economic growth. In fact, one of the major ways we judge their effectiveness is how well, and how quickly they do just that. Since we have democratic representative governments, it must be reasonable to conclude that to be "Western" is to seek satisfaction and meaning in life through the dual goals of consumption and mass-production of tradable goods. Just in case we forget that this is the cause for which we all live, there is in place an effective propaganda system that very kindly bombards us with information specifically designed to help us remember our primary goal in life—to consume. The average person is subjected to nearly 3,000 advertisements every day—on TV, on the roads and highways, in storefronts, on the Internet, and even on the sides of cars, in the sky, and on restroom walls. Our governments openly admit that they aim to bring school curriculum into line with business needs, helping to produce effective candidates to enter into the competitive "corporate" reality of working life, thus making the country more effective in the globalized battlefield of big business.

In her paper, "School to Work, A Corporate Raid on Public Education,"[12] American school teacher Mary Ellen Cardella writes:

> If, as the oft quoted Thomas Jefferson and John Dewey, leading twentieth century education philosophers maintained, democracy resides in a well-informed electorate, then a system of public education rooted in the goals and behaviors of corporate America promises an electorate, a body politic, tooled to serve the narrow interest of the corporate model at the expense of a society of the people.

Huge transnational corporations dominate the workplace, and we should not be surprised then, that given the goals of capitalist society (maximum economic growth), that profit is the primary concern of these organizations—producing more for less and then getting us (that is, us in the rich North who can afford to pay extremely marked-up prices) to consume it. Thus it should also come as no surprise that worker's rights, the environment, even spiritual meaning in life should be at best only secondary goals, effective only insomuch as they aid and encourage the primary goal of making profit. The message drummed into our heads from the time of our birth is that you can find success, happiness, and contentment by "playing the game," and reaping the rewards of power, money, and the ability to consume anything we desire.

The Cost of Illusion

Most of us assume that the drive behind consumerism is the manufacturing of goods and services to satisfy individual needs and desires in order to have a more contented life. But consumerism is much more than that. It is a system for creating desires, and for progressively creating dissatisfaction. This can be witnessed at work today in an intense seventy-year-old global propaganda war waged against women to relieve them of their money through the manufacture of discontent, even, at times, at the cost of their lives.

From the early 1920s, at about the same time as women's political liberation, and following their essential contributions during the First World War and the associated rise of feminism, women began to feature much more prominently in the industrial economies. From 1945–1984, the number of women in employment in the U.S. rose from 32 percent to 53 percent. In Sweden the figure rose to 77 percent and in France to 55 percent. But the real changes in women's social roles started in the sixties: between 1960 and 1990 the number of U.S. women lawyers rose from 7,500 to 180,000; the number of doctors rose from 15,000 to 108,000 and of engineers from 7,000 to 174,000. Today 50 percent of entry management positions are held by women and 25 percent of middle management positions.

All this has led to a more meaningful, but still confined "liberation" of women from the role of doting housewife, so prominent in the nineteenth and early twentieth century, to a whole class of impulse buyers with far more disposable income. As David Edwards points out in his book *Free to Be Human*,[13] the manufacture of discontent has long been a standard marketing ploy. The technique essentially involves suggesting an unfavorable comparison between the inevitably flawed and imperfect individual of real life and an artificially perfected ideal who, it is implied, can be emulated by buying the advertised service or product. Advertisers have now focused on the "sexual revolution," combining it with an emphasis on female beauty.

Between 1968 and 1972 the number of diet related articles in women's magazines rose by 70 percent. By 1979 the number of diet related articles in the U.S. popular press per year had reached sixty. By January 1980 there were sixty-six in just one month. By combining their corporate assault on fat with an added attack focused on aging and complexion, the results they have achieved are staggering. By 1990 the global dietary industry had become worth $32 billion, the cosmetics industry $20 billion, and cosmetic surgery $300 million.

But we should not think that this success has just been an opportunist result of supplying an increasingly "liberated" woman with her beauty products. It has been a full assault on women's psyches designed to generate self-dissatisfaction in order to generate and increase sales. Between 1966 and 1969, and mirroring the new media emphasis on thinness, two U.S. studies showed that the number of teenage girls who thought they were fat rose from 50 percent to 80 percent. A later 1984 study by the University of Cincinnati showed that 75 percent of all women between eighteen and thirty-five believed themselves to be fat, while only 25 percent were medically overweight, and 45 percent of women classified as underweight thought they were fat. By 1985, 90 percent of all women thought they weighed too much. If we can believe Dr. C. Wayne of George Washington University, that the average model used by corporate advertisers is thinner than 95 percent of the population, then these figures prove the effectiveness of the corporate campaigns.

It is a sad fact though that because of this psychological onslaught, the *San Francisco Chronicle* was able to report that 33 percent of all women are "strongly dissatisfied" with their bodies. The real consequences of this growth industry —founded on women's discontent—has been the staggering eruption of physical and mental illness among women. Fully 10 percent of all U.S. women (and up to 20 percent of student-aged women) suffer from serious eating disorders. The American Anorexia and Bulimia Association reports that a million new women are stricken by these illnesses every year. Of these, 150,000 die each year (three times the number of deaths from fatal car accidents). Europe is starting to go the way of the U.S. with between 1–2 percent of all women in Britain, France, and Italy now suffering from either anorexia or bulimia.

Predictably, the University of Cincinnati report also showed that new generations are already limbering up to join their ranks—by the age of thirteen, 53 percent of girls are unhappy with their shape or size and this rises to 78 percent by age eighteen. Two million Americans have cosmetic surgery every year, fueling a $300 million industry, which is growing at 10 percent per year, while between 200,000 and 1,000,000 women have had breast implants, and 200,000 women have liposuctions every year.

But women are not alone in this highly structured corporate assault on life that we call capitalism. According to U.K. government figures, fully 25 percent of the population suffers from mental illness at any given time, and as June McKerrow, director of the Mental Health Foundation points out, "Mental illness affects one in four of the U.K. population at any one point in time and kills four times as many as road accidents. It is as prevalent as heart trouble and three times more common than cancer."

In the U.S., a hidden epidemic is taking place with one in four people dying from cancer. Obviously the situation deserves a much more in-depth investigation than I can hope to give here. More information and examples can be found in *Free to Be Human* by David Edwards (from where I drew these figures), but by now the questionable values and implications of Western life must be starting to become apparent.

Managing Chaos

So far I have only focused on some of the problems faced by the countries of the affluent North, but of course the headlong pursuit of economic growth we hold so dear in "civilized" Western culture has had some dire consequences for the rest of the planet as well.

Today over one billion people live in conditions of absolute poverty as described by the UN. The UN Human Development Program (UNDP) has reported that the gap between rich and poor nations has doubled between 1960 and 1989. While organizations such as the World Bank and the IMF help to implement the global environment for "favorable investment climates," ensuring massive wealth to transnational corporations and a handful of elites, the majority of the world is picking up the tab and living in an almost manifest hell. Even in countries as wealthy as Brazil, 40 percent of the populace goes hungry and seven million children work as slaves or prostitutes. In Guatemala 87 percent of the population of nine million live below the poverty line and millions of children have been orphaned due to (Western-backed) political violence. In Mexico 60 percent of households are unable to meet basic needs. In Venezuela 33 percent of the population cannot meet basic nutritional requirements. In El Salvador 90 percent live in poverty.

UNICEF reports that half a million children die each year as a result of scarcities caused by Third World debt repayment and eleven million from easily treatable diseases; this has been described as a "silent genocide" by World Health Organization Director General Nakajima. These debt repayment schemes or "structural adjustment programs" (SAPs) have been set up (and enforced) by the International Monetary Fund (IMF) and World Bank. So massive has been the decapitalization of South America that a former executive director of the World Bank exclaimed: "Not since the conquistadors plundered Latin America has the world experienced a flow in the direction we see today." If structural adjustment has brought neither growth nor debt relief, it has certainly intensified poverty.

In Latin America, according to Inter-American Development Bank president Enrique Iglesias, adjustment programs had the effect of "largely cancelling out the progress of the 1960s and 1970s." The numbers of people living in poverty rose from 130 million in 1980 to 180 million at the beginning of the 1990s. Structural adjustment also worsened what was already a very skewed distribution of income, with the result that today, according to Walden Bello and Shea Cunningham in their book, *The World Bank and the IMF,* the top 20 percent of the continent's population earn twenty times that earned by the poorest 20 percent. Even our own working classes here in the West are being affected— 40 percent of children in New York City and 36 percent of British children live below the poverty line. The *Wall Street Journal* reported that the number of full-time British employees with weekly pay below the Council of Europe "decency threshold" has risen from 28.3 percent in 1979 to 37 percent in 1994.

Our Pain Projected

With the Buddhist understanding that the condition of our minds directly affects the environment we perceive, it should not be too hard to conceive that this human misery, rooted in our drive for "maximized economic growth," should be mirrored in the environment about us. Northern Europe experienced a 20 percent ozone depletion in January 1992 and 40 percent in January 1993.

Data collected by the British Antarctic Survey Team indicates that the "greening of Antarctica" has begun, with one of the only two flowering grasses found in the region twenty-five times more common than it was thirty years ago, and summer temperatures present for 50 percent longer than in the seventies. In September 1993, Norwegian scientists reported that the polar ice cap is melting 10 percent faster than it can be replaced. By 2020 there will be only fragments of the rainforest left untouched anywhere in the world.

Animal and plant species are disappearing at an unprecedented rate, with over-fishing pushing food chains close to collapse in the North Sea. Birdlife International has reported that 40 percent of all bird species are in decline with 10 percent threatened with extinction, with the possibility of a hundred species disappearing within five years. Following this trend the same report suggests that up to ten million plant and animal species could be threatened globally.

As David Edwards[14] wrote so compellingly:

> The reality is that the world is on fire, that the natural systems of life are collapsing beneath the weight of the industrial killing machine. After only fifty years of total industrial war against the needs of humanity and the natural environment, both are starting to show signs of collapse.

And he concludes:

> We are, after all talking about the torture, mutilation, and genocide of hundreds of thousands, even millions of innocent people as the result of the actions of individuals hell-bent on personal gain [maximum economic growth].

A Necessary Illusion?

So we can see that the "Western" approach to meaningful life, "freely" chosen by the majority, by "democratic" process is actually failing the majority of those it is meant to serve, even here in the West. In fact only a very small elite are "benefiting" (this is of course only by their analysis of events, since from a Buddhist perspective you could argue that they are in fact a lot worse).

This brings me back to the original question I posed at the start, namely what does it mean to make our approach to Buddhism "more Western"?

Political Interdependency

Within Buddhism we are told that by succumbing to the "threefold poisons" of greed, hatred, and ignorance we continually perpetuate our own and others' suffering. This is not brought about by some external "god" or authoritarian force, but by a complex series of causes and effects (karma). As this ancient wisdom so clearly points out, all too often the things we cling to for our happiness are in fact the causes of our suffering.

It would seem fair to me to say that with the turning of the New Millennium these very three Buddhist poisons are not just manifest right within the root of capitalist consumerist society, they are the Root! We can, with a little analytical investigation, find these poisons motivating the obscene situations mentioned above. It is ours and others' manufacturing of greed and desires that fuel our own continual dissatisfaction, which is such an integral part of the consumerist society. This is achieved often at a great expense to Third World countries as shown above.

Holistic Engagement

Buddhist doctrine suggests that all beings from the loftiest corporate executive, the most radical of radicals, or even the legendary "couch potato" of modern society, are equal in one matter. We all desire to be happy and free from suffering. The methods by which we try to avoid distress differ and, as we have seen, have varying degrees of success.

As Buddhists we may feel that it is enough just to find our own liberation, so we need not be too concerned with the individual manifestations of the "three poisons" in the outside world. And as political activists, such metaphysical ramblings and spiritual dreaming may pale into insignificance when we are faced with such horrors as East Timor, Cambodia, Iraq, or any number of catastrophes currently plaguing the world. But I feel that a link between these two approaches is vital. When we see the repercussions of our cultural drive to achieve maximum economic growth, and the incredible cost to our mental, physical, environmental, and spiritual life, we might begin to truly grasp some of the profound implications of Buddha's wisdom and its relevance in the modern Western world.

Thich Nhat Hanh has said, "The lotus grows best when planted deep in the mud." The sometimes controversial Buddhist teacher Geshe Kelsang Gyatso said that we should not underestimate the far-reaching consequences of our self-cherishing, which is the main cause of all our suffering. I believe this cultural self-cherishing can be seen today to reach far into the established social and economic institutions of the West. Until we can realize just how far these "poisons" are penetrating into our daily lives and even our perception of these lives, we will be severely obstructed in our attainment of true happiness.

Conversely though, by developing an acute understanding of the "necessary illusions" of Western life and their negative effects, one can truly be motivated to work for the benefit of both oneself and others. As Stephen Batchelor wrote:

> ... the contemporary social engagement of Dharma practice is rooted in awareness of how self-centered confusion and craving can no longer be adequately understood only as psychological drives that manifest themselves in subjective states of anguish. We find these drives embodied in the very economic, military, and political structures that influence the lives of the majority of the people on Earth.[15]

As long as we neglect to perceive these "three poisons" of greed, hatred, and ignorance within Western cultural life we are subjecting ourselves to massive indoctrination by an institution diametrically opposed to that of Buddhism. We might argue that it is simply people's karma to suffer like that and there is nothing you can do about it, except for maybe easing your nagging conscience by saying prayers on their behalf, and you would be partly right. The primary cause of their suffering is their own negative karma, but the secondary cause is our very own wants and needs as chosen "democratically" by the majority of the West. One must not think that this is some elaborate conspiracy though, it is simply the result of choosing "maximum economic growth" as the defining goal of our culture. All of the tragic developments enumerated above flow from this. But just as greed, hatred, and ignorance are the root of our predicament, their opponents, generosity, loving-compassion, and understanding are the keys that could set us free.

Defined by Belief Not Borders

I would like to propose that we not "become more Western" in our approach towards Buddhism, but instead that we strive to "become more Buddhist about our Westernness." We do not need violent opposition of power or even a more even distribution of "wealth" (material gain) to overcome suffering. Through the generation of love and understanding, through generosity and compassion, we can cut through the root of much of our own pain and find real meaning in life, something that is lacking in today's hedonistic culture. By understanding the implications of our cultural desires we might find it easy to develop compassion for those who suffer as a result. With this deep understanding we might be driven by our conscience to abandon such empty pursuits and actually open the way to replace them with the real causes of happiness. We might even develop a deeper understanding of emptiness when we understand that things are not always as they seem.

This is what *Lam rim* (the gradual path to enlightenment) means to me; and this is what is meant by incorporating Buddhism into our daily lives and activities—not in some intellectual way, but in real, mutually beneficial ways. There is real potential in this approach to combat the troubles that face us all. After all, Buddha advised us that we are able to achieve freedom from suffering for both ourselves and others.

Even Western applied logic validates this approach. "The suffering I and others experience at this time is rooted in greed, hatred, and ignorance. If I apply the antidotes of generosity, compassion, and understanding this will defiantly counter their effect. The two cannot exist together." In this sense Buddhism really is political and global activism. As people suffer and the Earth's complex eco-structure crumbles before our eyes, the wisdom contained within this ancient tradition may well be our only hope, regardless of race or creed. I am not saying that the whole world should become Buddhist, merely that if, as I believe, these three poisons are the source of our woes, then surely their opposites must be the antidote.

Minds of Compassion and Understanding

The arrival of Buddhism in the West is an amazing opportunity to address many of our own cultural dilemmas. But in accepting this task we will need to make many decisions about how to interpret the real meaning and implications of these invaluable teachings. If we allow ourselves to be influenced by the weight of propaganda within our cultural environment, I fear this opportunity could soon go the same way as "Green Consumerism" or "Sustainable Growth." Both have become effective ways of appearing to be doing something while not threatening the cultural agreement on the desirability of endless growth and increasing profits.

Conversely, to "become more Buddhist about our Westernness" may prevent this degeneration. The real beauty of this approach may be that the more we take this path, the less power is given to the other with all its disastrous results, until eventually it must negate it altogether.

A Systems View of Overconsumption

by Riane Eisler

IT'S UP TO YOU AND ME to care for the place where we all live—our natural environment. There are many things we can do to this end. The first, and simplest, is to help those around us understand that our environmental problems cannot be solved by the same system that's creating them.

We are used to thinking of economic systems in terms of capitalism vs. communism, industrial vs. pre- or postindustrial, hi-tech vs. technologically undeveloped. But economic and technological systems are inextricably interconnected with the larger cultural system in which they operate. So we need to look at the underlying cultural models that inform the construction of economics.

There are two fundamentally different models for constructing human cultures: the *partnership* model and the *domination* model. The degree to which a culture orients to one or the other of these two underlying models molds all our relationships—from relationships between parents and children and between women and men to the relations between governments and citizens and between us and nature. It profoundly affects how we structure all our institutions, from the family, and education, to economics, and politics.

In the domination model, somebody has to be on top and somebody has to be on the bottom. Those on top control those below them. People learn, starting in early childhood, to obey orders without question. They learn to carry a harsh voice in their heads telling them they're no good, they don't deserve love, they need to be punished. Families and societies are based on control that is explicitly or implicitly backed up by guilt, fear, and force. The world is divided into in-groups and out-groups, with those who are different seen as enemies to be conquered or destroyed. It is a model that makes it difficult to meet our most basic human needs for caring connection. And it tends to inhibit and even suppress our innate capacity for empathy and compassion.

In contrast, the partnership model supports mutually respectful and caring relations. It resonates deeply with the Buddhist truths of the interdependence of all life. It also resonates deeply with the Buddhist teaching of not doing harm. Because there is no need to maintain rigid rankings of control, there is also no built-in need for abuse and violence in cultures that orient primarily to the partnership model. Partnership relations free our innate capacity to feel joy, to play. They enable us to grow mentally, emotionally, and spiritually. This is true for individuals, families, and whole societies. Conflict is an opportunity to learn and to be creative, and power is exercised in ways that empower rather than disempower others.

Societies modeled on the partnership blueprint can be very different from each other. Societies that orient more to this configuration—a democratic and egalitarian social structure, partnership between women and men, and less social acceptance of violence—transcend differences based on technological development and geography. For example, we find orientation to the partnership configuration today in some tribal societies and in the industrialized, technologically advanced Scandinavian nations. We find this same pattern in Western and Eastern prehistoric societies, as described in my work and in the work of scholars at the Chinese Academy of Social Sciences.[16] And if you look around, you can see movement everywhere toward family and social structures that are closer to the partnership than domination blueprint.

Domination and Overconsumption

Our present economic system comes out of more rigid dominator times when chieftains, kings, and feudal lords controlled not only economic resources but also the bulk of the population. The economic system we inherited from these times was a dominator system, beginning with the slave societies of the ancient world and later manifesting itself in serfdom and the turning of factory workers into mere cogs in the industrial machine for the benefit of those on top. A foundation of this kind of economic system is a family structure also based on economic domination—one in which women as well as children were seen as basically male possessions with their labor owned by the male head of household by law.

This system involved overconsumption by those on top, with scarcity for those on bottom. And to our day, to the degree that we continue to have a dominator system of economics be it capitalist or communist, this system depends largely on a cycle of overconsumption and wastefulness by some, exploitation of others, and environmental despoliation. This cycle is at the root of many environmental woes.

Overconsumption and waste by those on top is a perennial feature of dominator societies, whether preindustrial or industrial, ancient or modern. In these societies, conspicuous consumption is a symbol of power. And control over possessions and other humans is a substitute for the emotional and spiritual fulfillment missing from a system rooted in fear and force.

Today's mass marketing capitalizes on these unmet human needs by telling us that our yearning for love, fulfillment, and joy will be met if we buy and buy and consume and consume. In a Haagen-Dazs ad, Bernardette Peters practically has an orgasm eating ice cream. The implied promise of sex with gorgeous women or men is used to sell everything from soft drinks to cars. Love is promised in ads for deodorants and diamonds, and so forth. So the rich buy ever more costly luxury goods and the poor jam the aisles of discount stores to buy ever more gadgets.[17] And all these useless, even harmful, objects clutter up our planet, while depleting our finite natural resources.

We have to make people aware of how our most basic emotional needs are manipulated by commercial interests. Above all, we have to change the economic rules that encourage pathological cycles of overconsumption, exploitation, and environmental despoliation.

Dominator Economics

I want to emphasize that when we talk about dominator economics the issue is not bad people. It is bad economic rules — rules that come out of, and help maintain, dominator economic relations.

Certainly, some corporate executives are aware of the damage they cause, and deliberately conceal this knowledge as long as they think they can get away with it. There have been well-documented cases in the petrochemical, utilities, and other industries. The movie *Erin Brockovich* tells a true story. Pacific Gas & Electric executives deliberately deceived families about the health and environmental consequences of plant operations in their neighborhood. They said that an epidemic of failing health, including high rates of cancer and serious respiratory problems, had nothing to do with PG&E—until Ms. Brockovich exposed them. Bill Moyer's documentary *Trade Secrets* tells how executives at Dow Chemical, Chevron, Ethyl, Conoco, and other petrochemical giants deceived their employees. They never informed them of studies showing that working in petrochemical plants was slowly killing them, causing brain tumors, bone disintegration, and cancer.[18] As the tobacco company scandals demonstrate, unfortunately this kind of deception is not uncommon. And, more recently, the Enron scandals are showing how contaminated our entire economic system is by patterns of uncaring domination, deception, and exploitation.

Still, I believe that most people are well-meaning and would like to make a living for themselves and their children without causing harm to others. As the Buddha said, "Like a bee collecting nectar, one acquires wealth by harming none."[19] But all too often people are caught in dominator economic rules. And these rules effectively support psychological predispositions of denial and fear of change. They also support lack of empathy and compassion. And they make it difficult for people to meet their most basic needs for caring relationships.

For instance, current rules governing profits and losses for businesses do not include in the cost of manufacturing what economists call "externalities," such as the cost to our health and to our natural environment of many old industrial processes. Until we change these rules, we can't effectively curtail activities that pollute our air and water, since these activities are rewarded rather than penalized. People will continue to suppress their capacity for caring to function and survive within such an economic system.

One thing we need fundamentally is a different system of accounting. Calculations of profit and loss should include the cost to our environment and health caused by industrial processes and products. As it stands, consumers and taxpayers pay these costs, and there is little incentive for business to be more responsible. Taxes on "externalities" such as environmental and health damage, and tax credits for companies that change to more environmentally and socially responsible processes and products, can also make a huge difference.

Changing rules may seem a daunting prospect. But economic rules and business practices are human creations—and hence can be changed. We need rules that support relations of partnership/respect. We need corporate charters that require environmental and social responsibility. We need international treaties that protect nature. And we need new economic rules that recognize and accord real value to the work of caring and caregiving—including caring for Mother Earth.

We can promote partnership economic policies by talking with our friends and colleagues. We can start by pointing out that economic rules and business practices depend on human choices, and it's up to us to change the cultural values that determine these choices. We also can point out that technology itself is not the problem: the real issue is what kinds of technologies are funded, how they are developed, and how they are used.

We can further point out that while we hear a lot of rhetoric about meeting basic human need by caring and caregiving, since these activities are not economically valued, there is little social and economic support for them. So we have a vicious cycle of more overconsumption rather than meeting basic human needs.

Caregiving Has Value

In accordance with the valuations inherent in dominator cultural and economic systems, the work of caregiving that is essential for human survival and welfare is not even included in measures of economic productivity such as Gross National Product (GNP)—which instead counts work such as building and using weapons, making and selling cigarettes, and other activities that destroy rather than nurture life.[20]

Even when caregiving work is done for pay, the pay is much less than for work in other professions. Childcare workers, the people to whom you entrust your child, get lower wages than parking lot attendants, the people to whom you entrust your car. This makes absolutely no sense.

Why is the work of caregiving given so little economic value? We would be in very bad shape if our day-to-day needs for food, clean clothes, and a habitable place to live weren't cared for. There wouldn't even be a labor force to go to their jobs or businesses if it weren't for the work of caregiving. So clearly the reason this essential work is given little or no value has nothing to do with logic.

Again, to understand the devaluation of caring work, we have to look beyond logic to what has, and has not, been considered valuable in rigid dominator societies. Here we come back to the enormous impact of cultural beliefs and economic rules that we've inherited from more rigid dominator days.

A mainstay for the domination model of relations is the ranking of the male half of humanity over the female half. We see this in both religious and secular traditions, including Buddhism, which is today trying to break free from this cultural heritage. But this heritage has led to the devaluing of anything stereotypically associated with women, including the "women's work" of caring and caregiving. The results were economic systems—tribal, feudal, capitalist, and communist—that give little or no value to the work of caring and caregiving.

Obviously both men and women are able to give care. Some men do so better than some women. But according to the belief system we've inherited, this work is unfit for "real men." In rigid dominator societies, caregiving is supposed to be done by women for free in male-controlled households. It's simply taken for granted as men's due, like the air they breathe, so it has no visibility.

Caregiving work, particularly mothering, is sometimes idealized in rhetoric, as in the American myth of "motherhood and apple pie." But in reality, mothering is not valued. For example, in programs to aid families with dependent children, no economic value whatsoever is given to the work of caregiving. Professions that involve caregiving such as childcare and elementary school teaching, where women predominate, are typically lower paid than those where caring and caregiving are not integral to the work, such as plumbing and engineering, jobs in which men predominate. Workers in childcare centers often still work for minimum wages, with no benefits.

As is characteristic of dominator mindsets, current economic rules and practices are heavily based on denial. They are based on the systematic denial that caregiving has tangible economic value, that it is in fact the most indispensably valuable human activity. These rules are also based on another characteristic dominator bias: stereotypically masculine activities are given greater attention in education and economics than stereotypically feminine ones.

So we have been taught to think it strange to have government-funded training and pensions for those who perform the "women's work" of caring for children and the sick. And we're still taught this—even though high-quality caregiving is essential for children's welfare and development. Of course, this is illogical. It's also inhuman. It prevents us from imbuing our lives and our communities with what we all want—more caring.

Building Caring Homes, Workplaces, and Communities

Politicians give us catchy slogans like "a more gentle, caring world" and "compassionate conservatism." But when it comes to caring for children, for the sick, the elderly, and the homeless, their policies are far from caring.

And why would these policies be caring when the devaluation of the "women's work" of caring and caregiving is deeply embedded not only in our unconscious minds but in the economic rules and models most politicians unconsciously accept? How realistic is it to talk about a more equitable economic system as long as the indispensable, life-sustaining caring work is given a lot of lip service but few if any economic incentives or rewards? Indeed, how can we seriously talk of more caring communities, when we continue to go along with these old dominator rules?

Take a moment to consider all the pain you would have been spared if everyone around you had learned to truly value caring. Think of all the pleasure you would have had if everyone learned the skills for caring and caregiving. Think of what kind of communities, and what kind of world, we would have if we really gave value in our education and our economics to caring and caregiving.

But can we seriously talk about providing better care for children as long as childcare is paid so little in the labor market, and caregiving at home is not given any economic value at all? Is this a realistic expectation? What needs to change so that caregiving work is no longer systematically devalued? And what needs to change so that people can meet their basic human needs for caring connections rather than trying to compensate through overconsumption?

Overconsumption As Compensation

The issue of consumption is usually framed around personal choices in the marketplace. These are important and it is true that every purchase we make is a vote for the kind of society we live in. But we need to look deeper at the underlying dynamics that drive these choices and make it so difficult for people to break with habitual patterns of consumption.

As we have briefly explored, overconsumption is rooted in a system of domination we inherited. If we want to change behaviors, we have to also change the institutions and beliefs that guide them. This means working to accelerate the movement to the partnership model across the board—beginning with the foundational parent-child and woman-man relations that are distorted so that we do not get our basic needs for caring adequately met. We also need to work on the larger economic and political institutions, as well as our system of values and beliefs.

A primary step is to promote economic inventions that give real value to caring and caregiving. We already have a few, such as parental leave, pioneered in the more partnership-oriented Scandinavian world. But we need many more. It is peculiar that our schools teach everything except the essential life skills of caring. For example, I propose in my book *Tomorrow's Children,* that caring for life—for self, others, and our Mother Earth—be a thread running through the educational curriculum from preschool to graduate school. It should be an integral part of every child's education.

When we begin to value caring and caregiving not just rhetorically but economically, we will be creating the conditions where people's emotional needs can be met much more effectively than through overconsumption in the marketplace. We will also be creating the conditions where everyone's basic physical needs are met. Because empathy and caring will no longer be distorted and suppressed by dominator beliefs and rules, we will leave behind the misdistribution of resources characteristic of dominator economics. And because people thrive mentally, emotionally, and physically when they are cared for, we will be creating a much more truly productive economy.

A New Economics to Save the Earth:
A Buddhist Perspective

by Shinichi Inoue
translated by Duncan Ryuken Williams

THE WEST AND THE EAST developed rather different ideas on money and the economy. In the West, money has been viewed from one of two extremes. On the one hand, based on egocentric greed, there has been a tradition of uninhibited pursuit of money. But on the other hand, an extremely negative evaluation of moneymaking appears in such texts as Shakespeare's *The Merchant of Venice*, where money lending and money itself is viewed with suspicion. Buddhism, or the "Middle Way," which is found mainly in the East, disavows extremes and advocates a moderate view of materialism that allows for basic economic subsistence, but at the same time prohibits materialistic indulgences. The goal in a Buddhist approach to economics is, therefore, to provide for the basic comfort of all beings, not just oneself.

But this economic goal of creating wealth for both oneself and for others is, in fact, a part of a long tradition in economic theory. Adam Smith (1723–1790), the so-called father of modern economics, began to develop an economics coupled with morality. We often have an image of Smith, through his *The Wealth of Nations,* advocating a laissez-faire economics unhampered by morality. His book, believed by many to be the Bible of economics, also contains the popular axiom that as each economic player, whether as individuals or as companies, acts for his or her own self-interest, wealth will naturally increase and society as a whole will prosper. Though at first his theory seems to be simply an economics of egocentric desires, in fact, Smith's earlier work *The Theory of Moral Sentiments* connects self-interest with morality. For him, morality comes not from God, but from "reason" and "conscience."

Although Smith sought to conjoin morality and economic activity, he knew that being materially comfortable—which for him included good health and freedom from debt and bad conscience—involved competition. He was also aware of the drawbacks of competition in that people, when caught in the endless fervor of competition, can become warped and miserable as their aim shifts from affluence to the pursuit of more profit, or simply to competition for competition's sake. For example, towards the end of Smith's lifetime when the Industrial Revolution was in full force, landlords drove peasants off the land, pushing them to the cities where, instead of finding good health and freedom from all debts and worries, the workers found themselves struggling to eke out an existence amid heightening competition.

But Smith believed that this "myth of competition" was crucial to economic growth. He truly believed that as more wealth was created in an economy, more and more people would be able to secure happiness. This "myth of competition," though, has fortunately been questioned by Smith's successors starting with J.S. Mills (1806–1873), Alfred Marshall (1842–1924), on down to J.M. Keynes (1883–1946), all of whom have emphasized more strongly the tradition of connecting economic activity with morality.

The British economist Joan Robinson (1903–1983) once said that the purpose of studying economics is to learn how not to be fooled by the myths of economics. We ought to take up her challenge to reevaluate our basic approach to economics as we stand at the pinnacle of the new millennium. The greatest challenge we face as a human race today is the environmental crisis that has been, in no small part, engendered by our previous economic activity. We have increasingly come to see that if developing nations grow in the same fashion as the so-called First World nations, the world's environment will be completely destroyed. Further, if people in the already industrialized countries continue their culture of consumption, the result will be the same. Although we have, since the late nineteenth century, relied on science and technology to deal with problems such as the environmental one, is not the fundamental problem a moral one, a question of how to reduce our seemingly uncontrollable appetite for consumption? How might we build a sustainable economics, a zero-emissions society?

Capitalism Made in Japan: A Buddhist Approach to Economics

As a Japanese, to answer the above questions, it is appropriate to reflect on moral and philosophical resources from the ancient tradition of Buddhism in order to develop a new economics, a new capitalism. The life story of the Buddha is itself a very valuable lesson as we ponder the theme of Buddhist economics. Buddhism is sometimes called the "Middle Way" because the Buddha rejected the two extremes of asceticism and the indulgence of desire. Though he refused to be seduced by the material comforts of a royal life, he also realized the futility of asceticism and the denial of natural physical needs. Thus, he walked a fine line between materialism and denial of the world, and this middle way, or moderate standpoint, is fundamental to Buddhist economics. Though immediately after his death, many of the Buddha's disciples tended to be conservative and some even elitist, as time went on, a more inclusive school called the Mahayana tradition, which emphasized the salvation of not only monks but laypeople as well, developed.

This broader Mahayana tradition came to Japan in the form of Buddhist scriptures and teachers from mainland East Asia. One of the first proponents of Buddhism in Japan was Prince Shotoku (574–622). Considered the author of the first Japanese constitution, his "Seventeen-Article Constitution" includes Buddhist ideas such as harmony and religious tolerance (particularly between Shinto and Buddhism) as well as caring for the welfare of all, including the poorest people in the nation.

During this period, Buddhism came to rely heavily on the support of the merchant classes. Its teachings, having an ethical, but positive view of money-making, encouraged merchant support throughout the medieval period. By the Tokugawa era (1600–1868), Japan entered a period characterized by ever-increasing levels of economic production and the widespread development of a monetary economy. The American Japanologist Edwin O. Reischauer (1910–1990) describes this period as the one in which Japan developed its own version of capitalism. Another student of this period, the sociologist Robert Bellah, has found parallels between the Weberian Protestant work ethic and capitalism and the rise of Japanese capitalism of this period.

One of the key figures in this made-in-Japan capitalism was a Buddhist monk, Suzuki Shosan (1579–1655). He believed that each man's work—regardless of what he does—is deeply worthwhile and is itself a pathway to Enlightenment. He is remembered for his words: "Those who are engaged in economic activity must derive profit from their endeavors through working as if the work itself was spiritual practice." Suzuki encouraged merchants to reflect on their spiritual lives, to be honest in their dealings, and to develop the mind of a bodhisattva, a being who cares for and saves other beings. If his many merchant adherents sincerely persevered in such spiritual practices, he said, they would all be assured of a spiritual life and would also be financially rewarded—a view reminiscent of the Protestant work ethic. And just as a bodhisattva is a being free from all attachments, he encouraged merchants to freely engage in economic activity without regard to class or borders, perhaps an important lesson for us as we enter an ever-increasing global economy. Like Smith, Suzuki must have believed that if individual merchants conducted their business with moral principles, the society as a whole would benefit.

Another important figure in the development of Japanese capitalism was Rennyo (1415–1499), the "second founder" of the Jodo Shinshu sect of Pure Land Buddhism. He is said to have given merchants the advice: "When engaged in business, do it as the work of the Buddha." This advice was followed by the merchants across Japan, but particularly in the Ohmi (Shiga) and Osaka regions, where Rennyo's teachings had a strong influence. Even today, firms that started in that area, such as Itochu, one of the top Japanese trading companies, have prospered by adopting this philosophical approach in their business dealings.

The Zero-Emissions Society of the Tokugawa Period

As mentioned above, Japanese capitalism began in the Tokugawa period. But the capitalism of that period was, unlike today, characterized by both economic and environmental sustainability despite requiring the basic capital and natural resources necessary for a growing economy. Though it would be natural to think that a resource-poor nation like Japan requires a sustainable, zero-emissions society, in the modern period, Japan has adopted a mass production model that creates tremendous waste. We might therefore look back upon the Tokugawa period for clues on how to build a society in the future.

The Tokugawa period was headed by the Tokugawa shogunate based in the capital city of Edo (present-day Tokyo). The shogunate, or the military government, feared the growing influence of the Western powers in their region as they saw one Asian country after another being colonized both politically by Spain, Portugal, and other Western powers and spiritually by Christian missionaries. Thus the government instituted a "closed country policy" restricting foreign trade to the Dutch and only through the single port city of Nagasaki. Within the context of this rather insular society, the capital city of

Edo was the focal point for the expansion of the domestic economy as the government instituted a policy which required the regional governors to move back and forth between the capital and the provinces. Thus began the ever-increasing movement of personnel, goods, money, and the economy more generally.

Though agriculture was, at that time, still the center of economic life, the sustainable model of economics developed in the capital city of Edo, which was one of the world's most populated cities at that time, spread as the provinces became increasingly interconnected. The zero-emissions economy developed as the following policies and customs took root: (1) Human waste from household toilets was collected periodically and sold to farmers from the outlying regions who used it for fertilizer. The payment was often made in the form of vegetable produce and this practice continued until World War II; (2) Well water was the primary form of water usage and was efficiently distributed using wooden pipes; (3) While most garbage was incinerated by the city, much of the resulting ash was recycled back as fertilizer for household use; (4) To make products last longer, a wide array of repair businesses (from tobacco utensils to large furniture) developed; (5) Waste water was not directed to the river, but treated naturally by letting it seep into the ground. These practices from the Edo period continued in modern Japan through such entrepreneurs as Shuzo Nishihara, who headed a research institute (Nishihara Eisei Kenkyujo, founded in 1916) that developed recycling techniques to turn raw sewage from major urban centers into fertilizer.

At the base of all of these principles of a sustainable economy is the idea of *"mottainai."* This word in Japanese includes both the meaning of being in awe of nature as well as being thankful for its blessings, which give rise to the concept of "not wasting." These ideas have their root in the Buddhist teaching that all beings, and even inanimate objects, have life and Buddha-nature.

The Essence of Buddhist Economics

It is generally well-known that economics as a field of study includes both natural science and humanities approaches. However, mainstream economics, as symbolized in Nobel Economics Prize winners for example, has tended to be heavily dominated by the Anglo-American quantitative, econometric paradigm. While more humanistic approaches have been offered by such Nobel Prize winners as Gunnar Myrdal and Friedrich von Hayek, they have not been accepted by the mainstream. However, an economics which focuses almost exclusively on quantitative analysis cannot possibly reveal to us a way to develop a more sustainable culture. Buddhist economics, therefore, must emphasize the human element, the vicissitudes of the human heart, in the economic equation in order to develop a new economics that can save the Earth.

Several key ideas form the basis of Buddhist economics. The first is the idea that in economics one can "benefit oneself and others" simultaneously. Though the phrase "benefiting oneself and others" comes from Shinran (1173–1263), the founder of the Jodo Shinshu sect of Pure Land Buddhism, the notion of self-gain occurring simultaneously with the benefit of others is a broader Buddhist doctrine. For example, the medieval Zen master Dogen (1200–1253) wrote, "In accomplishing the Way, there is no distinction between self and other." Here Dogen is talking about Buddhist practice, but if we think about economics through his words, can we not envision an economics in which profit is not exclusively a personal matter, but a collective one that does not distinguish between self and other? This idea of collective or mutually-benefiting economics was something E.F. Schumacher picked up in his days in Myanmar and wrote about in the chapter "Buddhist Economics" in his best-seller *Small Is Beautiful*.

However, can such a concept really function in a capitalist society? One good example of someone who used this idea and made it work is none other than Henry Ford (1863–1947), the "king of the automobile industry." A typical capitalist of his age, Ford recognized that pure self-interest in automobile production would involve hiring labor as cheaply as possible and selling the products as expensively as possible. However, despite the business ethic common at the time, he went one step further and realized that everyone—from worker to customer to society—could profit if he paid workers high enough wages so that they themselves could afford to buy automobiles, at the same time keeping the costs of the cars down through mass production. In line with Walt Rostow's concept of "mass consumption," Ford's approach to economics did provide a mutually-beneficially economics for his time.

A Japanese example would be Tadao Yoshida (b. 1908), the founder of YKK, well-known for its production of fasteners and zippers. He was famous in industry circles as a diligent and thrifty businessman, and earned a reputation for directing most of his profits toward making innovations in the design of his products and simultaneously making his products more affordable. He called this flow of capital "the circulation of good works" and made his commitment to quality and affordability a fundamental company policy. Eventually, his company became the leading fastener-maker with a worldwide reputation.

The second key idea in Buddhist economics is "an economics of tolerance and peace." One distinguishing feature of Buddhism as a religion is that it has never directly engaged in a religious war. While other religions have similar ethical principles, an emphasis on peace is based on the first ethical precept of Buddhism: Do not kill. Although we witnessed in World War II a degree of complicity with the war on the part of some Buddhists, and some justification offered by Zen teachers for killing in the Samurai era, for the most part Buddhism appears to be one of the few religions to have actually put into practice the precept of *ahimsa* (or non-harming), made famous by Gandhi's nonviolence movement.

One example of this economics of peace can be seen in India in the third century B.C.E., during the reign of Ashoka, the third emperor of the Mauryan dynasty that unified the land. The misery and suffering brought upon all those who fought in the wars of unification caused the emperor to reevaluate the idea of conquest by the sword. Drawn increasingly toward Buddhist beliefs, he felt that in order to govern he needed to publicly atone for all the killing done during the wars, though in a religiously tolerant way. He embarked on the experiment of creating a peaceful nation by first creating the conditions necessary for domestic stability. Because Ashoka believed that poverty eroded the social fabric, one of his first acts was to fund social welfare and other public projects, such as road construction.

In Japan, this sentiment toward an economics of peace has been expressed most forcefully by an eminent Buddhist scholar who has stated that as a Buddhist country, Japan should not engage in trade with countries that produce and sell weapons of war. Though this perspective is surely a minority one, the tradition of a Buddhist approach to peace has a long history in Japan. For example, in 792, despite constant threats from the Korean Peninsula, Emperor Kammu (r. 781–806), basing his actions on Buddhist principles, abolished the hundred-year-old national army, save for one regiment to guard the region near Korea. In its stead, the sons of local clan leaders maintained local security forces somewhat similar to the present-day police. In addition, from the beginning of the ninth century, the death penalty was abolished for nearly three and a half centuries, and Japan was effectively without an army until the emergence of the new warrior class before the Kamakura shogunate (1192–1333). Mahatma

Gandhi often talked about the creation of a peacekeeping force (Shanti Seva), and an early prototype could be seen in Japan a thousand years earlier.

An Economics that Respects the Environment

At the end of each year, *Time* magazine selects a "Man of the Year" to feature in a special edition. In 1989, however, the magazine broke with tradition and instead selected Earth as the "Planet of the Year." In this issue were numerous articles highlighting ways to improve international cooperation in response to the environmental crisis. Among the articles, there was an article, remarkable to me, which quoted a U.S. senator suggesting that certain interpretations of the Bible may have played a role in abusing the Earth through its seemingly anthropocentric view of human domination over other creatures. Certainly if we look at the Bible, we find passages such as Genesis 1:27–28:

> So God created male and female in his own image, in the image
> of God. And God blessed them, and said unto them: "Be fruit-
> ful, and multiply, and replenish the Earth and subdue it; and have
> dominion over the fish of the sea, and over the fowl of the air,
> and over every living thing that moveth upon the Earth."

Although there are many ways to decipher this, it isn't surprising that some people have interpreted passages such as this one literally: they see it as giving divine sanction to dominate the Earth for the benefit of human beings inasmuch as they are superior to all other creatures on Earth.

Buddhist sacred texts may be somewhat more modest on behalf of humans, as revealed in phrases such as *Issai shujo bussho ari, somoku kokudo mina jobutsu,* which suggest that plants, trees, and sentient beings, and even non-sentient beings, are equally bound up in the nature of the Buddha or cosmic life itself. For example, the Great Buddha in the ancient temple of Todaiji in Nara is depicted sitting on a large lotus flower. If you inspect the petals of the flower closely, you will see that they are covered with small Buddha images, implying that the Great Buddha (or the cosmos) includes all the small Buddhas (such as human beings and other living things) in its vastness. In other words, humans and other living creatures coexist to maintain the cosmos, and the cosmos in turn supports them.

In the Buddhist view, human beings, rather than being masters of the Earth, simply make up one tiny element in a vast cosmos. Though the culture of the twentieth century has been characterized by the destruction of the environment to fulfill human greed, in the twenty-first century, we will come to regret what we have done to the Earth and must learn to respect the bounty that it provides for us.

These three key ideas of Buddhist economics — "an economics to benefit both self and other," "an economics of peace," and "an economics to save the Earth" — form the foundations for a sustainable society for the new millennium.

Work, Play, and Consumption

The Western attitude toward work can perhaps be summed up by the phrase "work is pain," or to use the words of the popular Buddhist commentator Sachiya Hiro, "work is punishment." One Genesis account of Adam and Eve being driven out of the Garden of Eden and made to work suggests that the ideal world is a world without work.

The Buddhist view of work is that it is an integral part of Buddhist life. The Buddha recognized this by highlighting "livelihood" as one of the components of his eightfold path of practice. The Buddhist scriptures also use the phrase "playful *samadhi*" or a liberative, joyous meditation to describe the way in which a Buddhist practitioner works. In other words, work and play are not two separate spheres, as in the West, but are intertwined in an unbroken thread. In Japan, for instance, even the busiest of people — such as the emperor himself — will find time to compose playful *waka* poems, engage in agricultural harvest festivals, or fold birds or flowers out of paper (*origami,* a popular children's activity).

But the Western view of work has spread throughout the world and has been responsible for the idea of working to consume more and more things or, as Rostow suggests, an ideal of a mass consumption society. But this shift into a mass production and mass consumption society has worried people like Ragnar Nurkse (1907–1959) who have feared the effects of such a culture and exponential growth it presumes on the predominantly agricultural nations of Buddhist Asia. Schumacher, too, had his worries about how the cultural fabric might be broken if Buddhists lost their positive view of work and exchanged it for a view of work as hardship or burden. Work, he suggests, must lead to the kind of consumption, not of the mass consumption variety, that can ensure the happiness of others in the community. This approach to work and consumption is based on the consideration of others, including nature, and can be the basis of a stable and sustainable economy, rather than one that has quick growth spurts and dips and destroys the environment in the process.

An Economics of Simplicity

There is a phrase in the medieval Zen master Dogen's writings: *shoyoku chisoku*, to lessen desires and know it's enough. In the West, the general orientation has been to attain happiness by increasing wealth so that one can get more of what one desires. In contrast, Buddhism emphasizes the happiness that comes from being detached from desires, i.e., happiness is increased by reducing our desires.

In the Tokugawa period when Japanese capitalism began to flourish, as money began to circulate in ever larger amounts, there were those who flaunted their wealth with lavish gold accessories or flashy clothes. As economies develop, displaying wealth and grandeur seems to come as part of the package. However, not only are there social and environmental consequences of excessive consumption, but Buddhism suggests that true happiness cannot come without reducing the desire to gain and display more wealth. Buddhist economics is an economics of simplicity. Just as an impressively large gas-guzzling limo symbolizes excess, surely what we really need is a simpler and smaller, more fuel-efficient and non-polluting vehicle that can drive us to a more sustainable and brighter future.

The Practice of Generosity

by Stephen Batchelor

ENEROSITY IS CENTRAL to Buddhist practice and manifests in many ways: giving of material support to those in need; giving of spiritual advice to those in despair; giving of love to those who are abandoned; or giving of protection to those who are threatened. Beginning with the recognition that they are not yet generous, Buddhists engage in a way of life that cultivates generosity. The practice of Buddhism is an ethical, psychological, and philosophical challenge to the habit of selfishness. It embraces the whole of one's life, is humbly aware of one's mortality, and aims at contentment for oneself and others.

The first questions are those arising from the unavoidable facts of birth, sickness, aging, and death, concerning the nature, origins, and transcendence of which Buddhists seek enlightenment. Buddhists all over the world follow both the example of the historical Buddha, as well as that of subsequent teachers, to find a way to reach such enlightenment. These ways and the philosophies that underlie them differ according to the cultures in which the traditions have arisen. Gautama, the historical Buddha, emphasized the importance of both self-reliance and pragmatism in defining one's own practice. Historically, the major developments in Buddhist thought and practice have come about as responses to the specific demands of new situations. Today, as Buddhism encounters a world transformed by science and technology, it is challenged to draw on its insights in a way that responds effectively to the crises of our times while remaining true to the values of its traditions.

The task of Buddhists is to create, sustain, and exemplify a way of living that embodies Buddhist values. This is particularly important at a time when religious and spiritual values—simplicity, generosity, and kindness—are seen by many as irrelevant to tackling the world's problems. Buddhists have the responsibility not only to keep alive but also to make the flame of such values burn more brightly.

The principal Buddhist values are concerned with directing one's life around the Buddha, the Dharma, and the Sangha. "Buddha" refers to the state of wisdom and compassion realized by Buddha Gautama who lived in India around the sixth century B.C.E., and subsequently by his followers. The realization of such wisdom and compassion is a possibility open to all human beings—irrespective of their social position, sex, race, etc. As long as there exist people in the world who personify these values, Buddhism can be said to be a living spiritual tradition.

The way of life the Buddha personified and taught is the "Dharma." Two and a half thousand years ago Gautama taught that temporary material welfare is not the be all and end all of human existence; that the aim of human life is the transformation of the individual from a self-centered, greed-driven way of being to one that is other-centered and greed-free. For change to be genuine, it must begin with an authentic change in the human heart. The Dharma is the way whereby Buddhists seek to realize such change. It is revealed in words through the recorded teachings of the Buddha and his interpreters and through experience by the actualization of those instructions in one's own life. Although Buddhist practices vary from tradition to tradition, they are all concerned with effecting such a liberating transformation of the individual.

"Sangha," the third central value in Buddhism, means "community." The realization of the wisdom and compassion taught by the Buddha is not a solitary affair but one grounded in living relationships with those likewise committed to such a way of life. In a narrow sense, "Sangha" refers to the communities of ordained monks and nuns, i.e., those who symbolize the values of Buddhism by their very vocation. In a broader, practical sense it refers to those around one—friends, teachers, colleagues—who affirm and clarify one's spiritual values. And in the widest sense, such a community encompasses all living beings, implying that the potential for wisdom and compassion are present in every relationship into which one enters, and that all human beings can turn from delusion and greed towards enlightenment and detachment.

The Buddhist view of the kind of world we live in is based on an understanding of the nature and origin of suffering. The suffering we experience has its origin in the delusion of perceiving oneself as an isolated and independent being, existing in a world of isolated independent things. Such a sense of separation of oneself from the world is the basis for the innate belief that by amassing quantities of things which one associates with pleasure, one will eventually secure a lasting and stable happiness. This is the assumption from whence greed develops into an insatiable habit. It has as its corollary aversion to whatever is seen to stand in the way to such happiness. Since this selfishness and greed are based on an irrational basis (although this may be supported by sophisticated rationalizations), to undermine it requires spiritual practice. Adopting a worldview that sees life in this way will help, but without committed practice will have little effect on habitually entrenched ways of behavior. Buddhism seeks a middle way between the extremes of sensual indulgence and life-denying asceticism.

To lead fulfilled lives, human beings require the provision of basic necessities: nutritious food, warm and dry housing, adequate clothing, medical care, etc. It is only when one is driven by the insatiable demands of greed to believe that additional wants to these are in fact needs, that problems begin. Buddhism criticizes consumerism on precisely these grounds: that the level of greed is stimulated to a degree that is not only unnecessary to meet one's needs but, contrary to its avowed claim to bring happiness, actually increases dissatisfaction, frustration, and suffering. Moreover, such a lifestyle is damaging to the natural environment, leads to exploitation of the underprivileged, and in the long term is unsustainable.

At the time of the Buddha, the simple fact of accumulating wealth did not entail large-scale environmental destruction or social injustice. The Buddhist approach emphasizes enhancing the quality of life without damaging either the present environment or the prospects of others. This is not an appeal to poverty, but rather the advocating of simplicity—a quality that becomes increasingly attractive the more one's life accords to the values taught by the Buddha. Traditionally, Buddhism spoke of greed, aversion, and delusion as the three mental poisons. In Asian agrarian economies, such poisons could largely be contained within the immediate environment of human beings. Now it is as though they have spilled beyond the borders of the human mind to poison, quite literally, the Earth, the seas and rivers, the very air we breathe. A Buddhist economic agenda therefore emphasizes a profound reevaluation of needs over wants.

Action in Buddhism is understood by the often-misconstrued term "karma." Work, or labor, as forms of action, is therefore to be understood in the context of Buddhist teachings on karma. The primary value of any action lies in its ethical consequences. For the way we act determines not only the future quality of life but also establishes the tendencies and habits which influence subsequent behavior. Far from being a doctrine of fate, the teaching on karma insists on the centrality of choice. On many occasions the Buddha defined "action" as "intention." But this does not mean that the value of an action is subjectively determined solely by the quality of one's intentions. Action is ethically evaluated by the entire context in which it takes place: the intentions behind it, its impact on others, the nature of the act itself, as well as whether or not it reaches completion. Meaningful work, therefore, is that which is both freely chosen and entered into with a sense of ethical responsibility.

As principles of action, there are five basic ethical precepts in Buddhism: Refraining from (1) killing, (2) stealing, (3) sexual misconduct, (4) lying, and (5) intoxication. These could also be interpreted as a framework for developing an understanding of economic activity. To refrain from intentionally taking life has implications from agricultural policy to military spending. From a Buddhist perspective harmlessness should characterize all relations between people and all relations between humans and nature. To refrain from stealing invites a reflection on the conservation of scarce resources for the benefit of others, including future generations, whose absence from today's markets cannot be interpreted as silent consent for high rates of present consumption. As the world's population grows and its natural resources are depleted, to refrain from sexual misconduct demands that individuals and governments accept responsibility for planning the size of the global family. Refraining from unskillful speech condemns the deliberate stimulation of desires by, for example, high-pressure advertising, and the unrealistic raising of economic expectations. Likewise, to refrain from intoxication cautions against allowing consumer spending to become either a personal addiction or the single criterion for macroeconomic success.

Although traditionally phrased in terms of restraint, the precepts implicitly encourage the positive virtues of cherishing life, respecting the property of others, maintaining sexual integrity, being honest and truthful in one's dealings with others, and valuing clarity and coherence of consciousness. Generosity, as the preeminent Buddhist virtue, is both a spontaneous expression of selfless, impartial concern for the well-being of others, and a deliberate means of enhancing the quality of one's own life. Melford Spiro, in his study of Buddhism in rural Burmese society, observes that the formal practice of generosity—particularly religious giving—is a powerful motive for work and for moderating one's own personal consumption. As savings are "invested" in religious generosity rather than in risky capital accumulation, the rate of economic growth is held in check.

Taken to extremes, this could prove an obstacle to economic development; the Buddha's advice, cited below, concerning the optimal proportions of saving, spending and reinvesting, and donating one's income can thus be seen as a wise counterbalance. Foregoing excessive present consumption in favor of long-term investment in environmental assets is an act of generosity to future generations. Generosity between nations, rich to poor, reduces inequalities in economic growth. As exemplified by the Edicts of King Ashoka, one of the classical virtues of a good king or government is to implement a compassionate welfare policy towards the most disadvantaged members of society. Finally, generosity is included among the *havatthu* (qualities which make for Sangha integration) or social cohesion, together with *atthaeariya* (voluntary service)—so that paid and voluntary work are of equal value—and *samanattata* (equality, impartiality, and participation).

Buddhism recognizes that a life committed to the ending of suffering involves far more than just personal transformation through silent contemplation. Although such contemplation may be the preeminent value in Buddhist life, the Buddha understood that to be meaningful, even possible, it requires a philosophical and ethical context. And as part of this ethical context, he spoke of "Right Livelihood." Traditionally, right livelihood has been explained as avoiding those kinds of work that evidently entail harm being caused to oneself and others: e.g., working as a slaughterer, an arms-manufacturer, a publican, a dealer in poisons, or a trader in human life.

Today, however, as we live and work in a world of far greater complexity, where the apparently simple acts of buying and selling have repercussions on people's lives around the world, the ethics of right livelihood must be accordingly reevaluated. The implications of even driving a car or drinking a cup of coffee have social, environmental, and economic consequences far beyond the limits of our immediate experience, which we are morally obliged to take into account. From this perspective, inner spiritual transformation is just as dependent upon the effect of our economic life upon the world as transformations in the world are dependent upon spiritual re-orientation. Buddhism holds that economic behavior is a manifestation of social attitudes, and these in turn reflect social values. The ideal social values are the four qualities termed *brahmavihara*, the sublime states of:

1) loving kindness, the wish for the welfare and happiness of others;

2) compassion, empathy with those afflicted with suffering;

3) sympathetic joy, rejoicing in the success and happiness of others; and

4) equanimity, the capacity to regard all beings equally, free from favoritism and bias.

Although originally taught as exercises in meditation, they can also be viewed as positing the ideal relationships that the individual should establish with his or her fellows in society. As applied to economics, they imply an order where competition and exploitation are replaced by cooperation in the pursuit of shared goals and the alleviation of misery. The Buddha himself did not speak at length about the actual tasks of social change or economic reform. On many occasions, however, the Pali Canon—the earliest record of the Buddha's teaching—records his giving advice about how to conduct one's economic relationships in a way that accorded with the Dharma. He said that in his or her work, a Buddhist should be energetic, industrious, diligent, skillful, proficient, and prudent. People should protect their earnings, keep good company, and live within their means. Wealth, he taught, provided that it is lawfully obtained, brings four kinds of happiness: economic security; having enough to spend generously on oneself and others; the peace of mind that accompanies freedom from debt; and the leading of a blameless life. Meeting one's material responsibilities to family, friends, and employees is emphasized. Instead of squandering or hoarding wealth, a quarter should be used for consumption, a quarter saved for an emergency, and a half used for one's business—a very high rate of reinvestment if taken literally.

From such examples, it is clear that Buddhist ethics are not antagonistic to the development of material prosperity. Right Livelihood is as much concerned with the spirit in which work is done as with the economic results of the work. Such livelihood would seek to create in the workplace an atmosphere of kindness and cooperation, mindfulness and generosity, where not only the workers' material requirements are catered to but also their spiritual needs. The quality of work should reflect the spirit in which it is done. The challenge, especially in a competitive, free-market economy, is to find a balance between making enough to live on and sustaining a workplace that is spiritually nourishing.

The key to understanding economic activity from a Buddhist perspective is the recognition of the interrelatedness of all things, traditionally addressed through the doctrine of "Co-dependent Emergence" (*pratitya samutpada*). Suffering comes about both through the individual and collective failure to understand this fact and the construction of a distorted sense of reality that assumes that living beings and things are intrinsically unrelated. The frequently misunderstood doctrines of "nonself" and "emptiness" are pointing not to some transcendent void, entirely disconnected from the concerns of the world, but to the absence of a fictitious world of discrete, reified entities. The concept of emptiness *(sunyata)* is a means to realize that one's limited ego is not the inescapable center of the world in constant battle with other egos competing for the same impossible preeminence, but part of a network of relationships upon which it depends for its own unique identity. The ethical implications of emptiness likewise do not lead to world-denial but to compassionate participation in the plight of others, with whom one empathetically recognizes a shared destiny.

Buddhism invites us to consider its claim that acquisitiveness originates as much in the root insecurity and anxiety of the human being as it does in physical needs. This is amply illustrated both by the conspicuous consumption throughout history of wealthy, privileged yet nonetheless discontented minorities, as well as by the compulsive behavior found in our present affluent societies. The habit of acquisitiveness is sustained by delusion: psychological entrapment in the fantasy of lasting happiness being achievable through the acquisition of material goods, money, status, etc. The impossibility of unlimited acquisitive growth in a world of finite resources is unlikely ever to be accepted by people still attached to the illusion that final happiness is found through compulsive acquisition—precisely the illusion fostered by the powerful worldwide advertising industry. Whether Buddhists see the need for a specifically Buddhist economic theory depends on a clear understanding not only of Buddhism but also of economic theory. One view is that mainstream economic theory is in itself "value free" and able to incorporate and reflect any system of values, including a Buddhist one. An alternative view is that mainstream economic theory is inherently unable to reflect adequately the Buddhist "practice of generosity," for instance, as part of economic activity.

Buddhism emphasizes the need to relate all human activity, including labor, to a daily practice which can enable individuals to understand their interrelatedness with every manifestation of the conditions around them and hence to find contentment at a truer level of experience. This practice is an ongoing challenge to greed, hatred, and delusion, since such traits of mind preclude recognition of the interconnectedness of all life by reinforcing the individual's sense of isolation. The resultant view of life leads to a diminution of personal wants and to a higher valuation of simplicity for its own sake.

Given its view of the power of delusion and greed to dominate and corrupt the human mind, Buddhism is certainly not optimistic about a sane ordering of the world and has for the most part resisted positing a utopian vision. Traditionally, this view has led to reluctance by Buddhists to involve themselves too closely with social and political change. But now it is simply a question of trying to save the world from the disastrous consequences of delusion and greed run amok. Today Buddhism is presented with the challenge to make its wisdom accessible for the world as a whole. In his book *Small Is Beautiful* the economist E.F. Schumacher included a chapter on Buddhist Economics which he concluded with the words: "It is a question of finding the right path of development, the Middle Way between materialist heedlessness and traditionalist immobility, in short, of finding Right Livelihood." Such an approach is associated with the emergence in recent decades, both in Asia and the West, of an eco-socially engaged Buddhism, which seeks to combine the work of transforming social structures and processes with the ancient practices of mindfulness and meditation, in a single mutually supportive spiritual practice. It seeks, for example, to combine the wisdom of personal insight into our restless acquisitive itch with a compassionate nonviolent social activism aimed at transforming the institutions of delusion and acquisitiveness.

It would be arrogant to claim that the views expressed here would be shared by all people who call themselves Buddhists. For Buddhism is a rich and diverse set of traditions, between which there have existed and continue to exist a wide range of tensions. There are many Buddhists who would place primary emphasis on the value of adhering to time-honored traditions of doctrinal interpretation and spiritual practice, while others would lay greater stress on the need to reinterpret and modify traditional thought and practice to make the Dharma more accessible to the modern world. Yet most would agree that Buddhism is more of a practice than a creed, a way of life that emphasizes the possibility of spiritual experience rather than dogmatic adherence to the letter of sacred texts. Buddhists are fully aware of how grandiose solutions to the world's problems fail to appreciate the complexity of concrete situations, which by their nature are rooted in a network of relationships that the unenlightened mind only dimly perceives. Yet through their practice of ethics, meditation, and wisdom, Buddhists also understand that generosity is not an option but an imperative. How they will express their generosity, as the world shifts and changes in the flux of time, remains to be seen.

PART TWO

Self As Consumer

The wise and moral man
Who does not hurt the flower,
Shines like a fire on a hilltop.

Such a man makes his pile
As an anthill, gradually.
Grown wealthy, he thus can help
His family and firmly bind his friends to himself.

He should divide his money in four parts:
On one he should live, with the second,
He should expand his trade and give to the needy,
And with the fourth, save for a rainy day.

—*from the* Singalovada Sutta

Looking Deeply at the Nutriments

by Thich Nhat Hanh

THIS MORNING I picked up a branch of flowers on the path of walking meditation and I gave it to a monk who was on my left. I told him, "This belongs to the Pure Land of the Buddha. Only the Pure Land of the Buddha has such a beautiful branch of flowers. Only the Kingdom of God has such a miracle as this branch of flowers." The blue skies, the beautiful vegetation, the lovely face of your child, the song of the birds, all of these things belong to the Pure Land of the Buddha. If we are free enough we can step into the Kingdom of God and enjoy walking in it. It is my practice to enjoy walking in the Kingdom of God every day, to enjoy walking in the Pure Land of the Buddha every day. Even if I am aware that suffering is there, anger and hatred are there, it is still possible for me to walk in the Kingdom of God every day. I can tell you that there is no day when I do not enjoy walking in the Kingdom of God.

Every step should bring me peace and joy. I need it in order to continue my work, my work to build up more brotherhood, more understanding, and more compassion. Without that kind of nourishment, how can you continue? Go back to the present moment, become fully alive. Don't run anymore. Go back to the here and the now and get in touch with the wonders of life that are available for our nourishment and healing. This is the basic practice of peace. If we can do that we have enough strength and joy to help repair the damage caused by war, by violence and hatred, by misunderstanding. And we will know exactly how to live our daily life in order not to contribute to the kind of action that leads to more discrimination and more war, to more violence. Living in such a way that we can embody peace, that we can be peace in every moment of our lives. It is possible for everyone to generate the energy of peace in every step. Peace is every step. If you know that the Kingdom of God is available in the here and the now, why do you have to run anymore?

In the Gospels there is a parable of a person who discovered a treasure in a field. After that he got rid of everything in order to buy this field. When you are able to touch the Kingdom of God, to get in touch with the wonders of life that are available in the here and the now, you can very easily release everything else. You do not want to run anymore. We have been running after the objects of our desire: fame, profit, and power. We think they are essential to our happiness. But we know that our running has brought us a lot of suffering. We have not had the chance to live, to love, and to take care of our loved ones because we cannot stop running. We run even when we sleep. That is why the Buddha advises us to stop. According to the teaching, it is possible to be happy right in the here and the now. Going back to the here and the now with your mindful breathing and mindful walking, you will recognize many conditions of happiness that are already available. You can be happy right here and now.

You know that the future is a notion. The future is made only with one substance, that is the present. If you are taking good care of the present moment, why do you have to worry about the future? By taking care of the present you are doing everything you can to assure a good future. Is there anything else to do? We should live the present moment in such a way that peace and joy may be possible in the here and the now—that love and understanding may be possible. That is all that we can do for the future.

When we are capable of tasting true happiness and peace, it is very easy to transform the anger in us. We don't have to fight anymore. Our anger begins to dissolve in us because we are able to bring into our body and into our consciousness elements of peace and joy every day. Mindfulness helps us not to bring into our body and into our consciousness elements of war and violence. That is the basic practice in order to transform the anger, the fear, and the violence within us.

Mindful Consumption

The Buddha spoke about the path of emancipation in terms of consumption. Perhaps you have heard of a discourse called the *Discourse on the Son's Flesh*. In that discourse the Buddha described four kinds of nutriments. If we know the nature of our food, if we are aware of what we are consuming every day, then we can transform the suffering that is inside of us and around us.

I would like to tell you a little bit about this discourse. I wish to translate it and offer concrete exercises of practice.

The first kind of nutriment the Buddha spoke about is edible food. He advised us to eat mindfully so that compassion can be maintained in our heart. He knew that compassion is the only kind of energy that helps us relate to other living beings, including human beings. Whatever we eat or drink, whatever we ingest in terms of edible food should not contain the toxins that will destroy our body. He used the example of a young couple who wanted to flee their country and live in another country. The young couple brought their little boy and a small quantity of food with them. But halfway through the desert they ran out of food. They knew that they were going to die. After much debate they decided to kill the little boy and eat his flesh. They killed the little boy and ate one piece of his flesh and then preserved the rest on their shoulders for the sun to dry. Every time they ate a piece of their son's flesh they asked the question, "Where is our beloved son now? Where are you, our beloved son?" They beat their chests and pulled their hair. They suffered tremendously. But finally they were able to cross the desert and enter the other country.

The Buddha turned to his monks and asked, "Dear friends, do you think the couple enjoyed eating the flesh of their son?" And the monks said, "No, how could anyone enjoy eating the flesh of their own son?" The Buddha said, "If we do not consume mindfully we are eating the flesh of our own son or daughter."

This body has been transmitted to us by our parents. If we bring into it poisons and toxins we destroy this body, and we are eating the flesh of our mother, our father, and our ancestors. If we destroy our body by unmindful eating and consuming we eat the flesh of our son and daughter and their children also. UNESCO reported that 40,000 children die every day because they do not have enough to eat. And many of us overeat in the West. We are eating the flesh of these children. We have been using a lot of wheat and oats in order to feed animals for food, and the way we raise animals for food is very violent. We destroy Mother Earth. You see, the simple act of eating can be very violent.

Report on U.S. Resources

I have a report on how we use our land and water and forests in the United States of America for food.

Land: Of all agricultural land in the U.S., 87 percent is used to raise animals for food. That is 45 percent of the total landmass in the U.S.

Water: More than half of all the water consumed in the U.S. is used to raise animals for food. It takes 2,500 gallons of water to produce a pound of meat. It takes 25 gallons of water to produce a pound of wheat. That is 25 versus 2,500 gallons of water. A totally vegetarian diet requires 300 gallons of water per day, while a meat eating diet requires 4,000 gallons of water per day.

Pollution: Raising animals for food causes more water pollution in the U.S. than any other industry. Animals raised for food produce 130 times the excrement of the entire human population, 97,000 pounds per second. Much of the waste from factory farms and slaughterhouses flows into streams and rivers, contaminating water sources.

Deforestation: Each vegetarian saves one acre of trees every year. More than 260 million acres of the U.S. forests have been cleared to grow crops to feed animals raised for meat. An acre of trees disappears every eight seconds. The tropical rainforests are being destroyed to create grazing land for cattle. Fifty-five square feet of rainforest may be cleared to produce just one quarter-pound burger.

Resources: In the U.S. animals raised for food are fed more than 80 percent of the corn that we grow and more than 95 percent of the oats. The world's cattle alone consume a quantity of food equivalent to the caloric needs of 8.7 billion people, more than the entire human population on earth.

Mindfulness helps us to be aware of what is going on. Our way of eating and producing food can be very violent. We are eating our mother, our father, and our children. We are eating the Earth. That is why the Buddha proposed that we look back at our situation of consumption. We should learn to eat together in such a way that compassion can remain in our hearts. Otherwise we will suffer and we will make ourselves and all species around us suffer deeply. A Dharma discussion should be organized so that the whole society can sit down together and discuss how we produce and consume food. The way out is mindful consumption.

The Second Nutriment

The second kind of food that the Buddha spoke about is sensory impressions. We also eat with our eyes, our ears, nose, tongue, body, and mind: our six sense organs. A television program is food. A conversation is food; music is food; radio is food. When you drive through the city, even if you don't want to consume, you consume anyway. What you see, what you hear is the food. Magazines are food. And these items of consumption might be highly toxic. An article in a magazine or a television program can contain a lot of violence, a lot of anger, a lot of despair. We continue to consume these poisons every day and we allow our children to consume these toxins every day. We are bringing into our consciousness a lot of poisons every day. The seeds of violence, of despair, of craving and hatred in us have been nourished by what we consume and have become so important. The country is getting angrier and angrier every day.

When a child finishes elementary school she has watched about 100,000 acts of violence on television, and she has seen 8,000 murders on television. That is too much. That is the second kind of food that we consume. We consume thoughts of despair. We consume ideas of craving, of hatred, of despair every day. The Buddha advises us to be mindful, to refuse the items that can bring craving, despair, hatred, and violence into our consciousness. He used the image of a cow with skin disease. The skin disease is so serious that the cow does not seem to have any skin anymore. When you bring the cow close to a tree all the tiny living beings will come out and suck the blood on the body of the cow. When you bring the cow close to an ancient wall, all the tiny animals living inside the wall will come out and suck the blood of the cow. The cow has no means for self-protection. If we are not equipped with the practice of mindful consumption we will be like a cow without skin and the toxins of violence, despair, and craving will continue to penetrate into us. That is why it is very important to wake up and to reject the kind of production and consumption that is destroying us, destroying our nation, and our young people. Every one of us has to practice. As parents, as schoolteachers, as filmmakers, as journalists we have to practice looking deeply into our situation and see if we are creating violence every day and if we are offering that not only to the people in our country, but also to people around the world.

The Third Nutriment

The third nutriment that the Buddha spoke of is volition. Volition is what you want to do the most, your deepest desire. Every one of us has a deepest desire. We have to identify it, we have to call it by its true name. The Buddha had a desire; he wanted to transform all his suffering. He wanted to get enlightened in order to be able to help other people. He did not believe that by being a politician he could help many people; that is why he chose the way of a monk. There are those of us who believe that happiness is only possible when we get a lot of money, a lot of fame, a lot of power, and a lot of sex. That kind of desire belongs to the third category of food spoken of by the Buddha.

The Buddha offered this image to illustrate his teaching: There is a young man who loves to be alive—he doesn't want to die. And yet two very strong men are dragging him to a place where there is a pit of burning charcoal and want to throw him into the glowing embers so he will die.

He resists but in the end he dies because the two men are too strong. The Buddha said, "Your deepest desire will bring you either to a place where there is happiness or to hell." That is why it is very important to look into the nature of your deepest desire, to look deeply into volition. The Buddha said that craving will lead you to a lot of suffering, whether there is craving for wealth, sex, power, or fame. But if you have a healthy desire—like the desire to protect life, to protect the environment, or to help people live a simple life with time to take care of yourself, to love and to take care of your beloved ones—that is the kind of desire that will bring you to happiness. But if you are pushed by the craving for fame, for wealth, for power, you will have to suffer a lot. And that desire will drag you into hell, into the pit of glowing embers and you will die there.

There are people everywhere in the world who consider vengeance as their deepest desire. They become terrorists. When we have hatred and vengeance as our deepest desire, we will suffer terribly also, like the young person who has been dragged by the two strong men to be thrown into the pit of glowing embers. Our deepest desire should be to love, to help, and not to seek revenge, not to punish, not to kill. And I am confident that New Yorkers have that wisdom. Hatred can never answer hatred: all violence is injustice. Responding to violence with violence can only bring more violence and injustice, more suffering, not only to other people but also to ourselves. This is wisdom that is in every one of us. We need to breathe deeply, to get calm in order to touch the seed of wisdom. I know that if the seed of wisdom and of compassion of the American people could be watered regularly during one week or so, it would bring a lot of relief, it would reduce the anger and the hatred. And America would be able to perform an act of forgiveness that would bring about radical relief to America and to the world. That is why my suggestion is the practice of being calm, being concentrated, watering the seeds of wisdom and compassion that are already in us, and learning the art of mindful consumption. This is a true revolution, the only kind of revolution that can help us get out from this difficult situation where violence and hatred prevail.

Looking Deeply

Our Senate, our Congress has to practice looking deeply. They should help us by making laws that prohibit the production of items full of anger, full of craving and violence. We should be determined to talk to our children, to make a commitment in our family and in our community to practice mindful consumption. These are the real practices of peace. It is possible for us to practice so that we can get the nourishment and healing in our daily life. It is possible for us to practice embracing the pain, the sorrow, and the violence in us in order to transform.

The basic practice is to be aware of what is going on. By going back to the present moment and taking the time to look deeply and understand the roots of our suffering, the path of emancipation will be revealed to us. The Buddha said what has come to be does have a source. When we are able to look deeply into what has come to be and to recognize its source of nutriment we are already on the path of emancipation. What has come to us may be our depression, our despair, and our anger. We have been nourished by the kinds of food that are available in our market. We want to consume them. It is not without reason that our depression is there. We have invited it in by our way of unmindful consumption. Looking deeply into our ill-being, the ill-being of our society, and identifying the source in terms of consumption — that is what the Buddha recommended. Looking deeply into our ill-being and identifying the source of nutriment that has brought it into us — that is already the beginning of healing and transformation.

We have to practice looking deeply as a nation if we want to get out of this difficult situation. And our practice will help the other nations practice. I am sure that America is very capable of punishment. You can send us a bomb; we know you are very capable of doing so. But America is great when America knows how to act with lucidity and compassion. I urge that in these days of post 9-11, when we have not been able to overcome the tremendous shock yet, we should not do anything, we should not say anything. We should go home to ourselves and practice mindful breathing and mindful walking to allow ourselves to calm down and to allow lucidity to come, so we can understand the real roots of our suffering and the suffering of the world. Only with that understanding can compassion arise. America can be a great nation if she knows how to act with compassion instead of punishment. We offer peace. We offer the relief for transformation and healing.

Buddhist Perspectives on Economic Concepts

by Ven. P. A. Payutto

Value

THE ENGINE of all economic activity is desire. In the Buddhist canon, two distinct types of desire are identified: *chanda* and *tanha*. Tanha is directed toward feeling. It leads to the seeking of objects which pander to self-interests and is supported and nourished by ignorance. Chanda, however, is directed toward what is of true benefit, it leads to effort and action, and is founded on intelligent reflection.

It follows that there are two kinds of value, which we might term true value and artificial value. True value is created by chanda. In other words, a commodity's true value is determined by its ability to meet the need for well-being. Conversely, artificial value is created by tanha—it is a commodity's capacity to satisfy the desire for pleasure.

To assess an object's value, we must ask ourselves which kind of desire— tanha or chanda—defines its worth to us. Fashionable clothes, jewelry, luxury cars, and other status symbols contain a high degree of artificial value because they cater to people's vanity and desire for pleasure. A luxury car may serve the same function as a cheaper car, but it commands a higher price largely because of its artificial value. Many of the pleasures taken for granted in today's consumer society—the games, media thrills, and untold forms of junk foods available—are created solely for the purpose of satisfying tanha, have no practical purpose at all, and are often detrimental to well-being. For the most part, advertising promotes this artificial value. Advertisers stimulate desires by projecting pleasurable images onto the products they sell. They induce us to believe, for example, that whoever can afford a luxury car will stand out from the crowd and be a member of high society, or that by drinking a certain brand of soft drink we will have lots of friends and be happy.

The true value of an object is typically overshadowed by its artificial value. Craving and conceit, and the desire for the fashionable and sensually appealing, cloud our reckoning of the true value of things. How many people, for instance, reflect on the true value or reasons for eating food or wearing clothes?

Consumption

The question of consumption is similar to that of value. We must distinguish which kind of desire our consumption is intended to satisfy: is it to answer the need for things of true value, or to indulge in the pleasures afforded by artificial value? Consumption is said to be one of the goals of economic activity. However, economic theory and Buddhism define consumption differently.

Consumption is the alleviation or satisfaction of desire, that much is agreed. Modern economics defines consumption as simply the use of goods and services to satisfy demand. Buddhism, however, distinguishes between two kinds of consumption, which might be termed "right" consumption and "wrong" consumption. Right consumption is the use of goods and services to satisfy the desire for true well-being. It is consumption with a goal and a purpose. Wrong consumption arises from tanha; it is the use of goods and services to satisfy the desire for pleasing sensations or ego-gratification.

While the Buddhist perspective is based on a wide view of the stream of causes and effects, the specialized thinking of economics identifies only part of the stream: demand leads to consumption which leads to satisfaction. For most economists that's the end of it—there's no need to know what happens afterwards. In this view, consumption can be of anything whatsoever, so long as it results in satisfaction. There is little consideration of whether or not well-being is adversely affected by that consumption.

Consumption may satisfy sensual desires, but its true purpose is to provide well-being. For example, our body depends on food for nourishment. Consumption of food is thus a requirement for well-being. For most people, however, eating food is also a means to experience pleasure. If in consuming food one receives the experience of a delicious flavor, one is said to have satisfied one's desires. Economists tend to think in this way, holding that the experience of satisfaction is the end result of consumption. But here the crucial question is: What is the true purpose of consuming food: satisfaction of desires or the attainment of well-being?

In the Buddhist view, when consumption enhances true well-being, it is said to be successful. On the other hand, if consumption results merely in feelings of satisfaction, then it fails. At its worst, consumption through tanha destroys its true objective, which is to enhance well-being. Heedlessly indulging in desires with no regard to the repercussions often leads to harmful effects and a loss of true well-being. Moreover, the compulsive consumption rampant in consumer societies breeds inherent dissatisfaction. It is a strange thing that economics, the science of human well-being and satisfaction, accepts, and indeed lauds, the kind of consumption that in effect frustrates the realization of its own objectives.

By contrast, right consumption always contributes to well-being and forms a basis for the further development of human potentialities. This is an important point often overlooked by economists. Consumption guided by chanda does much more than just satisfy one's desire; it contributes to well-being and spiritual development. This is also true on a global scale. If all economic activities were guided by chanda, the result would be much more than just a healthy economy and material progress—such activities would contribute to the whole of human development and enable humanity to lead a nobler life and enjoy a more mature kind of happiness.

Moderation

At the very heart of Buddhism is the wisdom of moderation. When the goal of economic activity is seen to be satisfaction of desires, economic activity is open-ended and without clear definition—desires are endless. According to the Buddhist approach, economic activity must be controlled by the qualification that it is directed to the attainment of well-being rather than the "maximum satisfaction" sought after by traditional economic thinking. Well-being as an objective acts as a control on economic activity. No longer are we struggling against each other to satisfy endless desires. Instead, our activities are directed toward the attainment of well-being. If economic activity is directed in this way, its objectives are clear and its activities are controlled. A balance or equilibrium is achieved. There is no excess, no overconsumption, no overproduction. In the classical economic model, unlimited desires are controlled by scarcity, but in the Buddhist model they are controlled by an appreciation of moderation and the objective of well-being. The resulting balance will naturally eliminate the harmful effects of uncontrolled economic activity.

Buddhist monks and nuns traditionally reflect on moderation before each meal by reciting this reflection:

> Wisely reflecting, we take almsfood, not for the purpose of fun, not for indulgence or the fascination of taste, but simply for the maintenance of the body, for the continuance of existence, for the cessation of painful feeling, for living the higher life. Through this eating, we subdue old painful feelings of hunger and prevent new painful feelings (of overeating) from arising. Thus do we live unhindered, blameless, and in comfort.[21]

The goal of moderation is not restricted to monastics: whenever we use things, be it food, clothing, or even paper and electricity, we can take the time to reflect on their true purpose, rather than using them heedlessly. By reflecting in this way we can avoid heedless consumption and so understand "the right amount," the "middle way."

We also come to see consumption as a means to an end, which is the development of human potential. With human development as our goal, we eat food not simply for the pleasure it affords, but to obtain the physical and mental energy necessary for intellectual and spiritual growth toward a nobler life.

Nonconsumption

Lacking a spiritual dimension, modern economic thinking encourages maximum consumption. It praises those who eat the most—three, four, or more times a day. If someone were to eat ten times a day, so much the better. By contrast, a Buddhist economics understands that nonconsumption can contribute to well-being. Though monks eat only one meal a day, they strive for a kind of well-being that is dependent on little.

On Observance days, some Buddhist laypeople also refrain from eating after midday and, in so doing, contribute to their own well-being. Renunciation of the evening meal allows them to spend time in meditation and reflection on the Buddha's teachings. The body is light and the mind easily calmed when the stomach is not full. Thus Buddhism recognizes that certain demands can be satisfied through nonconsumption, a position which traditional economic thinking would find hard to appreciate. Refraining from eating can play a role in satisfying our non-material, spiritual needs.

It's not that getting down to eating one meal a day is the goal, of course. Like consumption, nonconsumption is only a means to an end, not an end in itself. If abstinence did not lead to well-being, it would be pointless, just a way of mistreating ourselves. The question is not whether to consume or not to consume, but whether or not our choices lead to self-development.

Overconsumption

Today's society encourages overconsumption. In their endless struggle to find satisfaction through consuming, a great many people damage their own health and harm others. Drinking alcohol, for instance, satisfies a desire, but is a cause of ill-health, unhappy families, and fatal accidents. People who eat for taste often overeat and make themselves ill. Others give no thought at all to food values and waste money on junk foods. Some people even become deficient in certain vitamins and minerals despite eating large meals every day. Apart from doing themselves no good, their overeating deprives others of food.

So we cannot say that a thing has value simply because it provides pleasure and satisfaction. If satisfaction is sought in things that do not enrich the quality of life, the result often becomes the destruction of true welfare, leading to delusion and intoxication, loss of health and well-being.

A classic economic principle states that the essential value of goods lies in their ability to bring satisfaction to the consumer. Here we may point to the examples given above where heavy consumption and strong satisfaction have both positive and negative results. The Buddhist perspective is that the benefit of goods and services lies in their ability to provide the consumer with a sense of satisfaction at having enhanced the quality of his or her life. This extra clause is essential. All definitions, whether of goods, services, or personal and social wealth, must be modified in this way.

Contentment

Contentment, while not technically an economic concern, is a virtue that has often been misunderstood and, as it relates to consumption and satisfaction, it seems to merit some discussion. The tacit objective of economics is a dynamic economy where every demand and desire is supplied and constantly renewed in a never-ending and ever-growing cycle. The entire mechanism is fueled by tanha. From the Buddhist perspective, this tireless search to satisfy desires is itself a kind of suffering. Buddhism proposes the cessation of this kind of desire, or the realization of contentment, as a more skillful objective.

Traditional economists would probably counter that without desire, the whole economy would grind to a halt. However, this is based on a misunderstanding of the nature of contentment. People misunderstand contentment because they fail to distinguish between the two different kinds of desire, tanha and chanda. We lump them together, and in proposing contentment, dismiss them both. A contented person comes to be seen as one who wants nothing at all. Here lies our mistake.

Obviously, people who are content will have fewer wants than those who are discontent. However, a correct definition of contentment must be qualified by the stipulation that it implies only the absence of artificial want, that is tanha; chanda, the desire for true well-being, remains. In other words, the path to true contentment involves reducing the artificial desire for sense-pleasure, while actively encouraging and supporting the desire to improve the quality of life.

These two processes—reducing tanha and encouraging chanda—are mutually supportive. When we are easily satisfied in material things, we save time and energy that might otherwise be wasted on seeking objects of tanha. The time and energy we save can, in turn, be applied to the cultivation of well-being, which is the objective of chanda. When it comes to developing skillful conditions, however, contentment is not a beneficial quality. Skillful conditions must be realized through effort. Too much contentment with regards to chanda easily turns into complacency and apathy. In this connection, the Buddha pointed out that his own attainment of enlightenment was largely a result of two qualities: unremitting effort, and lack of contentment with skillful conditions.[22]

Work

Buddhist and conventional economics also have different understandings of the role of work. Modern Western economic theory is based on the view that work is something that we are compelled to do in order to obtain money for consumption. It is during the time when we are not working, or "leisure time," that we may experience happiness and satisfaction. Work and satisfaction are considered to be separate and generally opposing principles.

Buddhism, however, recognizes that work can either be satisfying or not satisfying, depending on which of the two kinds of desire is motivating it. When work stems from the desire for true well-being, there is satisfaction in the direct and immediate results of the work itself. By contrast, when work is done out of desire for pleasure-objects, then the direct results of the work itself are not so important. With this attitude, work is simply an unavoidable necessity to obtain the desired object. The difference between these two attitudes determines whether or not work will directly contribute to well-being. In the first case, work is a potentially satisfying activity, and in the second, it is a necessary chore.

Work performed in order to meet the desire for well-being can provide inherent satisfaction, because it is appreciated for its own sake. Achievement and progress in the work lead to a growing sense of satisfaction at every stage of the work's development. In Buddhist terminology, this is called working with chanda. Conversely, working out of desire for pleasure is called working with tanha. Those working with tanha are motivated by the desire to consume. But since it is impossible to consume and work at the same time, the work itself affords little enjoyment or satisfaction. It should also be pointed out that work in this case postpones the attainment of satisfaction, and as such will be seen as an impediment to it. When work is seen as an impediment to consumption it can become intolerable. In the developed, as well as the developing, countries this is readily seen in the extent of debt and corruption, and where consumers cannot tolerate the delay between working and consuming the objects of their desires.

In modern industrial economies, many jobs preclude satisfaction, or make it very difficult to realize even a modicum of satisfaction by their very nature. Factory jobs can be dull, undemanding, pointless, even dangerous to health. They breed boredom, frustration, and depression, all of which have negative effects on productivity. However, even in menial or insignificant tasks, there is a difference between working with tanha and working with chanda. Even in the most monotonous of tasks, where one may have difficulty generating a sense of pride in the object of one's labors, a desire to perform the task well, or a sense of pride in one's own endeavors, may help to alleviate the monotony, and even contribute something of a sense of achievement to the work: even though the work may be monotonous, one feels that at least one is developing good qualities like endurance and is able to derive a certain enthusiasm for the work.

As we have seen, the fulfillment of tanha lies with seeking and obtaining objects which provide pleasant feelings. While this seeking may involve action, the objective of tanha is not directly related in a causal way to the action undertaken. Let's look at two different tasks and examine the cause and effect relationships involved:

(1) Mr. Smith sweeps the street, and is paid $500 a month;
(2) If Little Suzie finishes the book she is reading, Daddy will take her to the movies.

It may seem at first glance that sweeping the street is the cause for Mr. Smith receiving his wage; that is, sweeping the street is the cause, and money is the result. But in fact, this is a mistaken conclusion. According to Buddhist understanding, one would say: the action of sweeping the street is the cause for the street being cleaned; the cleanness of the street is a stipulation for Mr. Smith receiving his wage, based on an agreement between employer and employee.

All actions have results that arise as a natural consequence. The natural result of sweeping the street is a clean street. In the contract between employer and employee, a stipulation is added to this natural result, so that sweeping the street also brings about a payment of money. This is a man-made, or artificial, law. However, money is not the natural result of sweeping the street: some people may sweep a street and get no money for it, while many other people receive wages without having to sweep streets. Money is a socially contrived or artificial condition. Many contemporary social problems result from confusion between the natural results of actions and the human stipulations added to them. People begin to think that a payment of money really is the natural result of sweeping a street, or, to use another example, that a good wage, rather than medical knowledge, is the natural result of studying medicine.

As for Little Suzie, it may seem that completing the book is the cause, and going to the movies with Dad is the result. But in fact finishing the book is simply a stipulation on which going to the movies is based. The true result of reading the book is obtaining knowledge.

Expanding on these examples, if Mr. Smith's work is directed solely by tanha, all he wants is his $500, not the cleanness of the street. In fact, he doesn't want to sweep the street at all, but, since it is a condition for receiving his wage, he must. As for Little Suzie, if her true desire is to go to the movies (not to read the book), then reading will afford no satisfaction in itself; she only reads because it is a condition for going to the movies.

When people work solely out of tanha, their true desire is for consumption, not action. Their actions — in this case, sweeping and reading — are seen as means of obtaining the objects of desire — the salary and a trip to the movies. When they work with chanda, on the other hand, Mr. Smith takes pride in (i.e., desires) the cleanness of the street and little Suzie wants the knowledge contained in the book. With chanda, their desire is for action and the true results of that action. Cleanness is the natural result of sweeping the street and knowledge is the natural result of reading the book. When the action is completed, the result naturally and simultaneously arises. When Mr. Smith sweeps the street, a clean street ensues, and it ensues whenever he sweeps. When Little Suzie reads a book, knowledge arises, and it arises whenever she reads the book. With chanda, work is intrinsically satisfying because it is itself the achievement of the desired result.

Thus, the objective of chanda is action and the good result which arises from it. When their actions are motivated by chanda, Mr. Smith applies himself to sweeping the street irrespective of his monthly wage, and little Suzie will read her book even without Daddy having to promise to take her to the movies. (In reality, of course, most people do work for the wages, which are a necessity, but we also have the choice to take pride in our work and strive to do it well, which is chanda, or to do it perfunctorily simply for the wage. Thus, in real life situations, most people are motivated by varying degrees of both tanha and chanda.)

As we have seen, actions motivated by chanda and actions motivated by tanha give rise to very different results, both objectively and ethically. When we are motivated by tanha and are working simply to attain an unrelated object or means of consumption, we may be tempted to attain the object of desire through other means which involve less effort. If we can obtain the objective without having to do any work at all, even better. If it is absolutely necessary to work for the objective, however, we will only do so reluctantly and perfunctorily.

The extreme result of this is criminal activity. If Mr. Smith wants money but has no desire (chanda) to work, he may find working for the money intolerable and so resort to theft. If Little Suzie wants to go the movies, but can't stand reading the book, she may steal money from her mother and go to the movies herself.

With only tanha to get their salary but no chanda to do their work, people will only go about the motions of performing their duties, doing just enough to get by. The result is apathy, laziness, and poor workmanship. Mr. Smith simply goes through the motions of sweeping the street day by day until payday arrives, and Little Suzie reads the book simply to let Daddy see that she has finished it, but doesn't take in anything she has read, or she may cheat, saying she has read the book when in fact she hasn't.

When sloppiness and dishonesty of this type arise in the workplace, secondary checks must be established to monitor the work. These measures address the symptoms but not the cause, and only add to the complexity of the situation. For example, it may be necessary to install a supervisor to inspect Mr. Smith's work and check his hours; or Little Suzie's brother may have to look in and check that she really is reading the book. This applies to employers as well as employees: workers' tribunals must be established to prevent greedy or irresponsible employers from exploiting their workers and making them work in inhumane conditions or for unfair wages. When tanha is the motivating force, workers and employers are trapped in a game of one-upmanship, with each side trying to get as much for themselves as they can for the least possible expense.

Tanha is escalated to a considerable extent by social influences. For instance, when the owners of the means of production are blindly motivated by a desire to get rich for as little outlay as possible, it is very unlikely that the workers will have much chanda. They will be more likely to follow the example of their employers, trying to get as much as they can for as little effort as possible. This tendency can be seen in the modern workplace. It seems, moreover, that the more affluent a society becomes, the more this tendency is produced—the more we have, the more we want. This is a result of the unchecked growth of tanha and the lack of any viable alternative. Meanwhile, the values of inner contentment and peace of mind seem to have been all but lost in modern society.

In rare cases, however, we hear of employers and employees who do work together with chanda. This happens when the employer is responsible, capable, and considerate, thus commanding the confidence and affection of employees, who in return are harmonious, diligent, and committed to their work. There have even been cases of employers who were so caring with their employees that when their businesses failed and came close to bankruptcy, the employees sympathetically made sacrifices and worked as hard as possible to make the company profitable again. Rather than making demands for compensation, they were willing to take a cut in wages.

Production and Nonproduction

The word "production" is misleading. We tend to think that through production new things are created, when in fact it is merely changes of state which are effected. One substance or form of energy is converted into another. These conversions entail the creation of a new state by the destruction of an old one. Thus production is always accompanied by destruction. In some cases the destruction is acceptable, in others it is not. Production is only truly justified when the value of the thing produced outweighs the value of that which is destroyed. In some cases it may be better to refrain from production. This is invariably true for those industries whose products are for the purpose of destruction. In weapons factories, for example, nonproduction is always the better choice. In industries where production entails the destruction of natural resources and environmental degradation, nonproduction is often the better choice. To choose, we must distinguish between production with positive results and production with negative results; production that enhances well-being and that which destroys it.

In this light, nonproduction can be a useful economic activity. A person who produces very little in materialistic terms may, at the same time, consume much less of the world's resources and lead a life that is beneficial to the world around him. Such a person is of more value than one who diligently consumes large amounts of the world's resources while manufacturing goods that are harmful to society. But modern economics could never make such a distinction; it would praise a person who produces and consumes (that is, destroys) vast amounts more than one who produces and consumes (destroys) little.

In the economics of the industrial era the term production has been given a very narrow meaning. It is taken to relate only to those things that can be bought and sold — a bullfight, where people pay money to see bulls killed, is seen as contributing to the economy, while a child helping an elderly person across the street is not; a professional comedian telling jokes on stage, relaxing his audience and giving them a good time, is taken to be economically productive because money changes hands, while an office worker with a very cheerful disposition is not considered to have produced anything by his cheerfulness toward those around him. Nor is there any accounting of the economic costs of aggressive action and speech that continually create tension in the workplace, so that those affected have to find some way to alleviate it with amusements.

Competition and Cooperation

Modern economics is based on the assumption that it is human nature to compete. Buddhism, on the other hand, recognizes that human beings are capable of both competition and cooperation.

Competition is natural: when they are striving to satisfy the desire for pleasure—when they are motivated by tanha—people will compete fiercely. At such times they want to get as much as possible for themselves and feel no sense of sufficiency or satisfaction. If they can obtain the desired object without having to share it with anyone else, so much the better. Inevitably, competition is intense; this is natural for the mind driven by tanha.

This competitive instinct can be redirected to induce cooperation. One might unite the members of a particular group by inciting them to compete with another group. For example, corporate managers sometimes rally their employees to work together to beat their competitors. But this cooperation is based entirely on competition. Buddhism would call this "artificial cooperation."

True cooperation arises with the desire for well-being—with chanda. Human development demands that we understand how tanha and chanda motivate us and that we shift our energies from competition towards cooperative efforts to solve the problems facing the world and to realize a nobler goal.

Choice

"Whether a given want is a true need, a fanciful desire, or a bizarre craving is of no matter to economics. Nor is it the business of economics to judge whether such wants should be satisfied," say the economics texts,[23] but from a Buddhist perspective the choices we make are of utmost importance, and these choices require some qualitative appreciation of the options available. Choice is a function of intention, which is the heart of *kamma,* one of Buddhism's central teachings. The influence of kamma affects not only economics but all areas of our lives and our social and natural environment. Economic decisions, or choices, which lack ethical reflection are bad kamma—they are bound to bring undesirable results. Good economic decisions are those based on an awareness of the costs on the individual, social, and environmental levels, not just in terms of production and consumption. These economic decisions are kamma. Every time an economic decision is made, kamma is made, and the process of fruition is immediately set in motion, for better or for worse, for the individual, for society, and the environment. Thus it is important to recognize the qualitative difference between different courses of action and to make our choices wisely.

Life Views

I would now like to take a step back and look at economics from a somewhat wider perspective. We have discussed the various economic activities. We may now ask: What is the purpose of these activities? What are we striving for in all this buying and selling, producing and consuming? Or we may ask an even grander question: What indeed is the purpose of life?

Everybody holds views on these matters, although most of us are unconscious of them. Buddhist teachings stress that these views exert a tremendous influence on our lives. The Pali word for view is *ditthi*. This term covers all kinds of views on many different levels—our personal opinions and beliefs; the ideologies, religious and political views espoused by groups; and the attitudes and worldviews held by whole cultures and societies.

Views lead to ramifications far beyond the realm of mental states and intellectual discourse. Like ethics, views are linked to the stream of causes and conditions. They are "subjective" mental formations that inevitably condition events in "objective" reality. On a personal level, one's worldview affects the events of life. On a national level, political views and social mores condition society and the quality of day-to-day life.

The Buddha warned that views are potentially the most dangerous of all mental conditions. Unskillful views can wreak unimaginable damage. The violence of the Crusades, Nazism, and Communism, to name just three disastrous fanatical movements, were fueled by extremely unskillful views. Skillful views, on the other hand, are the most beneficial of mental conditions. As the

Buddha said: "Monks, I see no other condition which is so much a cause for the arising of as yet unarisen unskillful conditions, and for the development and fruition of unskillful conditions already arisen, as wrong view. . . ."[24]

This begs the question: what view of life is behind modern economics? Is it a skillful or an unskillful one? At the risk of oversimplifying, let us say that the goal of modern life is to find happiness. This view is so pervasive in modern societies that it is rarely even recognized, let alone examined or questioned. The very concept of "progress" — social, economic, scientific, and political — assumes that society's highest goal is to reach a state where everyone will be happy. The United States' Declaration of Independence poetically embodies this ideal by asserting mankind's right to "life, liberty, and the pursuit of happiness."

While certainly a goodhearted aspiration, the view that happiness is the goal of life betrays a fundamental confusion about the truth of life. As often said, "happiness" is never more than an ill-defined, elusive quality. Many people equate happiness with sense pleasure and the satisfaction of their desires. For these people, happiness remains a remote condition, something outside themselves, a future prize that must be pursued and captured. But happiness cannot be obtained through seeking, only through bringing about the causes and conditions which lead to it, and these are personal and mental development.

From the Buddhist point of view, people often confuse tanha — their restless craving for satisfaction and pleasure — with the pursuit of happiness. This is indeed an unskillful view, because the craving of tanha can never be satisfied. If the pursuit of happiness equals the pursuit of the objects of tanha, then life itself becomes a misery. To see the consequences of this unfortunate view, one need only witness the depression and angst of the citizens in so many modern cities filled with limitless distractions and pleasure centers. Rather than leading to contentment and well-being, the pursuit of happiness so often leads to restlessness and exhaustion in the individual, strife in society, and unsustainable consumption of the environment.

By contrast, the Buddhist view of life is much less idealistic but much more practical. The Buddha said simply, "There is suffering."[25] This was the first of his Four Noble Truths, the central tenets of Buddhism. He went on to describe what suffering is: "Birth is suffering; old age is suffering; sickness is suffering; death is suffering; sorrow, lamentation, pain, grief, and despair are suffering; separation from the loved is suffering; getting what you don't want is suffering; not getting what you want is suffering. . . ."

There is little question that these things exist in life and they are all unpleasant, but the tendency of our society is to deny them. Death, in particular, is rarely thought of or spoken about as a personal inevitability. Denying these things, however, does not make them go away. This is why the Buddha said that suffering is something that should be recognized. The first Noble Truth is the recognition that all things must pass and that ultimately there is no security to be had within the material world. This is the kind of truth the Buddha urged people to face—the painfully obvious, fundamental facts of life.

The second Noble Truth explains the cause of suffering. The Buddha said that suffering is caused by craving based on ignorance (that is, tanha). In other words, the cause of suffering is an internal condition. Old age is inevitable; craving is not. The Buddha said that craving can be eliminated, which brings us to the third Noble Truth, which concerns the cessation of suffering. With the complete and utter abandonment of craving, suffering ceases. But how to do that? In the fourth Noble Truth the Buddha tells how. It is the Noble Eightfold Path for the cessation of suffering, through training of body, speech, and mind in accordance with the Buddhist code of Right View, Right Thought, Right Speech, Right Action, Right Livelihood, Right Effort, Right Mindfulness, and Right Concentration.

It is fairly obvious from the Four Noble Truths that the Buddhist view of life is very much at odds with the view common to modern societies. Whereas Buddhism says, "There is suffering," modern societies say, "There is happiness, and I want it now!" The implications of this simple shift in perception are enormous. A society that views the purpose of life as the pursuit of happiness is one that is recklessly pursuing some future dream. Happiness is seen as something that is inherently lacking and must be found somewhere else. Along with this view comes dissatisfaction, impatience, contention, an inability to deal with suffering, and a lack of attention to the present moment.

On the other hand, with a view of life that appreciates the reality of suffering, we pay more attention to the present moment so that we can recognize problems when they arise. We cooperate with others to solve problems, rather than competing with them to win happiness. Such a view also influences our economic choices. Our production and consumption are geared less toward the pursuit of sense gratification (tanha) and more toward relieving suffering (chanda). If this Buddhist view were taken up on a national or global scale, rather than seeking to satisfy every demand, our economies would strive to create a state free of suffering, or a state which is primed for the enjoyment of happiness (just as a healthy body is one which is primed to enjoy happiness).

Only through understanding suffering can we realize the possibility of happiness. Here Buddhism makes a distinction between two kinds of happiness: dependent happiness and independent happiness. Dependent happiness is happiness that requires an external object. It includes any happiness contingent on the material world, including wealth, family, honor, and fame. Dependent happiness, being dependent on things that can never be ours in an ultimate sense, is fickle and uncertain. Independent happiness, on the other hand, is the happiness that arises from within a mind that has been trained and has attained some degree of inner peace. Such a happiness is not dependent on externals and is much more stable than dependent happiness.

Dependent happiness leads to competition and conflict in the struggle to acquire material goods. Any happiness arising from such activity is a contentious kind of happiness. There is, however, a third kind of happiness which, while not as exalted as the truly independent kind, is nevertheless more skillful than the contentious kind. It is a happiness that is altruistically based, directed toward well-being, and motivated by goodwill and compassion. Through personal development, people can appreciate this truer kind of happiness—the desire to bring happiness to others (which in Buddhism we call *metta*). With this kind of happiness, we can experience joy at the happiness of others, just as parents feel glad at the happiness of their children.

This kind of happiness might be called "harmonious happiness," as distinct from the contentious kind of happiness. It is less dependent on the acquisition of material goods and arises more from giving than receiving. Although such happiness is not truly independent, it is much more skillful than the happiness resulting from selfish acquisition.

The most assured level of happiness is the liberation resulting from enlightenment, which is irreversible. But even to train the mind, through study and meditation practice, to achieve some inner contentment is a powerful antidote to the dissatisfaction of the consumer society. And with the clarity of inner calm comes an insight into one of life's profound ironies: striving for happiness, we create suffering; understanding suffering, we find peace.

The Religion of Consumption:
A Buddhist Perspective

by Jonathan Watts & David R. Loy

Introduction: Expanding the Discourse on Social Change

ERHAPS THE MOST disturbing trend in public debates over issues like economic globalization, development, democracy, human rights, and so forth, is the way the issues themselves are framed. Over the last four hundred years, scientific rationality has become the increasingly dominant view by which we envision the world and the ways we try to live in it. This standpoint tends to see the world, including ourselves, as machines that can always be improved with better engineering. Although "social engineering" may have its merits in constructing safer and more convenient societies, such an approach is incomplete, because it does not take into sufficient account the very purpose of material development: human happiness, which is a more subjective consideration that includes our spiritual concerns.

Spiritual viewpoints on personal and collective transformation are important resources for deepening the discussion of social issues. To assert the importance of a religious perspective is not to argue for committing to Buddhism or some other traditional faith. The point is simply that we cannot escape spiritual questions insofar as we cannot escape the deepest questions about the meaning of our lives. Rather than dismiss religion as a narcotic for the politically naive, we need to become more aware of the potentials for personal transformation (and in turn social transformation) that reside in its teachings and institutions. Religious engagement remains an enormously powerful social force that should not be surrendered to fundamentalists.

This highlights the importance of personal transformation (including techniques to assist that) as much as group or structural transformation. To pursue the latter without the former is to risk reenacting the social tragedies of the last several centuries, in which revolutions have for the most part merely replaced one gang of thugs with another. All of our attempts to engineer human happiness—from industrial development to all sorts of preventative legislation—will remain incomplete until we get to the root of human happiness: realizing meaning in our lives.

The greatest expression of this drive to engineer human happiness in today's world is economic globalization. In the last few years, it has become apparent to an increasing number of people throughout the world that this system of economic engineering is not very rational, not very scientific, and not very just. However, the problem is not simply that our present economic system exploits people in underdeveloped countries and destroys their once self-sufficient economies. From a Buddhist perspective, globalization is far more insidious than that. The problem of most underdeveloped societies today is not so different from the problem with the developed world: an impoverished worldview that privileges consumption over other values and other meaning-systems.

Although so much of our drive to create happiness seems to be preoccupied with the material dimension, with the desire for a comfortable or luxurious life, closer inspection reveals something in our spirits that is driving us to consume our Earth into ruin. Since so many of us are now able to satisfy our basic material needs, our desire for "ever more" must be motivated by something more than just a desire for comfort. That motivation is what drives "consumerism": and consumerism is the dominant culture of a modernizing invasive industrialism which stimulates—yet can never satisfy—the urge for a strong sense of self to overlay the angst and sense of lack intrinsic to the human condition. As a result of this sense of lack, goods, services, and experiences are consumed beyond any reasonable need. This undermines the ecosystem, the quality of life, and particularly traditional cultures and communities, as well as the possibility of spiritual liberation.

More simply, consumerism is a way of living in which the meaning of one's life becomes the acquisition and consumption of things and experiences. From a socially engaged Buddhist perspective, it is necessary to look beyond approaches that seek to economically engineer human prosperity and consider the role of consumerism in the way we construct the meaning of our lives. While we may be skeptical of religion, and there is good reason to be suspicious of most religious institutions, we also need to realize that consumerism functions as a religion for a rapidly increasing number of people worldwide.

Step I—Awareness of Consumerism's Distortions

Buddhism is unique among the major religions in the way it focuses on questioning the nature of the self and unpacking its illusions. The *anatta* (not-self) teaching is difficult to understand, but in more contemporary terms, one might say that Buddhism implies that our sense of "I" is a social construction. From this standpoint, the important issue becomes how that sense of self is constructed and who constructs it.

The Buddhist critique of the self-construct implies that we need to understand the Western psychological concept of repression (like fear of death) in a more fundamental way. Fear of death is fear of what will happen in the future; but fear of not-self—that my sense of self is not real—is fear of what "I" am (or am *not*) right now. Perhaps all of us have some sense of this problem, but our feeling of being "unreal" is repressed. In other words, our sense of self, because it is an ungrounded construct, is inherently insecure and uncomfortable. The result is that we become obsessed with constructing our own identity—that is, with making ourselves real in one or another symbolic fashion. As with fear of death, repressed fear of my "emptiness" returns as a preoccupation with symbolic immortality and reality—with "making my mark on history so I will not be forgotten."

What is the relevance of this for consumerism? Traditionally, self-identity has usually been a matter of identifying with one's religion, nation, race, class, occupation, etc. This has often involved intolerance of other religions, nations, races, etc.—something that we can see persists in both the developing and developed worlds. However, today we are increasingly conditioned to construct our self-identity through another means, consumption. From a Buddhist perspective, our lives are now saturated with a new religious message that promises a different kind of salvation—that is, a different way to become truly happy. The primary agent of its proselytizing is, of course, advertising, which now envelops us so completely that we tend not to be aware of its effects. The basic problem, however, is that consumerism does not work and cannot work, in the deepest and most important sense—as a way to give our lives satisfactory meaning. Essential to any genuine solution, therefore, is the process of becoming more aware of how the false promise of consumerism distorts our own lives and the lives of those around us.

Buddhism sees desire or "greed" as a fundamental motivating factor in our consumer societies. Through the ever-increasing domination of market values like competition and hyper-individualism, we become increasingly confused about how to relate to the world. With the market perpetually designing new "needs" for the individual, "needs" and "wants" have become virtually synonymous. Poverty has taken on the purely quantifiable meaning of material underdevelopment. It has come to mean not so much hunger or homelessness but relative "under-consumption" of the "essentials" of a developed lifestyle—i.e., car, TV, a university education, etc. At the same time, we have become blind to what our real needs are. So we see teenagers in the United States living on food stamps while lusting over (and acquiring) $150 Nike basketball shoes, or squatter families in Bangkok living in corrugated steel shacks while owning TVs and motorbikes.

Buddhist psychology teaches that greed naturally concocts "dispersion" and "delusion." When the mind is unable to distinguish between desire and genuine need, the door is opened to a numbing preoccupation with consumer goods and consumed experiences. Myriad worlds of lowest-common-denominator entertainment are the bait, but the hook is the distraction of commercials, fueled by advertising dollars, that spread the ethic of greed. The consumption of novel experiences in the leisure industries has become another major arena of delusion and dispersion. From mega-media to professional sports and tourism, leisure activities have become a significant component of most national economies. The consequences of dispersion and delusion are twofold. First, the individual is left distracted and disconnected from him/herself and his/her surroundings. With so many games to watch, so much shopping to do, so many trips to take, we have less and less time to connect with and relate to our families, our partners, our neighbors and, most importantly, ourselves. From turning on the TV first thing in the morning, to the car stereo or Walkman on the way to work, to falling asleep in front of the TV at night, the opportunities to reflect on life and to consider more meaningful alternatives are washed away.

With the ever-increasing speed of technology, our disconnection deepens into the next level in the Buddhist causal chain, despair and disempowerment. There remains little hope for changing our lives when the "democratic" politics of "developed" countries involve image adjustment rather than policy review, and when people from Tokyo to New York fear for their livelihoods as corporations "downsize" in the struggle for a competitive edge. The political consequences of our consumerist way of life, in a world dominated by corporations and the state—or, more precisely, the corporate-state—lead us more deeply back into the dispersion and numbness of consumer experience.

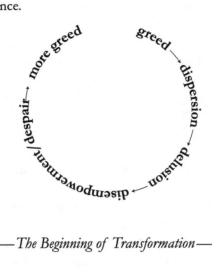

Step II—The Beginning of Transformation—Personal

Buddhism provides many integrated systems of practice for the "structural adjustment" of the spirit. Perhaps the most straightforward yet profound encapsulations are the three interconnected practices of *sila-samadhi-panna* (proper action-mindfulness-wisdom).

In the face of unlimited greed and our inability to distinguish between needs and desires, *sila* provides us with a starting point in a system of discipline and ethics. Buddhism elaborates on this in some detail, but in order to come to grips with its meaning, perhaps sila is best understood as "renunciation." In essence it is letting go of certain pleasures in order to experience a higher meaning or to accomplish a more important goal. A traveling musician renounces a settled home in search of the inspiring muse. A student limits his/her "partying" in order to graduate on time. The variations on this theme are endless, because renunciation does not mean going hungry in the woods. We remember that correct Buddhist practice does not involve extremism but rather the middle way of moderation.

By adopting basic practices of renunciation, we begin to reassert the social value of simplicity. Then, those in poverty will not be seen as only half-human "under-consumers." Without such a disempowering view of poverty, or a paternalistic approach that tries to bring less fortunate people into the fold of our consumer values, those who are materially poor may rediscover their powers of self-determination and find their true priorities in their own quest for material and spiritual stability for themselves. The materially rich will be transformed as well. Traditional Buddhist societies evaluated people of wealth not by how much they had accumulated but by how many soup kitchens or shelters they had established. When renunciation and generosity are recognized as essential social values, it becomes clearer to the rich what they actually need for a comfortable life. The rest is excess to be shared with subordinates and those of lesser means.

In the space and simplicity of a life with a certain level of renunciation, the second component of Buddhist practice enters, namely, *samadhi* or mindfulness. With the Walkman and TV cleared away or used only at certain times, the nature of our situation comes more evident. We begin to notice how other family members spend their time. The subtleties of a loved one's state of being become more apparent, and neighbors become more like colleagues or extended family rather than simply the unknown faces next door. More generally, our body, our ways of thinking and feeling, our interactions with the world become more conscious. The relationships between physical well-being and emotional and mental well-being are more easily perceived. Chronic ailments might be ameliorated with simple adjustments. Connections in a disconnected world begin to be restored.

In the most basic method of Buddhist meditation, mindfulness with breathing *(anapanasati),* the long slow breath yields greater mindfulness, awareness, and well-being. Using this basic awareness technique, we can experience that action films and other multimedia entertainment, caffeine and nicotine, Internet surfing and computer use, sports thrills, and shopping mall dazzlements all tend to make our breathing shorter and quicker, and in turn make our thoughts faster, less connected, less mindful.

With the development of some restraint (renunciation) and some mindfulness, the third component of Buddhist practice arises, *panna* or wisdom. Renunciation opens our life up to different experiences in the present. Mindfulness enables us to become more aware of these moments and to enter into them more deeply. We begin to see the delusion of events surrounding us. We begin to see the bite of our greed and dispersion, which had seemed so pleasurable before. We begin to see the impermanence and instability of these pleasures, the frustrations they concoct as they fade and as we squirm and writhe to re-ignite them.

Wisdom, however, involves more than this. Some people view Buddhism as a value-free system for gaining mental power. It is indeed a very powerful tool for becoming aware of our attachments and cutting through them.

However, a Buddhism that uses sila and mindfulness to train corporate work-ers to be better employees, and to accomplish their tasks more ruthlessly, does not lead to genuine wisdom. Wisdom involves seeing the causes and conditions of events in our environment, yet it also implies using this wisdom for the benefit of others. Wisdom in the service of greed or power is not real wisdom. True wisdom harnesses the operative imperative of the human being, to spend a life supporting others as a vehicle free of defilement. Being free of attach-ments allows us to help ourselves by helping others.

METHODOLOGY 1: PERSONAL TRANSFORMATION

Step III—Expanding the Practice to the Social

The above discussion has outlined the process of personal transformation, yet, as we have just seen, wisdom (panna) includes a spontaneous desire to help others and society as a whole. This is envisioned as *Sangha* or community, the third pillar of Buddhism. When we reevaluate the Threefold Training in terms of its implications for community, we can see it as a means for con-fronting systems of exploitation resistant to individual challenges. The Three-fold training is the glue which brings and keeps community together.

First, sila (proper action) is the shared initiatives of the group. Sila is the expression of group solidarity, renouncing individual advantage and working for betterment of the community. Secondly, coming out of community solidarity (sila) is community mindfulness (samadhi) which finds expression in community awareness practices. Mindfulness takes form in religious communities as group prayer or meditation or ritual, traditional and powerful forms for maintaining community connections. In any community, mindfulness can also take form as the deepening of local and regional cultural heritage through the arts. Furthermore, mindfulness can take form in the preservation or re-awakening of knowledge of local plant and animal species which can offer the community sustainable resources for medicines, food, clothing, and shelter. Theoretically, mindfulness involves developing concentration into unity or one-pointedness. Thus, practically, in terms of community, it means bringing individuals together in united awareness and feeling through the sharing of time, energy, and information.

Third, developing out of solidarity (sila) and sharing (samadhi) is wisdom (panna) and the strength of mind to cut through delusion. By developing group solidarity in sila and sharing group knowledge in mindfulness, the community becomes a powerful center for social action. In following the imperative of wisdom to benefit others, such a community will not become a self-centered entity narrow-minded in outlook and hostile towards other communities. Rather, the imperative to help others moves the community outwards towards other communities using the same energy of solidarity-sharing-communal resources (sila-samadhi-panna) that enables their own smaller community to prosper. In this way, local community is built and strengthened while plugging into an ever-widening web of community. In the end, a truly beneficial global society can emerge where community, bioregion, landmass, continent, and world are united in a cooperative social project.

In Thailand, many rural communities have been dislocated by economic globalization. The people have lost their traditional mode of livelihood, farming, due to the development of corporate agriculture and the exposure of their food staples to the pressure of international markets. The invasion of consumer products, such as electronic appliances and soft drinks, has broken down traditional systems of cultural sharing and health while further enticing villagers to abandon their farms for the bright lights of wage labor in Bangkok. Traditionally, Buddhist monks have been leaders of the community while their temples have acted as community centers. In the past twenty years, a charismatic group of "development" monks have begun to apply the Buddhist system of practice, as outlined above, to the social dimension. Working with groups of dedicated lay followers, they have sought to regain a modicum of community autonomy by using the power of local consumption.

New buffalo banks and rice banks, based in village temples, have enabled villagers to avoid purchasing unnecessary mechanized farming equipment and chemical fertilizers from national and international corporations, as well as rice at inflated prices from their own government (i.e., social sila). The financing systems for acquiring these goods, made necessary by outside economic manipulations of the local economy, had further indebted the farmers, forcing them into deeper poverty and eventually off their land. Such temples have integrated these community initiatives with personal development of the community. By establishing meditation classes, gambling and the consumption of expensive (and economically debilitating) local and foreign liquors have been reduced. By adapting traditional social events at the temple, such as robe-offering ceremonies for the monks, temples have been able to raise funds for community development projects. Monks and lay leaders have used these occasions to raise consciousness among villagers (i.e., social samadhi). Community-created initiatives such as cooperative stores keep local money in the local community, a twofold example of Right Consumption: such projects promote the diversion of excess money into community projects rather than into private consumption, and they also help to develop and maintain locally-run businesses that can be more accountable to the community (i.e., social panna). Finally, the expansion of such a vision beyond village empowerment can be seen in the coordination of the "development" monks into a national network called Phra Sekhiyadhamma. The network coordinates and shares material and spiritual resources in a movement for national transformation.

METHODOLOGY 2: SOCIAL TRANSFORMATION

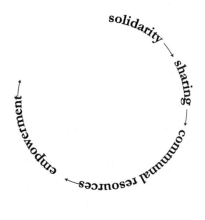

Conclusion: Imperatives Beyond Doubt

The results of such Buddhist initiatives towards community regeneration and social transformation nevertheless raise a number of issues. The above examples from Thailand involve mostly rural responses from societies relatively less integrated into the global economy. Such attempts, and others like the well-known Sarvodaya initiative in Sri Lanka, have not been immune to the powerful forces of the market and consumerism that eat away at communal solidarity. Two important questions, therefore, need to be addressed. How effective can religious, and specifically Buddhist, responses be in societies more deeply integrated into the global economy? And what role can this kind of socially engaged Buddhism serve in the larger world of institutionalized Buddhism?

For Buddhist societies more deeply integrated into the global economy, the prospects of such Buddhist engagement seem doubtful. In Japan, for example, although a number of consumer movements exist, they are rarely informed by Buddhist teachers or Buddhist communities. In general, Japanese Buddhism is more of a supporter of modern consumption patterns with expensive and elaborate funerals (Japan's third largest industry) and temple tourism. Indeed, throughout the Buddhist world, both East and West, mainstream Buddhism tends to support the modern drive for material wealth and spiritual sanctification through conspicuous consumption. In the West, there is the consumerism of expensive retreats and ritualistic paraphernalia. Further, there has been the rise of new schools of Buddhism which teach that material gain is a sign of spiritual blessing (Sokka Gakkai from Japan, and Dhammakaya in Thailand). There is plenty of evidence to support the conclusion that Buddhism is a specious practice for the personal and social transformation of our present economic and social injustices.

Buddhism, however, is not alone in this situation. The co-opting of every aspect of our humanity and spirituality by the consumerist "religion of the market" casts doubt on any method of social transformation so long as it is governed by market and consumer forces. This is where religion and spirituality as systems of humanity are able to rise above such material considerations and still have potential and meaning. One of the strengths of the socially engaged Buddhist approach is its basically nonsectarian character. Socially engaged Buddhism has become a nurturing ground for people of other faiths, as well as for people lacking any spiritual commitment, to discover a systematic method for personal and social transformation. Socially engaged Buddhism has been able to link with and be enriched by similar movements in other religions and other secular forms of human cooperation.

Envisioning social change as a matter of engineering a group of isolated nodes is limiting and, in the end, unsatisfactory. Consumerism is a vital issue which society needs to address. Buddhism is a spiritual "resource" that has much to offer on this issue. When we stop engineering and start transforming, we see that consumption cannot be treated as an isolated variable. Once we begin to examine socially engaged Buddhist and engaged spirituality approaches, we begin to realize that transforming consumption patterns is only part of a much more wide-ranging and fundamental transformation of our human psyche and our society.

How Not to Feast from the Poison Cake

by Bo Lozoff

A FRIEND OF OURS here in North Carolina recently lost her beautiful nineteen-year-old son to suicide. She told us he was the sixth among a small group of friends who had committed suicide in the past two-and-a-half years. Suicide is now the third leading cause of death among teenagers (murder is number two, car accidents are number one).

We need to start asking ourselves some searching questions about why life seems to be of so little value to our kids. From a spiritual perspective, one sentence can sum up the whole thing—not only our own and our kids' problems, but our planetary problems too, from pollution to wars—Human life is very deep, and our dominant modern lifestyle is not.

Life is inherently joyful, yet we're not enjoying it. We're caught in the details, in the "hundred other tasks" which will count for nothing if we don't wake up to our spiritual depth. Even the best, most loving people often seem to be working themselves into the ground, keeping up a frantic pace just to pay the bills and keep resolving each day's repairs, breakdowns, details, and little crises.

We seem to be knocking ourselves out in pursuit of a vague image of success and meaning, while the real quality of our everyday life with our families and communities steadily declines. We're asleep at the wheel, swept up in a fitful, agitated dream, and we're missing some gorgeous scenery that only passes by once.

When the Buddha experienced his great enlightenment, he got up from where he had been sitting and walked toward the village. The first person who saw him was awestruck by his radiance and power. The man approached him and said, "Sir, what *are* you? Are you a god?" The Buddha said, "No." The man said, "Well, are you a spirit or a demigod?" Again, the Buddha said, "No." "Are you a human being?" Once more, the Buddha said, "No." The man said,

"Well what *are* you, then?" The Buddha replied, "I am awake." And then he spent the rest of his life making it clear to us that we can awaken too. The joy is right here right now; we just need to wake up to it.

So what has gotten so out of whack in modern times? Why does it seem so complex and draining merely to pay the bills and just get by?

For one thing, our consumer culture encourages us from the time we're born to have *ceaseless* desires. To put it simply, we want so much, all the time, that we have not even noticed how much quality of life we have given up, how much peace of mind we have sacrificed, how much fun with our family we have forfeited in order to have the right shoes, cellular phones, TVs in every room, sexy cars—all the stuff that counts for zero in the deeper part of ourselves.

American life especially has been about "keeping up with the Joneses," but it is time we noticed that the Joneses are not happy. One of their kids is on drugs, the parents are in divorce court, Mr. Jones is on antidepressants, and Mrs. Jones is taking antianxiety medication. This is no joke; this is the reality of the American Dream for most people in the twenty-first century. Time to wake up from such a bad dream.

A second, related culprit of our imbalance is the role of "career" in our lives. Career seems to have become the accepted hub around which everything else revolves. We choose career over our health. We choose career over our mates and children. We choose career over our time to study, pray, walk, hike, meditate, participate in community life. We fuss over our children's potential careers like it's the most important thing in the world. If our child wants to take a year or two off between high school and college, we freak out. We worry they'll "get behind." What does that mean? What's the message?

Career is not deep enough to be the center of life. Career is not who you are. It's something you do for twenty or thirty years and then you stop. If you sink all your identity into it, then your life hasn't started until your career begins, and it's basically over when your career ends. An astounding percentage of American men die within three years of retirement. That's sad, foolish, and unnecessary. Career hardly scratches the surface of who you are. Character and virtue and wisdom and joy are the mark of a person, not one's choice of career. Contentment is a virtue. A lack of materialistic ambition is not such a bad thing.

The most valuable form of activism in this day and age may be to explore a lifestyle based around simple living and simple joy. It may take toning down our materialistic demands and figuring out how to live on less income, but that process itself will begin to save some of the world's resources and thereby address many of the world's pressing problems, as well as giving us more time with our families and communities.

In cultures where people must share limited resources—TVs, power tools, vehicles—their sense of community is much stronger. We have bought in to a model of progress and personal choice that has isolated us as individuals and has actually damaged our family and community life a great deal. Is that really progress?

So these days, it is political activism to go against that tide. Share tools with our neighbors, cut down to one TV in our home (and cut down our use of it greatly), eat meals with our families, go for walks, do daily readings of spiritual stories, occasionally play hooky together, and go skip stones across a pond. It is activism to slow down and move through the day more gracefully; activism to explain to our kids the hype and deceit involved with the endless ads that incite them to buy something new or follow the latest craze. Our kids may be deeper if we treat them with depth. Our kids may be deeper if we are.

Perhaps the saddest, most disturbing consequence of the "let's buy something new" mentality is personal consumer debt. While on a flight to Nebraska to do some talks and workshops recently, I read a cover story in *USA Today* about the problem of personal debt. The average American is something like $10,000 in debt, mostly on credit cards. Most people pay the minimum monthly payment. A graph in the article showed that with a debt of $10,000, paying the minimum of $200/month—which is a pretty big chunk of most people's salary—it would take fifty years to pay off the total. That's $120,000 to pay off $10,000. Is that okay with you? Are you willing to pay $6,000 for that $500 washing machine? $4,800 for that $400 television set? That's how much you're really paying when you buy things on time.

Peddling credit cards to college students is also a big new industry. The article said modern students no longer want to live "on the cheap" while in school. No more old jalopies, or mattresses on the floor. Now, minimum monthly payments enable them to live in whatever style they like. But again, at what cost? Their whole lives? Besides such credit debt, according to the *Boston Globe,* American college students also have an average debt of $18,000 in student loans upon graduation with a bachelor's degree, and $40,000 average debt for masters' degrees or Ph.D.s.

Amazing. Millions of people, young and old, are rushing to enslave themselves to big corporations for the rest of their lives, to support a lifestyle that has little to do with joy or truth or freedom.

There is certainly an alternative to being consumer sheep fattened for the slaughter. We can step away from the "let's buy something new" impulse both internally, through simple spiritual practices which clear our vision and cultivate our courage and faith; and externally, through creating a simpler lifestyle which not only requires a lot less money, but also gives us more time for the things that really do matter. We can go from "loving things and using people," back to "loving people and using things."

It takes work, of course. Any time we step aside from the crowds there will be work involved. Maybe people trying to discourage us. Fellow slaves mock our efforts to be free. Mahatma Gandhi called his autobiography, *My Experiments with Truth*. That is the opportunity each of us has — not just what we read in the evening, not just in church on Sundays — to make our everyday lives a grand, noble, good-humored experiment in truth. Where what we do for a living (and how much time we spend doing it), where we live, how our children are educated, the causes we embrace and support, how we spend our free time are all one thing. An undivided whole. A deliberate life. This is a rare thing in today's world.

Many people say, "Oh, I could easily live in a simpler way or dedicate my life to a cause I believe in, but it would be unfair to my children. What about health care? What about their college education? I don't want to limit their opportunities."

Raising our kids to be indentured servants of the credit card companies and prostitutes to the dollar seems extremely limiting to me! I know perfectly healthy people in their twenties taking jobs they don't like because the employers offer the most "bennies" — benefits like health insurance and retirement plans. Do we want our kids to sell their lives to the highest bidder? Is that all life is about? We have seriously lost a "Big View."

The truth is, no matter how we live, we risk limiting our children's experience. Poor kids think there are no bad parts to being rich; rich kids think there are no good parts to being poor. Kids on a farm don't know the benefits of traveling, and kids who have seen the world may not have the deep connection to one place they can call home. Our personal interests and values necessarily define much about our kids' lives, so we must make sure we have deliberate and deep values rather than the "default" values of a dysfunctional, unhappy culture.

If family life doesn't provide a deep view about our purpose for being alive and the importance of respecting all beings, then our children may grow up like

Lord of the Flies—feasting on a poison cake—which seems to be exactly what's happening for a great number of modern children who are lost, selfish, close-minded, angry, violent. Without lots of joyful guidance from us, they meet a confusing and frightening world.

I find it sweetly ironic that the Great Activism of our day—inspiring our children to stay alive, and to live and behave in civilized ways—requires us to rediscover the simple joy of life for ourselves as well. We have to do it. Nothing less will do.

What Then Must We Do?

by David Edwards

A S WE BEGIN to become aware of the true scale and causes of suffering, we quickly find ourselves confronted by the central question: What can we do to make a difference?

There is, I think, more to this question than meets the eye. If we were as intent on kindly behavior as this question suggests, the question itself would surely be redundant—good causes in need of urgent assistance are hardly in short supply or difficult to find. In full, the real question perhaps should read: Is there some way I can reconcile my desire for personal happiness with my desire to do something about the suffering and destructiveness that afflicts our world? That is, I want to do something but not at the expense of my own happiness. How, then, can I find the motivation?

The problem of motivation is surely resolved by the Buddhist conception of compassion. When we realize that a compassionate life dedicated to relieving the suffering of others is also far more conducive to our own happiness than a life of self-destructive greed, then we have discovered the motivation, the means, and the goal.

The standard Western objection to doing something is, of course, the assertion that the problems facing us are just too big and too entrenched for us to be able to make any real difference. Why support Amnesty International by writing letters about despots in Tibet when the world is overflowing with torture and misery? Why campaign to protect the environment, when greed is so entrenched and so ably assisted by corporate power? Why try to reform the factory-farming system when every year hundreds of millions of animals are killed or die of natural causes all over the world? What is the point of doing something kind when the world is awash with pain? Why do any of these things, when all of us share the fate to grow ill and die—that is, to suffer?

Another similar objection is the idea that to seek to be a little kinder without being a perfect saint is hypocritical: to stop swatting flies while continuing to eat meat, for example. But whether or not we can become fully enlightened beings, or whether the world can be turned into some kind of utopia, is beside the point. The Buddhist assertion is that by reducing our selfishness and increasing our compassion and kindness we will make life better for ourselves and for those around us. We do not refuse to keep ourselves clean because the world is full of unwashed bodies or because we will someday die. We wash because it is conducive to our current and future health and happiness. So, too, generosity and kindness can wash away some of the self-destructive selfishness and cruelty from our minds to the benefit of all. The difference is that, unlike physical washing, as we practice compassion we can become better at it, stronger, more all-inclusive, with increasing benefits for everyone.

The answer to the question of what we should do is found in the nature of the problems facing us, which fall into two categories. Firstly, the ultimate source of the destruction of the Third World and environment is in the individual human tendency to greed, hatred, and ignorance. Secondly, these destructive forces have become institutionalized in political, economic, and media forces which depend upon the promotion of these same forces for their survival. Both aspects of the problem need to be tackled simultaneously. As Stephen Batchelor writes :

> The contemporary social engagement of Dharma practice is rooted in awareness of how self-centred confusion and craving can no longer be adequately understood only as psychological drives that manifest themselves in subjective states of anguish. We find these drives embodied in the very economic, military, and political structures that influence the lives of the majority of people on earth.[26]

I agree that if we are serious about relieving suffering, we need to combat greed, hatred, and ignorance as manifested in ourselves as individuals but also as manifested in these institutions. The two tasks are inseparable: understanding the goals and nature of the institutions of power is a key factor in combating greed, hatred, and ignorance in ourselves. For example, to rely on the corporate media as a credible source of news about the world is to lay ourselves open to massive indoctrination. Political deceptions such as the notion that we are free, that the West supports human rights around the world (in fact it very often supports profits at the expense of human rights), that real action is already being taken to protect the environment (in fact action on global warming remains trivial) will impair our critical and compassionate faculties. We will also be ensnared by deep self-deception promoted by corporate consumerism, such as the idea that unrestrained satisfaction of personal desires is conducive to happiness, social harmony, environmental security, and the economic well-being of our country. Trained to stand in awe of our superiors and experts generally, we may have great difficulty taking ourselves seriously, and the idea that we might have some role to play in helping to respond to these problems may strike us as an embarrassing and presumptuous fantasy.

An ability to appreciate the true nature and drives of corporate capitalist institutions frees us from the business-friendly version of reality, allowing us to take a genuinely critical look at the nature of what is and is not conducive to happiness and social reform. We can come to appreciate, for example, that the idea that a more compassionate society is impractical and unrealistic from an economic point of view, is a deception designed to perpetuate inequality.

The Myth of "Tough Love": Sacrifice, Ancient and Modern

In his book *The Buddha,* Trevor Ling notes that the Brahmanical sacrificial system into which the Buddha was born was based on the idea that the world "was kept in existence, and the important aims of human life were achieved, by the operation of the sacrifice."[27]

Because the brahmans alone understood how the sacrifice was to be effectively performed, they deemed it their duty to perform this task and consequently considered themselves to be the most essential class in society. Both of these claims were rejected by the Buddha. He is said to have criticized the tradition of sacrifice "on the grounds of economic wastefulness, cruelty to animals, forced labor, with harsh treatment of the laborers, and oppressive taxation of the people in order to pay for it all."[28]

Buddhists have rightly argued that this attitude to sacrifice is indicative of the Buddha's rationalism, his rejection of all unfounded superstition. We could also interpret his rejection in another way, however, by considering the practice of sacrifice in the modern context. After all, is not our entire social, economic, and political system built on the idea of the need for sacrifice? We are all of us aware that our nation is filled with poor, disadvantaged people, and families struggling to survive. We know also that the world's two hundred richest people possess as much wealth as 40 percent of the world's population. We know that a billion people are living in abject poverty, suffering the effects of starvation, disease, and other miseries. So why do we not do something to help those who need help? Because, as in the Buddha's time, we are told (and are convinced) that the world is kept in existence, that the important aims of human life are achieved by an economic and political system dependent on this necessary sacrifice. To tinker with this system too much, to spend too much on the poor, to spend too much on housing, education, and health, would bring the whole structure crashing down. It is possible, we are told, to be too kind: compassion for all would simply lead to disaster.

Thus Britain's role as a supplier of five billion dollars worth of arms a year, constituting almost a quarter of total world sales, is defended on the basis of the need to preserve "jobs" (actually profits), regardless of the possibilities of conversion to peaceful production and the complete moral redundancy of an argument that pits lives against jobs. After disingenuously declaring that Labour would put "human rights at the heart of our foreign policy,"[29] Foreign Secretary Robin Cook announced that "the government is committed to the maintenance of a strong defense industry, which is a strategic part of our industrial base,"[30] which, of course, puts arms manufacturers' profits at the heart of our foreign policy.

Corporate attempts to block limits on greenhouse gas emissions are ultimately based on the same notion of the need to sacrifice others for the sake of "jobs" and "economic growth" (for which read, once again, profits). Consider the following letter sent by the Executive Vice President of the U.S. National Association of Manufacturers in May 2001:

> Dear Mr. President:
> On behalf of 14,000 member companies of the National Association of Manufacturers (NAM)—and the eighteen million people who make things in America—thank you for your opposition to the Kyoto Protocol on the grounds that it exempts eighty percent of the world and will cause serious harm to the United States.[31]

This letter was sent four years after Nobel Laureate Henry Kendall, chairman of the Union of Concerned Scientists, warned in 1997:

> Let there be no doubt about the conclusions of the scientific
> community that the threat of global warming is very real and
> action is needed immediately. It is a grave error to believe that we
> can continue to procrastinate.[32]

The basic principle at work is the idea that some people have to be sacrificed, that not everyone can be treated compassionately if basic stability and prosperity are to be maintained.

It is exactly this idea that the Buddha rejected. His insistence was always that happiness could not be built on the suffering of others: "Don't try to build your happiness on the unhappiness of others. You will be enmeshed in a net of hatred."[33]

As we have seen, the Buddhist view is that individual happiness can only be based on the promotion of happiness for all.

In one tale of the Buddha's former lives, the Buddha-to-be is said to have ruled over a land afflicted by great drought and disaster. In the tale, ministers and religious advisors insisted that a large sacrifice (that is, "tough love") was required to save the people (that is, "our industrial base"). The Buddha was unimpressed; he might almost have been referring to our own political and economic leaders when he said:

> Truly, those who are proclaimed the best refuge among men are
> often those who do the most harm, all in the name of religion
> [in our time, "national prosperity"]. Alas for any who follow such
> a path, for they end in desperate straits, surrounded by the evils
> they think to avoid! What connection can there possibly be
> between virtuous behavior and the killing of animals?[34]

Instead, the Buddha had a different kind of sacrifice in mind:

> The protection of my subjects has always been my highest aim.
> Now. . . my people have themselves become worthy to receive
> the gifts of sacrifice. . . . Let anyone who seeks to fuel his happiness by wealth come and accept all he wishes from my hand.[35]

As a result of his great kindness and generosity, "all his subjects grounded their lives in virtue, and the powers of evil faded away."[36] For how could a nation not prosper where the people were inspired by an example of generosity on this scale?:

> The people of that land indeed enjoyed the wonders of a Golden Age, for their practice of virtue, self-control, good conduct, and modesty continued unabated. The strength of the king's sacrifice, performed in accordance with the spirit of the law, put an end to the sufferings of the poor. The country teemed with a thriving and happy populace. . . .[37]

Significantly for our own time, the story notes that this revolution in generosity and virtue also had the effect of resolving all the environmental problems: "The seasons succeeded one another in due course, gladdening everyone with their regularity. The Earth produced all kinds of food in abundance."[38]

This is a kind of deep libertarian view, arguing that the growth of compassionate values in society has effects that go far beyond what we might immediately expect or imagine, even to the point of healing the environment. These profound effects, though hard to divine and impossible to quantify, are very real, and the same is true for individual acts of compassion. Superficially, giving money to other—maybe unknown—people might seem a kind of waste. But the effects of such actions on our lives can go far beyond merely having less money to spend. To be more generous consistently will radically affect the kind of thoughts and emotions we experience, the kind of impression we make on other people, the kind of reception we receive, the kind of relationships we develop. According to Buddhism, the same is equally true for whole societies and their relationship with their environments.

This deep libertarian view rejects the idea that suffering is an unfortunate necessity that must be tolerated. No one needs to be sacrificed for some spurious notion of "stability," or "strategic" necessity. The stability that exists in our own time is stability for a wealthy few, and chaotic instability for the rest of us. Stability nowadays means maintaining state and corporate pipelines of exploitation, stifling critical thought and compassion with ceaseless propaganda, and the systematic repression of impoverished, men, women, and children in the Third World. This is the stability of a prison regime.

Real personal, social, and global environmental stability can only be rooted in a commitment to kindness and compassion for all. The world is not maintained by economic management alone: it is maintained by kindness and compassion. To strengthen that understanding and commitment is to improve and strengthen all human relations, including economic relations, immeasurably.

Re-Imagining the American Dream

by Elizabeth Thoman

L IKE MOST MIDDLE-CLASS children of the fifties, I grew up looking for the American Dream. In those days there were no cartoons in my Saturday viewing, but I distinctly remember watching, with some awe, "Industry on Parade." I felt both pride and eager anticipation as I watched tail-finned cars rolling off assembly lines, massive dams taming mighty rivers, and sleek chrome appliances making life more convenient for all.

When I heard the mellifluous voice of Ronald Reagan announce on GE Theatre that "Progress is our most important product," little did I realize that the big box in our living room was not just entertaining me. At a deeper level, it was stimulating an "image" in my head of how the world should work: that anything new was better than something old; that science and technology were the greatest of all human achievements and that in the near future—and certainly by the time I grew up—the power of technology would make it possible for everyone to live and work in a world free of war, poverty, drudgery, and ignorance.

I believed it because I could see it—right there on television.

The American Dream, however, was around long before television. Some believe the idea of "progress" goes back to when humankind first conceived of time as linear rather than cyclical. Certainly the Judeo-Christian heritage of a messiah leading us to a Promised Land inspired millions to strive for a better world for generations to come.

Indeed, it was the search for the "City on the Hill" that brought the Puritans to the American colonies and two centuries later sent covered wagons across the prairies. In 1835, Alexis de Tocqueville observed that Americans "never stop thinking of the good things they have not got," creating a "restlessness in the midst of prosperity" that drives them ever onward.

Even the U.S. Constitution only promises the pursuit of happiness. It doesn't guarantee that any of us will actually achieve it. It is this search for "something-more-than-what-we've-got-now" that is at the heart of the consumer culture we struggle with today. But the consumer culture as we know it could never have emerged without the invention of the camera and the eventual mass production of media images it made possible.

Reproducing Pictures

In 1859 Oliver Wendell Holmes described photography as the most remarkable achievement of his time because it allowed human beings to separate an experience or a texture or an emotion or a likeness from a particular time and place — and still remain real, visible, and permanent. He described it as a "conquest over matter" and predicted it would alter the physics of perception, changing forever the way people would see and understand the world around them. Holmes precisely observed that the emergence of this new technology marked the beginning of a time when the "image would become more important than the object itself and would in fact make the object disposable."

Contemporary advertising critic Stuart Ewen describes the photographic process as "skinning" the world of its visible images, then marketing those images inexpensively to the public. But successive waves of what might be called reality-freezing technology—first the photograph, followed by the phonograph, and then the motion picture camera—were only some of the many nineteenth century transformations that paved the way to our present image culture. As the wheels of industrialization began to mass-produce more and more consumer goods, they also increased the leisure time available to use these products and the disposable income required to buy them. Soon the well-being of the economy itself became dependent on an ever-expanding cornucopia of products, goods, and services. The Sears Roebuck catalogue and the department store emerged to showcase America's new abundance and by the turn of the century, as media critic Todd Gitlin notes, "production, packaging, marketing, advertising, and sales became functionally inseparable."

The flood of commercial images also served as a rough-and-ready consumer education course for the waves of immigrants arriving on America's shores and the thousands of rural folk lured to the city by visions of wealth. Advertising was seen as a way of educating the masses "to the cycle of the marketplace and to the imperatives of factory work and mechanized labor"—teaching them "how to behave like human beings in the machine age," according to the Boston department store magnate, Edward A. Filne. In a work world where skill meant less and less, obedience and appearance took on greater importance. In a city full of strangers, advertising offered instructions on how to dress, how to behave, how to appear to others in order to gain approval and avoid rejection.

Granted, the American "standard of living" brought an end to drudgery for some, but it demanded a price from all: consumerism. Divorced from craft standards, work became merely the means to acquire the money to buy the goods and lifestyle that supposedly signified social acceptance, respect, even prestige. "Ads spoke less and less about the quality of the products being sold," notes Stuart Ewen, "and more about the lives of the people being addressed."

In 1934, when the Federal Communications Commission approved advertising as the economic basis of the country's fledgling radio broadcasting system, the die was cast. Even though early broadcasters pledged to provide free time for educational programs, for coverage of religion, and for news (creating the famous phrase: the "public interest, convenience, and necessity"), it wasn't long before the industry realized that time was money—and every minute counted. But it was not until the 1950s that the image culture came into full flower. The reason? Television.

Television was invented in the 1930s, but for many years no one thought it had any practical use. Everyone had a radio, even two or three, which brought news and sports and great entertainment right into your living room And if you tired of the antics of Fibber McGee and Molly or the adventures of Sergeant Preston of the Yukon, you could always go to the movies, which was what most people did at least once a week.

So who needed television? No one, really. What needed television, in 1950, was the economy. The postwar economy needed television to deliver first to America—and then to the rest of the world—the vision and the image of life in a consumer society. We didn't object because we thought it was, well, "progress."

Progress at What Price?

Kalle Lasn, a cofounder of the Canadian media criticism and environmentalist magazine *Adbusters,* explains how dependence on television occurred and how it continues today each time we turn on our sets:

In the privacy of our living rooms we made a devil's bargain with the advertising industry: Give us an endless flow of free programs and we'll let you spend twelve minutes of every hour promoting consumption. For a long time, it seemed to work. The ads grated on our nerves but it was a small price to pay for "free" television. What we didn't realize when we made our pact with the advertisers was that their agenda would eventually become the heart and soul of television. We have allowed the most powerful communications tool ever invented to become the command center of a consumer society defining our lives and culture the way family, community, and spiritual values once did.[39]

This does not mean that when we see a new toilet paper commercial we're destined to rush down to the store to buy its new or improved brand. Most single commercials do not have such a direct impact. What happens instead is a cumulative effect. Each commercial plays its part in selling an overall consumer lifestyle. As advertising executive Stephen Garey noted in a recent issue of *Media&Values,* when an ad for toilet paper reaches us in combination with other TV commercials, magazine ads, radio spots, and billboards for detergents and designer jeans, new cars and cigarettes, and soft drinks and cereals and computers, the collective effect is that they all teach us to buy. We are supposed to feel somehow dissatisfied and inadequate unless we have the newest, the latest, the best.

Just like our relatives at the turn of the century, we learned quickly to yearn for "what we have not got" and to take our identities from what we own and purchase rather than from who we are or how we interact with others. Through consuming things, through buying more and more, we continue the quest for meaning which earlier generations sought in other ways — conquering the oceans, settling the land, building the modern society, even searching for transcendence through religious belief and action. With few places on Earth left to conquer, the one endless expanse of exploration open to us is the local shopping mall.

Transcending Materialism

Thus the modern dilemma: Few of us would turn in our automatic washing machines for a scrub board or exchange our computers for a slide rule, and we cannot expect the images of the past to provide the vision for the future. We must recognize the tradeoffs we have made and take responsibility for the society we have created.

For many today, the myth of "progress" is stuttering to a stop. The economic slowdown of the early nineties presents only the most recent example of the human suffering created by the boom and bust cycles of the consumer economy. But even if some magic formula could make steady economic growth attainable, we can no longer afford it. Material limits have been set by the Earth herself. Unlimited exploitation in the name of "progress" is no longer sustainable.

True progress, in fact, would be toward a materially renewable lifestyle that would fulfill the physical, spiritual, and emotional needs of all—not just some—of the world's people, while allowing them to live in peace and freedom. Under such a system, communication's most important aim would be to bring people together. Selling things would be a part of its function, but not the whole.

Disasters like Chernobyl and the Alaskan oil spill raise hard questions about the long-term social impact of technological innovation. In the U.S., the loss of whole communities to the ravages of drugs, crime, and homelessness threatens the very principles that allow any humane society to flourish. At the same time, the global events of 1991—the breakup of the Soviet Empire, the struggles for national identity, even the rise of fundamentalist governments in many parts of the Third World—bear witness to a growing desire for meaningful connections as well as material and political progress.

In many ways we are living in a new world, and around that world hungry eyes are turning toward the Western democracies' long-standing promises of freedom and abundance—the promises the media has so tantalizingly presented. Yet behind the media culture's constantly beckoning shop window lies an ever-widening gap. West or East, North or South, the flickering images of the media remain our window on the world, but they bear less and less relationship to the circumstances of our day-to-day lives.

Reality has fallen out of sync with the pictures, but still the image culture continues. We'll never stop living in a world of images. But we can recognize and deal with the image culture's actual state, which might be characterized as a kind of midlife crisis—a crisis of identity. As with any such personal event, three responses are typical:

1) Denial. Hoping that a problem will go away if we ignore it is a natural response, but business as usual is no solution.

2) Rejection. Some critics believe they can use their television dials to make the image culture go away, and urge others to turn it off, too. But it's impossible to turn off an entire culture. Others check out emotionally by using drugs, alcohol, or addictions of all kinds to vainly mask the hunger for meaning that comes when reality and images don't converge.

3) Resistance. A surprisingly active counterculture exists and is working hard to point out the dangers of over-reliance on the image culture. But such criticism is negative by its very nature, and critics tend to remain voices crying in the wilderness.

A positive alternative is needed. What I have called media awareness—the recognition of media's role in shaping our lives and molding our deepest thoughts and feelings—is an important step.

The steps I have outlined above provide simple but effective tools for beginning to work through this process. Although they seem basic, they have their roots in the profound state of being that Buddhism calls mindfulness: being aware, carefully examining, asking questions, and being conscious.

Even a minimal effort to be conscious can make day-to-day media use more meaningful. Being conscious allows us to appreciate the pleasure of a new CD album and then later turn it off to read a bedtime story to a child. Being conscious means enjoying a TV sitcom while challenging the commercials that bait us to buy. Being conscious allows us to turn even weekend sports events into an intergenerational get-together. But however it is achieved, media awareness is only a first step. Ultimately, any truly meaningful attempt to move beyond the image culture needs to recognize the spiritual and emotional emptiness that material objects cannot fill.

To move beyond the illusions of the image culture we must begin to grapple with some deeper questions: Where is the fine line between what I want and what all in society should have? What is the common good for all? Or to rephrase Gandhi: How do we create a society in which there is enough for everyone's need but not everyone's greed?

Thousands of years ago Plato wrote of a cave of illusion in which captive humans were enraptured by a flood of images that appeared before them while they ignored the reality outside the cave. This prophetic metaphor contained its own solution. Once again we are summoned into the light.

A Quick Q & A on Buddhism & Materialism

by Joan Halifax

Question: What are your views about globalization?

Joan: From the point of view of interconnectedness, we are already globalized. From the point of view of diversity, plurality, and heterogeneity, we'd better be careful. In Buddhism, there are three *kayas,* or Buddha bodies: emptiness, interconnectedness, and uniqueness. Global health requires that these three bodies be in balance.

Question: How do we go about constructing criteria for "compassionate consumption"?

Joan: We should ask, "By consuming this, am I enlightening myself?" Be aware that whatever we consume entails loss and suffering. The Japanese call this: *mono non aware,* "the slender sadness," which means that by living we cause suffering and death to other beings. Look deeply at your vegetarian food. Many beings died for us to enjoy a carrot.

Question: Other than in terms of health and safety, what defines a product, idea, or image as toxic, and how do we transform the toxins in our collective consciousness?

Joan: Whatever reifies the sense of a separate self-identity is toxic, as toxic means the three root poisons of desire, hatred, and delusion. Ideally, practice shows us the way through the barrier gates of these three toxins to the wisdom found behind each.

Question: How does practicing right consumption in our own life benefit others?

Joan: How doesn't it?!

Question: Since we can't practice "compassionate consumption" perfectly, why is it important to practice it at all?

Joan: We are all headed down the highway of death, and with this in mind, ask yourself, what is it that is really worthwhile to do? Consume more things, or help others and wake up from our own delusion?

Question: How can mindfulness in the marketplace be an antidote to substance addictions?

Joan: If only we could see how we are not separate from any being or thing. Addiction is a deep hunger for what we seem to lack, but who is lacking, and how are we not connected?

Question: How does Buddhism distinguish between the desire for pleasurable objects and the desire for well-being?

Joan: To be free of suffering is to realize that we are not separate from any being or thing. What is lacking then?

Question: How do we transform the inevitable pain of modern existence so that it does not manifest in needless and damaging forms of consumption?

Joan: We first need to recognize our terrible loneliness and fear. Then, perhaps, with effort, we can accept it. Everything in our culture begs us to consume with a sense of separateness driving us. We are conditioned to grasp, from mother's breast to each other and our so-called resources. Can we accept that we needlessly and heedlessly consume, and then penetrate to the depths of that hunger? In this process, ask yourself, "How do I really want to die?" Saint Theresa of Avila said: "Thank God for all I do not own." Finally, can we appreciate our life in this moment, with each other, in our very situation?

Question: Is the cultivation of wealth outside the bounds of "compassionate consumption"?

Joan: Wealth should be shared and used to help relieve the suffering of others. That is all.

Question: Do monastics have a vested interest in the concentration of wealth so they might benefit from large gifts?

Joan: Monastics, in general, do not handle money, except insofar as it is used to feed and clothe them, and give them the simplest shelter. Monastics who are visionaries use money to create places of practice and healing.

Question: What is mindfulness of money and financial investments?

Joan: Helping others.

Question: What are some skillful ways to "let some cows go" in a materialistic society?

Joan: The Buddha did not advocate poverty; he advocated simplicity and felt wealth needed to be shared. Due to their karma, some people have more wealth than others. Those who have more need to help bring about economic justice through healing, practice, education, and other such good works.

Question: Why are consumer rights and access to adequate and honest information about goods and services necessary for compassionate consumption?

Joan: Who died for this tuna?

Question: Does nature or "biomimicry" model the way of "compassionate consumption"?

Joan: Nature is instinctual and non-biased in the ways of love and compassion. We, as humans with reflexive awareness, can cultivate compassion, love, and joy. What a gift to offer!

Question: Are democratic and participative structures of ownership and cooperation a prerequisite for a mindful consumer society?

Joan: Yes. We are equal and different.

Question: How does the Zen aesthetic of modesty, simplicity, and naturalness contribute to the elegance and attractiveness of "compassionate consumption"?

Joan: Perfectly, if possible.

Question: In what ways might "pop Buddhism" contribute to the excesses of a consumer driven society?

Joan: Many.

Question: How does Buddhism regard economic warfare—such as the strategy of consuming more in order to defeat those that would wage war against us?

Joan: Not well.

Question: When we are mindful of what has given us true joy and happiness in our life, what do we discover about the role that material things play?

Joan: A lot. It is often hard to let go of them, even as we are dying.

PART THREE

In the Market for Dharma

Contentment is the greatest wealth.
—*Buddha*

Ethical Economics

by His Holiness the Dalai Lama

I AM PLEASED to express my encouragement and support for dialogue about and exploration into the role of Buddhism in economics and the marketplace.

For a long time I have advocated the need for ethics or spiritual values in the world of politics and economics. In order to make this world a better, more humane, and safer place, we need to realize how interdependent we all are and therefore how we should take responsibility for one another. At the present time, globalization and advances in information technology have made our world so much smaller. This particularly applies to business leaders, whose actions affect the lives of many people, their employees, and the customers they serve all over the world.

Personally, I don't believe you need to be a religious or spiritual person to appreciate this reality and act accordingly. However, the world's religions all have in common an emphasis on developing qualities such as ethics, tolerance, and compassion. Some people may think that these sorts of ethical attitudes are not much needed within economic activity. I strongly disagree. The quality of all our actions depends on our motivation. In economics and business, as well as in the choices made by consumers, if you have a good motivation and seek to contribute to a better human society, you will be a good and honest businessperson or more conscious consumer.

On the global level, we must take immediate measures to create ethical codes in the worlds of business, finance, and the marketplace. For instance, global degradation of the natural environment and climate threatens life itself. We must also remember that economics is responsible for creating the unacceptable gap between the rich and the poor both among nations in the world and between different sections of society within a nation. If we continue along this path, the situation could become irreparable. The yawning gap between the "haves" and the "have-nots" is going to create a lot of suffering for everyone, including the world of finance and the global marketplace itself. Therefore, it becomes necessary for us to widen our perspective to include the well-being of the whole world and its future generations in our vision of economics, business, and the marketplace.

On a personal level, if you practice tolerance and compassion, you will immediately discover that these qualities are causes of happiness. There are many methods, some of them religious and others derived from what I think of as fundamental human values, that you can employ to develop these qualities and become a better person, and naturally you will also become a better and more effective businessperson (or a wiser and more satisfied consumer). There is no machine that can produce inner peace; there is no shop that sells inner peace. No matter how rich you are, there is no way you can buy inner peace. It is something that has to come from inside, through mental practice.

I am happy to learn that the goal of this book is to deal with all these questions. They are indeed big questions. I believe that the answers can be found on the basis of increased awareness: we should explore these issues more often and in this way we will gradually be able to create solutions. I am confident that the readers of this book will be inspired to take useful and practical steps.

Alternatives to Consumerism

by Sulak Sivaraksa

"CONSUMERISM" can be defined as the religion of consumption—attributing ultimate meaning to purchasing power. Economic growth at the cost of the poor has become the driving force of globalization even though world leaders try to hide this fact with cosmetic measures and rhetoric.

Undeniably, the fuel that keeps the capitalist engine running is profit: the more of it, the better, the argument goes. Hence, corporations must be free to pursue it—at all costs. The ends justify the means. It is also argued that the profit generated by the system will eventually trickle down to benefit the mass of humanity. The available evidence points otherwise. To be fair, capitalism does generate some benefits to humanity, but they are largely unintended byproducts of the system.

Capitalism works by exploiting labor and natural resources in order to concentrate wealth in the hands of an elite group. For maximum results, capitalism alienates humans from their communities, families, and ultimately, their spiritual selves by attributing worth solely in terms of economic value. The atomistic individual, rather than a larger community, is at the center of the capitalist system. Consumerism is able to dominate much of contemporary society because individuals have become alienated from their culture and from each other. The sense of community that led people to share scarce resources and work cooperatively has been supplanted by an anger, competitiveness, and fear that cause people to seek acquisitions at the expense of their neighbors. In sum, consumerism is a consequence of using greed and violence to regulate socioeconomic relations.

At the most profound level, consumerism owes its vitality to the delusion of the autonomous individual self; a self that exists independently of social relations and of human relations with nature—a human person thrown into the world. For the Buddha it was clear that the "self" constituted only a pattern of persistently changing experiences that had no more substance or permanence than those experiences.

We are deluded into seeking some transcendental subject; something that defines experience yet lies beyond the experience. We are exhorted to know ourselves and yet the "self" in this dualistic system remains unknowable. For the Buddhists, this delusion is the fundamental cause of suffering. Ontologically, we become estranged aspects of our experiences of others and ourselves. Hence we are precluded from any meaningful conception of identity.

Consumerism provides an artificial means to define our existence by suggesting that identity is realized through the process of acquisition. Put differently, consumerism is a perverse corollary of the Cartesian proof of personal existence: "I shop, therefore I am." Insatiable consumption is equated with ultimate happiness, freedom, and self-realization. As David Arnott, a British Buddhist and human rights activist, explains:

> By participating in the sacrament of purchase, sacrificing money, you can buy an object that is not so much an object as a focus of images which grants you a place in the system of images you hold sacred. For a while when you buy a car you also buy the power, prestige, sexuality, and success which the advertisements have succeeded in identifying with the car, or whatever the commodity is. Consumerism works by identifying the sense of unsatisfactoriness or lack *(dukkha)* we all hold at a deep level of mind. . . . and then [by corporations] producing an object guaranteed to satisfy that "need". . . .[40]

Corporatization depends on greed, delusion, and hatred in order to become entrenched in the global society and in the individual and is thus an anathema to the goals of Buddhism. When an individual places self-interest above all and negates the relational idea of "self," the result is greed and selfishness. Neoliberalist rhetoric deludes people and international organizations into believing that profits from multinational corporations will be fairly distributed in society and that any improvement in material conditions is an absolute gain for society. The ideology of consumerism deludes people into believing that constant acquisition of goods and power will lead to happiness. Lastly, competitive consumerism depends on callousness and hatred to prevent people from forming coalitions to challenge the existing system. Hatred is a force that paralyzes and prevents self-transformation and cooperative strategies.

In Buddhism, prosperity is defined as "more being." As such, it cannot be realized atomistically, only collectively, and with an emphasis on spirituality. Buddhism denounces and renounces greed, because it is seen as leading one down the perfidious road of aggression and hatred—in a word, of suffering. Greed can never lead to satisfaction, individually or collectively. Thus Buddhism seeks to show how to be content with changing oneself—that is, self-cultivation—and emphasizes the importance of caring about, promoting, and benefiting from one another's well-being. Whereas capitalism treats a person as only half-human—the economic dimension (e.g., greed, hatred, and selfishness) is cultivated to the exclusion of other considerations—Buddhism approaches a human person holistically. The mind and heart must be cultivated, and diversity must be nourished in social relations and in human relations with nature. A human person is an "interbeing" existing within a web of relations that includes all sentient beings.

In contrast to the modern notion of frantic, ceaseless consumption, the Buddha said that tranquility is the most important prerequisite for self-cultivation and self-criticism, for the true understanding *(prajña)* of the self. It should be pointed out that understanding is different from intellectual knowledge, since it is filtered through both the heart and the mind. Understanding helps the individual to recognize his or her limits and to be more humble. At the same time, it promotes loving kindness and compassion: the individual will be in a better position to witness the suffering of others and to help eliminate the cause of suffering. Of course, when one tackles the cause of suffering, particularly in an oppressive social system, one usually gets hurt. Here *bhavana* (mindfulness) facilitates the understanding of such danger as well as the forgiving of the oppressor. The oppressive system is hated and will be destroyed, but the oppressor will neither be despised nor executed. If one is aware of one's anger, then one can envelop it with mindfulness, thereby transforming it into compassion. Thich Nhat Hanh says that anger is like a closed flower; the flower will only bloom when deeply penetrated by the sunlight of bhavana. The constant radiation of compassion and understanding will eventually crack anger, enabling one to perceive its depth and roots. Likewise, bhavana will fully open the flower buds of greed, hatred, and delusion.

Compassion and competition are not mutually exclusive. His Holiness the

Dalai Lama says, "Any human activity carried out with a sense of responsibility, a sense of commitment, a sense of discipline, and a wider vision of consequence and connections, whether it be involved with religion, politics, business, law, medicine, science, or technology—is constructive." The emphasis is on the motivation for action. Given that motivation is deeply connected to worldview, a change in worldview, such as an understanding of interdependence or the universality of suffering, will lead to a change in motivation. As motivation shifts and the sense of responsibility and commitment are strengthened, broader changes can take place. For example, when a motivation for profit shifts to a sense of concern for the well-being, economic and spiritual, of the employees of a corporation, a cooperative relationship can start to replace a formerly exploitative one.

Similarly, competition is not a singularly negative force. In moderation and with a sense of direction it can be used to push us to become more generous and kind. His Holiness makes the distinction between two kinds of competition when he says that one kind of competition is only for individual glory and the other kind of competition includes an awareness that other people must also be fostered to succeed. Competition can be beneficial if it inspires us to be the best we can in order to serve others. Rituals and games are often built on competition but can serve also to strengthen the spirit. This discussion of competition and achievement parallels the discussion among Buddhist scholars about the purpose of nirvana. For some, spiritual enlightenment is a personal quest. For others, such as those in the Engaged Buddhist community, enlightenment is built upon wisdom and compassion and is intrinsically connected with the well-being of all others. The Mahayana tradition is particularly emphatic that all beings must be liberated before the bodhisattva can attain enlightenment. These discussions about the nature of competition and nirvana highlight how a seemingly minor difference in focus can shift the focus from an ego-centered attitude to a community-centered philosophy.

Instead of basing all interpersonal relations on social obligation or an economic calculation about what we can gain from another person, Buddhism uses the principles of *metta* (loving kindness), *karuna* (compassion), *mudita* (sympathetic joy), and *upekkha* (equanimity) to be the guiding forces in interpersonal relations. These Four Sublime Abodes *(Brahma Vihara)* are as follows:

1) Metta or loving kindness towards oneself and others. Yes, we all desire to be happy and have every right to do so. Nevertheless,

through practicing the precepts and meditation, a different state of happiness can be achieved. It is a state of happiness where the mind is in harmony with oneself as well as with others. It renders assistance and benefits without ill will and without the malice of anger and competition. Once one is tranquil and happy, these qualities will be spread to others as well.

2) Karuna or compassion can only be cultivated when one recognizes the suffering of others and, consequently, is driven to bring that suffering to an end. Undoubtedly a rich person who does not care about the miserable conditions of the poor lacks this quality. It is terribly difficult for him or her to develop into a better person. All those who lock themselves up in ivory towers in the midst of a shockingly unjust world cannot be called compassionate. In Mahayana Buddhism, one vows to become a bodhisattva and forgoes one's own nirvana until all sentient beings are free from suffering. In other words, one cannot remain indifferent; rather, one must endeavor to help others and alleviate or mitigate their suffering as much as one can. The essential characteristic of any healthy community/society is its principle of inclusion. As we become more attuned to compassion as the instrumentality of social organization, we can embrace the community.

3) Mudita or sympathetic joy is a mental condition whereby one genuinely rejoices when others are happy or successful in a number of ways. One feels this without the flame of envy even when a competitor gets ahead.

4) Upekkha or equanimity refers to the state in which the mind is cultivated until it becomes evenly balanced and neutral. Whether one faces success or failure, whether one is confronted with prosperity or adversity, one is not "moved" by it.

The Four Sublime Abodes are to be developed step by step from the first to the last. Even when one is not perfect, one must set one's mind toward this goal. Otherwise, in one way or the other, one's dealing with the self or with others will tend to be harmful. Moving towards happiness and tranquility rather than towards worldly success and material progress, a Buddhist is then in a position to develop his or her community—the family, neighborhood, village, etc. An individual who is awakened by these realities is called *purisodya*. When this awakening is shared with others, ultimately the whole nation may be awakened to the threats posed by capitalism, including its ethos.

Moreover, in a time of moral emergency like the present, the Buddhist teaching of the Four Wheels may serve as a useful antidote to the detrimental values of corporatization. As a cart moves steadily on four wheels, likewise human development should rest—and this point cannot be overemphasized—on the four dhammas, namely, Sharing, Pleasant Speech, Constructive Action, and Equality.

1) One must Share *(dana)* what one has with others—be it goods, wealth, knowledge, time, labor, etc. Corporatization, on the other hand, in Adam Smith's telling phrase, upholds the dictum "all for [ourselves] and nothing for other people." Powerful transnational corporations control access to essential commodities such as food, drugs, and technology. Yes they are all made available to us—for a high sum of course. To a large extent, dana is still practiced in most village cultures. We should strengthen the concept of dana and spread it to counteract the invasion of materialism and the ethos of competition by sharing, and by leading less commercialized lifestyles.

2) Pleasant Speech *(piyavaca)* not only refers to polite talk but also to speaking truthfully and sincerely. Its basic assumption is that everyone is equal. On the contrary, consumerism or the culture of corporatization posits that less commercialized lifestyles are inferior. People must be *deceived* to consume goods and services that they do not really need in the name of a "high standard of living."

3) Constructive Action *(atthacariya)* means working for one another's benefit. Here again it is antithetical to the dynamics of the corporation. A corporation does not work to benefit its employees or the town or city it is situated in. Rather, it is only geared towards enriching the large shareholders. For instance, it seems that every time a corporation "downsizes," the price of its shares skyrockets. Thereby new rules must be promulgated whereby investors who have high stakes in the well-being of their localities are rewarded.

4) And finally, Equality *(samanattata)* means that Buddhism does not recognize classes or castes, does not encourage one group to dominate or exploit the other. The global economy however creates a small caste of "winners" and mass hordes of "losers." The winners take all, and their action is deemed perfectly legitimate under the banner of "free trade" and "free competition." Hence, we urgently require "fair trade," not free trade.

The Four Sublime Abodes and the four dhammas are meant to act as guidelines for living a life consistent with a Buddhist understanding of freedom, drastically apart from a capitalistic notion of choice as the ultimate expression of freedom. Merely having a wealth of choices is not freedom. We must make the right choices—choices that show compassion for all and which are not motivated by greed. For Buddhists, the ideal of freedom is threefold: the first freedom is the freedom to be free from insecurities and the dangers of poverty, disease, famine, etc. The second freedom is social freedom and the freedom from human oppression and exploitation; such a state presupposes tolerance, solidarity, and benevolence. Lastly is the freedom of the inner life, the freedom from mental suffering, from impurities of the mind that propel people to commit all kinds of evil.

Engaged Buddhism (or "buddhism with a small b") has become a living alternative movement within Buddhism to put into practice the ideals of Buddhism and allow more people to have access to an alternate conception of freedom. We must let our common goal of creating an alternative guide us towards greater collaborative alliances. A fresh common effort to shape interreligious education—especially in the context of education reform now common in many countries, as well as joint outreach of emancipatory and community-based education fully involving the poor and underprivileged—should be undertaken without delay.

Buddhism and Poverty

by David R. Loy

DOES BUDDHISM have anything special to contribute to our understanding of poverty and how to alleviate it?

Like other religions, Buddhism is sometimes criticized for its idealism: for encouraging a non-materialistic way of life that goes against the grain of our desires and motivations. If we want to reduce poverty, we are referred instead to the science of economics, which has discovered the laws of economic growth, and to international development agencies, which apply those principles to improve the lot of "undeveloped" societies.

In fact, contemporary economics is much more "idealistic" in the sense that it presumes an unrealistic or ideal image of human nature. Economists today tend to live in an idealized, one-dimensional world of statistics and equations that do not accurately reflect human values and goals in the world we actually live in. Buddhism is more down-to-earth in its understanding of the sources of human ill-being and well-being. Its approach also happens to correspond more closely to the way most premodern communities have understood well-being, and the way "undeveloped" societies today still do. Let us consider the implications of Buddhist teachings for the problems of economic development. From a Buddhist perspective, it is not surprising that the institutional efforts of the last fifty years have actually aggravated the social problems they were supposed to solve. The development approach, still taken for granted today, is better understood to be the problem itself.

Shakyamuni Buddha summarized his teachings in the Four Noble Truths: ill-being *(dukkha),* its cause, its end, and its cure. When we try to understand economic "underdevelopment" according to this simple model, it helps to illuminate aspects of the issue that have often been overlooked.

What Is Poverty?

Buddhism values nonattachment towards material goods, and promotes decreasing desire, yet that is not the same as encouraging poverty. According to Buddhism, poverty is bad because it involves dukkha. The point of the path is to end dukkha, and it does not make any significant distinction between worldly dukkha and some other transcendental sort of suffering.

Poverty, as ordinarily understood in early Buddhism, consists in lacking the basic material requirements to lead a decent life free from hunger, exposure, and disease. Buddhism recognizes the importance of such minimum needs even in the case of those who aspire to its spiritual goal, and in fact the basic needs of a monk or nun provide a useful benchmark for measuring that level of subsistence below which human beings should not be allowed to fall. The four requisites of a Buddhist renunciate are food sufficient to alleviate hunger and maintain one's health, clothing sufficient to be socially decent and to protect the body, shelter sufficient for serious engagement with practices to cultivate the mind, and health care sufficient to cure and prevent disease. People who voluntarily renounce worldly possessions and pleasures in favor of a life of such minimal needs are viewed as belonging to the community of "noble ones" *(ariyapuggala).*

In the *Anguttara Nikaya* the Buddha teaches that some people are like the completely blind because they do not have the vision to improve their material circumstances, nor the vision to lead a morally elevated life. Others are like the one-eyed because, although they have the vision to improve their material conditions, they do not have the vision to live a morally elevated life; the third class have the vision to improve both. Such Buddhist teachings imply that when measuring poverty, it is not enough to evaluate just material conditions. For a more comprehensive evaluation of deprivation it is necessary to take into account the moral quality of people's lives.

But that is not to deny the importance of the first eye. According to the *Lion's Roar Sutra,* there is a causal relationship between material poverty and social deterioration. In that sutra, poverty is presented as a root cause of immoral behavior such as theft, violence, falsehood, etc. Unlike what we might expect from a supposedly world-denying religion, the Buddhist solution has nothing to do with accepting our (or others') "poverty karma." The problem begins when the king does not give property to the needy—that is, when the state neglects its responsibility to maintain what we today call distributive justice. Social breakdown cannot be separated from broader questions about the benevolence of the social order. The solution to poverty-induced crime is not to punish severely but to help people provide for their basic needs.

In another sutra, the Buddha speaks of the four kinds of happiness *(sukha)* attained by householders: possessing enough material resources, enjoying those resources, sharing them with relations and friends, and not being in debt. More important than any of them, he emphasizes, is the happiness of leading a blameless life. Elsewhere the Buddha teaches that the greatest wealth is contentment. There are said to be seven kinds of noble wealth: faith, moral conduct, the shame and the fear of doing something reprehensible, developing one's character, sacrificing one's possessions for the benefit of others, and insight into the three characteristics of existence (dukkha, impermanence, and no-self). The Buddha says that in the discipline of the noble ones who follow the Buddhist path, the absence of these seven may be called true poverty, a poverty even more miserable than that resulting from lack of material resources.

By redefining these moral qualities as "noble wealth," Buddhism draws attention to the fact that the single-minded pursuit of material wealth will not make human beings happy or even rich. A world in which envy *(issa)* and miserliness *(macchariya)* predominate cannot be considered one in which poverty has been eliminated. This follows from the Second Noble Truth of the Buddha: the cause of dukkha is *tanha,* "craving." When human beings gain an intense acquisitive drive for some object, that object becomes a cause of suffering. Such objects are compared to the flame of a torch carried against the wind, or to a burning pit of embers: they involve much anxiety but very little satisfaction—an obvious truth we repressed by immediately turning our attention to another craved object. For Buddhism such a proliferation of wants is the basic cause of unnecessary ill-being.

This implies that poverty can never be overcome by proliferating more and more desires which are to be satisfied by consuming more and more goods and services. While consumption may eliminate material poverty for some, it may be at the cost of promoting a different kind of poverty that is even more harmful. In short, there is a fundamental and inescapable poverty "built into" a consumer society. For that reason, development projects that seek to end poverty by "developing" a society into an economy focused on consumption are grasping the snake by the wrong end. From a Buddhist point of view we should not be surprised that such efforts in social engineering end up creating more problems than they solve.

This approach reflects the attitudes of most societies not already conditioned by advertising into believing that happiness is something you purchase. In economic theory, lack of income remains the basic criterion of ill-being, perhaps because some such numerical measurement is necessary to satisfy the economist's craving for statistical assessment. Gross National Product is a lot easier to gauge than General Well-Being.

As a result, development agencies have been slow to realize what many anthropologists have long since understood: in traditional societies, especially rural communities, income is not the primary criterion of well-being; sometimes it is not even a major one. When a master builder in a Bulgarian community was invited to rank people according to wealth, he "spontaneously enlarged the list of well-being criteria to emphasize the importance of children's education, good health and a good humored nature. Interestingly, the less well-off group included the most wealthy person in the village—an unhappy, bad tempered fellow who was put at the bottom of the pile along with the drunks and the sick." From his analysis of this study Robert Chambers concludes, "Income, the reductionist criterion of normal economists, has never, in my experience or in the evidence I have been able to review, been given explicit primacy."[41]

To assume that we in the "developed" world know something about worldly well-being which such peoples do not is a form of intellectual imperialism that looks increasingly dubious. Since our needs (or rather our wants) are now taken for granted as defining our common humanity as much as universal human rights do, we are encouraged to forget what in Buddhism is an essential human attainment if we are to be happy: the need for self-limitation.

The fundamental human problem is not the technological and economic dilemma of how to meet all our material "needs"—something psychologically as well as environmentally impossible—but the psychological and spiritual need to understand the nature of our own minds. Economics cannot avoid reducing the *good* to an *amount* because it factors all desires into its basic equation of scarcity, which derives from comparing limited means with potentially unlimited wants. Without having been seduced by the utopian dream of a technological cornucopia, however, it would never occur to most "poor" people to become fixated on fantasies about all the things they might have. For them, their ends are an expression of the means available to them. Insofar as they do this, we are imposing our own value judgments when we insist on seeing them as poor, or as living in a state of scarcity (again, except for the destitute unable to satisfy basic requisites for survival). It is presumptuous to assume that they must be unhappy, and that the only way to become happy is to start on the treadmill of a lifestyle dependent on the market and increasingly preoccupied with consumption.

All this is expressed better with a Tibetan Buddhist analogy. The world is covered with thorns and sharp stones (and now broken glass as well). What should we do about this? We can try to pave over the entire Earth or we can wear shoes. "Paving the whole planet" is a good metaphor for how our collective technological and economic project is attempting to make us happy. It will not be satisfied even when all the Earth's resources are transformed into products to be consumed. The other solution is for our minds to learn how to make and wear shoes, so that our collective ends become an expression of the renewable means that the biosphere provides.

Why do we assume that "income/consumption poverty" is the same as ill-being? That brings us to the heart of the matter. For us, material well-being has become increasingly important because of our loss of faith in any other possibility of fulfillment. Increasing our "standard of living" has become so compulsive for us because it serves as a substitute for traditional religious values — or, more precisely, because it has actually become a kind of secular religion for us.

What Are the Causes of Poverty?

According to the accepted development model, the cause of poverty is not a major issue. Poverty is the normal condition of "undeveloped" peoples, since it can be alleviated only by technological and economic development.

From a Buddhist perspective, however, there is something odd about this indifference to the causes of something we want to cure. This is reinforced by some intriguing discoveries that do not support the assumption that poverty is the normal premodern condition. Studies of "stone age economics" have concluded that the first humans in some ways had a comfortable life more leisurely than ours. Archeological research into early hunter-gatherers has found that they usually survived quite well on a few hours of work a day, with a diet more nutritious and varied than the farming settlements that supplanted them.

Agriculture meant harder work, but it could support a greater population density and still produce a surplus — the latter advantage usually restricted to those who had the power to appropriate it. Such appropriation led to the development of social classes. We view this appropriation as the origin of kings and priesthoods, but it was also the origin of the poor, now deprived of the fruits of their labors.

If social class continues to be our fundamental social problem, it is one that fifty years of "development" have done very little to alleviate, for, as many recent studies have shown, the share of human wealth owned by the rich worldwide has increased during this period, and continues to do so, while the share owned by the poor continues to decrease. According to the United Nations Development Report for 1998, 20 percent of the global population now accounts for 86 percent of consumption; the three richest people on the planet have assets that exceed the combined GNP of the forty-eight poorest countries. In "undeveloped" countries it is the powerful and wealthy classes that continue to benefit most from the efforts of development agencies such as the World Bank; and when projects fail, as many do, it is the poor that suffer the most from their failure. According to the same report for 1999, for example, the average African household consumes 20 percent less than twenty-five years ago.

In the early Buddhist texts the cause of dukkha is sometimes identified simply as craving, and sometimes as the three roots of moral evil. Human ill-being can be resolved only by transforming these roots: greed into generosity, ill-will into loving kindness, and delusion into wisdom.

The role of greed and ill-will in causing poverty is more or less obvious, but the function of delusion more subtle. One way to understand its role is to consider how we are misled by our own dualistic thinking. Dualistic categories divide things into opposites that are nonetheless dependent on each other because the meaning of each is the negation of the other. If I want to live a "pure" life, for example, I will be preoccupied with avoiding impurity. In the same way, a great desire for wealth is inevitably shadowed by fear of poverty. Psychologically they are indivisible, for each is dependent on the other.

This means there is no such thing as a "poverty problem" that can be understood separately from a "wealth problem." We are afflicted by a *wealth/ poverty dualism*. I would suggest that our concern for "attacking poverty" is the flip side of our aggressive preoccupation with wealth-creation. In this way we excuse the problems with economic globalization because, after all, we do want to address those problems. More insidiously, we rationalize a way of life preoccupied with economic growth, no matter what its costs. "Undeveloped" poor people must be miserable because that is how we would experience their circumstances of life. Mesmerized as we are by growth, we assume that everyone else must be too—or should be, especially if we are to have access to their resources and markets.

Global poverty is thus *conceptually* necessary if the world is to be completely commodified and monetarized. Otherwise one cannot rationalize the profound social reorientation (or social disorganization) that is required. Traditional cultures and lifestyles must be redefined as obstacles to be overcome, and local elites must become dissatisfied with them, in order to create a class of more individualistic and self-interested people that will serve as the vanguard of consumption.

The poverty of others is also necessary because it is the benchmark by which we measure our own achievements. Unless there are losers, we cannot feel like winners. If the "undeveloped" are not unhappy with their lot, we may come to doubt our own happiness with what we have, unable to rationalize the things we have had to put up with in order to get there, or to excuse the negative consequences of our economic development.

In all these ways, then, we need the poor. None of the above should be taken as making light of the situation of those many people in the world whose destitution needs to be alleviated as soon as possible. What it does suggest, though, is that among the causes of poverty today are the delusions of the wealthy—delusions that have very concrete effects on the well-being of many people, including the wealthy themselves. If so, we should not allow ourselves to be preoccupied only with the poverty side of the problem; to correct the bias, we should become as concerned about the wealth side: the personal, social, and environmental costs of our obsession with wealth-creation and collective growth.

What Is the End of Poverty?

It is, again, curious that development agencies such as the World Bank have said so little about what would constitute the end of poverty. If, however, aliens from another planet had been observing the World Bank's actual development practices over the last fifty years, without listening to any of its rhetoric about intentions, what would they conclude about the Bank's goals? On the basis of his own lengthy experience with Zimbabwe, Professor Colin Stoneman, an economic statistician at the University of York, concluded that the World Bank is an institution "whose overall intention, and increasing effect, is to promote the construction of a single world market, substantially on the basis of the present world division of labor. . . [a] role mediated through an ideology that is claimed to be a value-free science [i.e., economics]."[42] Doug Hellinger, a former Bank consultant, makes the same point more cynically:

> The Bank is saying that to join the world economy you have to become more efficient and you have to be able to compete against imports from around the world. But the purpose is not to develop Brazil or to develop Ghana. . . . The U.S. is trying to stay competitive with Europe and Japan and the Bank is helping to provide the government's friends in business with cheap labor, a deregulated atmosphere, and export incentives. It isn't a development strategy, it's a corporate strategy.[43]

In the same year that the World Bank and the IMF were established (1944), the economic historian Karl Polanyi published *The Great Transformation*. His account of the origins of capitalism remains one of the best accounts of the social consequences of a capitalist economy: a reversal of the traditional relationship between a society and its economy.

In premodern societies, and in traditional ones today, markets are limited in place, scope, and time, because they tend to disrupt social relations. Such societies make no clear distinction between the economic sphere and the social sphere, because economic roles are subordinate to social relationships. According to Polanyi, pre-capitalist man "does not act so as to safeguard his individual interest in the possession of material goods; he acts so as to safeguard his social standing, his social claims, his social assets. He values material goods only insofar as they serve this end." Today, however, our emphasis on "freeing markets" means that "instead of the economy being embedded in social relations, social relations are embedded in the economic system."[44]

Where there are no restrictions to protect social relationships, every potential resource tends to be commodified. This includes the very moral fabric of society, woven of innumerable personal relationships, now commodified into "social capital" or "moral capital"—ugly economist terms that describe how market forces rely upon but damage that fabric of interpersonal responsibility. A basic contradiction of the market is that it requires character traits such as honesty, trust, etc. in order to work efficiently, yet it is primarily motivated by a desire for profit that tends to erode such personal responsibility to others. The last few decades have made this more obvious. In the United States, massive "downsizing" and a shift to part-time workers demonstrate diminishing corporate concern for employees, while at the top astronomical salary increases and management buyouts reveal that the executives entrusted with managing corporations are becoming more adept at exploiting them for their own benefit. Internationally, the globalizing market has promoted more exploitative relationships with the poor and powerless in "undeveloped" parts of the world, where predatory governments often cooperate in keeping factory wages at subsistence levels.

These are examples of how the market itself "depletes moral capital" and therefore depends upon the community to regenerate it, in much the same way it depends upon the biosphere to regenerate natural capital. That is a good analogy, for the long-range consequences have been much the same: even as we have reached the point where the ability of the biosphere to recover has been damaged, our collective moral capital has become so exhausted that our communities (or collections of atomized individuals) are less able to regenerate it, with disturbing social consequences.

How do communities "generate moral capital"? Throughout history, religions have been the main source and repository for society's deepest values and goals, those most essential to a community's harmony and self-understanding. Not all of these have been goals or values we want to encourage today, but genuine religions have thrived because they have the potential to promote responsible personal relationships. Material values that emphasize income and consumption make it more difficult to resist corruption in the form of graft and bribes. True social development may require us to reverse the transformation Polanyi wrote about, re-embedding the economy in social relations, rather than letting economic forces determine what happens to our communities. Needless to say, this applies at least as much to the wealthy nations as to the "undeveloped" ones.

The moral role of religions is difficult for most Western-trained economists to accept, since their discipline is a legacy of the eighteenth-century Enlightenment project which contrasted scientific and social progress with the regressive weight of privileged churches. Today, however, it is necessary to recognize that the neoliberal economic understanding of what happiness is, and how that is to be achieved, is only one vision among many. There is a social price to pay for the comforts and commodities it offers, a price that should not be imposed on others who have their own worldviews and values.

All societies are confronted with the same basic tragedy of life, which for Buddhism is not primarily material poverty but illness, old age, and death. The main human response to this has been religion, which addresses it in various ways. From a perspective informed by the eighteenth-century Enlightenment, these responses are superstitious and escapist. From a Buddhist perspective, however, economic growth and consumerism are unsatisfactory alternatives because they are evasions, which repress the basic problem of life by distracting us with symbolic substitutes such as money, status, and power. Similar critiques of idolatry are explicit or implicit in all the great religions, and rampant economic globalization makes that message all the more important for our time.

How Do We End Poverty?

If we have to drive our people to paradise with sticks, we will do so
for their good and the good of those who come after us.
—Abel Alier, regional president of Sudan

Unfortunately, because the programs to end poverty so far implemented have not been based on an adequate understanding of what poverty actually is, we should not be surprised that the attempts have not been very successful.

The best answer to the poverty question may be quite simple, I think: let us admit that we do not know and cannot know. We should acknowledge that we are unable to determine what is the best course for other peoples to follow. If we are sensitive to what is happening in our own backyards, we will have enough trouble trying to determine what is best for our "developed" societies, all of which have major social problems.

I am suggesting, quite seriously, that one of the best things we can do for many "undeveloped" peoples is to leave them alone. Whether or not that is the very best thing, it is better than many poverty programs that have further diminished the ability of the "poor" to meet their own needs, often because they have involved divesting local people of their resources (e.g., diverting agriculture from self-consumption into monoculture for export). Letting-alone means allowing people to manage their own resources, deciding for themselves their own opportunities and capabilities.

Instead of simply "doing nothing," however, this can require intervention to restore local self-determination. And, to say it again, letting-alone is not something that should apply to the problem of genuine destitution, which morally obligates us to provide, at the very least, sufficient food, clothing, basic shelter, and medical care to all the world's people. This, it would seem, immediately brings us back to the onerous problem of devising economic development strategies to do so. In fact, these basic requisites could be met quite easily if our intentions were genuine and our motivation serious. Providing them to the needy would actually require a very small percentage of the world's present economic product. "It is estimated that the additional cost of achieving and maintaining universal access to basic education for all, basic health care for all, reproductive health care for all, adequate food care for all and safe water and sanitation for all is roughly $40 billion a year," according to the UN Development Report for 1998. "This is less than 4 percent of the combined wealth of the 225 richest people in the world." Probably the most effective way to provide those services would be through some revamped United Nations agencies.

I am reversing the usual metaphor and suggesting that instead of pretending to teach the poor how to fish, we give the most impoverished the fish they need. The dismal record of the last fifty years of development reveals the cruelty of the usual slogan: when we have taught the world's poor to fish, the effect has often been to deplete their fishing grounds for our consumption.

The problem, then, is not that we do not have enough resources to provide for the basic needs of everyone. We have much more than enough. The problem is a lack of collective compassion, enough collective will to overcome the simple fact that the people who have the most say about what happens to the Earth's resources do not care enough to help the world's destitute. It is just not a priority for them, and insofar as our own preoccupation with wealth accumulation encourages us to acquiesce, we are complicit with their indifference.

In conclusion, the solution to poverty is not primarily economic, because the cause is not primarily economic. Some "poverty," especially in rural areas, is not poverty at all, at least not by traditional standards. Often poverty is not solved but created by economic globalization, which dislocates people or divests them of their own resources. And I have suggested that genuine destitution is more a matter of our collective intentions and therefore our values.

This brings us back to religion, and the need for religious institutions which understand that market emphasis on acquisition and consumption undermines their most important teachings. The corrosive influence of economic globalization and its development institutions on other human values needs to be challenged.

Buddhist Economic Systems

by Frederic L. Pryor, Ph.D.

ALTHOUGH RIGHTEOUS RULERS may try to provide all people with a minimum income, the Buddhist canon places more stress on "radiation theory," which sees the economy prospering through the collective impact of virtuous actions of individuals who follow the moral law which includes the giving of alms to the poor. King Ashoka, one of the greatest of all Indian emperors, pursued a highly activist governmental budget policy, even though he believed only meditation could help people to advance in moral living. But canonical beliefs about economic activity, particularly by the government, are much more ambiguous than economic literature often indicates. Hence today there are rightist and leftist Buddhists, differing in interpretation of the canon.

Although the Buddhist canon places great stress on gift giving, it is primarily to the monks and the *Sangha* (monasteries). "There is," according to scholar David Little, "apparently, no. . . Theravadin literature on distributive justice, nor is it the poor as such who are for the Theravadas the primary object of beneficence."[45] Of course, through the laws of *kamma* (Sanskrit: *karma*) there is a distributive cycle of cosmic proportions, i. e., one's current social and economic position is due to one's good kamma accumulated in a previous existence. This does not mean indifference to the poor, for one's economic status is not only dependent on the laws of kamma, but is also complemented by the moral virtues of compassion and generosity. Alms giving to the poor is regarded as increasing one's merit.[46] The importance of our active intervention has some important implications for behavior of the "righteous ruler" as well.

It should be added that the revered Buddhist kings are also known for the financial aid that they provided for the poor; indeed, the *Cakkavatti-Sihanada Suttanta* of the Theravada canon advises kings to give their gifts to all who are poor. Moreover, gifts to the monks and to the monasteries assist them to provide a refuge for the destitute and redistribute such beneficence to the indigent.

Thus although there is little discussion of distributive justice, redistribution of income, either through the public, private, or monastery sectors, is certainly regarded in a favorable light. In order to favor the spiritual improvement of the population, the State is justified in taking steps to provide all people with a minimum income. Whether the motive for redistribution is to spread the Dhamma (in a Buddhist economy) or to increase distributive justice (in a Western economy) seems a bit irrelevant; in both cases, the limits of redistribution are difficult to determine.

Buddhists argue that since the economy can ultimately prosper only through virtuous action, ultimately the only hope for prosperity lies in a regeneration of humankind, e.g., through the cultivation of the Four Sublime Abodes (loving kindness, compassion, sympathetic joy, and equanimity). Buddhists generally hold that any appropriate dhammic action inevitably leads to an increase of the material wealth of the community.[47]

The major parts of the Buddhist canon do not appear to discuss any alternative means of distributing goods and services beyond the market. Thus their analysis of trade is quite straightforward. The Buddhist discussion on right livelihood prohibits trade in certain goods and services, which means that all other types of trade are apparently allowed (but not explicitly approved of). In an interesting comparison between trading and agriculture as means of livelihood, the Buddha also notes that both can bring high or low returns, depending on the circumstances; however, trading is an occupation with little to do, few duties, a small administration, and small problems, while agriculture is the reverse.[48] In other parts of the canon (e.g., *Anguttara Nikaya,* III, ii, 20) the capable merchant is approvingly said to know the value of goods and prices and the profits he obtains; and to buy where the price is low and to sell where the price is high.

One of the most favored of Buddha's disciples was Anathapidika, a merchant who was generous to the cause and who was highly praised for his piety. Some scholars claim that early Buddhism was particularly attractive to merchants, a marginal group adopting a marginal religion which had a strongly democratic nature.[49] In more recent times, some anthropologists have argued that Buddhists in some areas look unfavorably on merchants because they suspect that improper means were used in amassing wealth; however, this has nothing to do with the activity per se.

All of this raises a difficult point concerning Buddhist beliefs about the functioning of the market. Certainly Buddhism accepts competition in general in the sense that it is possible to compete without hurting others. We can lack attachment to our wealth and yet still experience considerable pain in the process of being deprived of our customary livelihood. It is important to stress the critical nature of motives in Buddhist ethical thought. Thus, if innovations are made, but not with the intention to ruin a competitor or to amass goods for personal use, but rather to supply goods to the population at a lower cost and to provide gifts to monks and the poor (including, perhaps, former competitors who were not flexible in responding), then innovation can be quite acceptable. Similar arguments can be made in the case of commercial rivalry.

The Buddha had little concern for society as such and little conviction of its possible improvability.[50] Certainly society was not to be destroyed and social conditions might help or hinder humans in their search for *nibbana,* but such conditions could never be fundamentally bettered. One receives the strong impression that early Buddhist writings generally accept existing political and economic institutions, even while providing a democratic social ethos which was revolutionary for its time. For instance, the Buddha did not appear to challenge the general framework of the kingship; and insofar as he did not strongly urge the freeing of slaves (who are mentioned in the canonical sources, even though they did not appear a numerically important group), he appeared to accept the institution of slavery.[51] The Buddha did represent a break from older social traditions in that he did not condemn urban institutions and seemed aligned with such groups as merchants.

According to the established rules of monastic life, however, the monks could not have slaves, which suggests that the institution of slavery was uncomfortable to them. In the writings of early Buddhists who are held in particularly high regard, e.g., King Asoka, there was no call to free slaves, but merely for the "proper treatment of slaves and servants."[52]

Economic Policies

The *Agganna Sutta* which described the origins of property also discusses the origins of the State. As crime increased after the division of the land, the people elected a king to maintain law and order, paying him for his troubles.

This suggests a type of social contract theory, which means that the king has important obligations toward the people. The *Kutadanta Sutta* speaks of the Royal Acts to increase prosperity which include giving of seed corn and food to farmers and of capital to merchants to start or increase their business. The particular source emphasizes that if prosperity increases, economic disorders and crime such as theft decrease.

The prototypical important righteous ruler was the revered King Asoka (ca. 274–232 B.C.E.), the grandson of the founder of the Mauryan dynasty in India and one of the greatest of the Indian emperors. From Asoka's edicts it appears that he generally accepted the economic and political institutions of his time. For instance, he did not condemn either torture (although he spoke of the necessity to avoid "unjust torture" or the killing of criminals, which seems peculiar with regard to his reverence for life, especially of animals).[53]

With regard to his capital expenditures, it appears King Asoka took it as the goal of the state to provide for the welfare and happiness of the people. For instance, he gave gifts to the aged and the needy, and to religious orders; he set up public education courses to teach the doctrines of the Dhamma; he cut back on large public festivals; he imported and planted medicinal herbs; and he carried out various public works projects including digging wells, planting trees, and constructing rest houses and animal watering stations along the main roads of the empire. Some of his edicts appeared to enforce traditional Buddhist beliefs, e.g., bans on slaughtering various animals. The funds spent on the maintenance of the crown and good works were high, and taxes were apparently about one fourth of the revenue of land.

However, a curious policy dilemma arises. Asoka quite specifically noted that "the people can be induced to advance in Dhamma by only two means: by moral prescriptions and by meditation. Of the two, moral prescriptions are of little consequence, but meditation is of great importance." In short, he saw limits of an activist government in promoting virtue. The definition of such limits has been a source of controversy among Buddhist writers ever since.

As many have suggested, a Buddhist economy comprised only of monks (and nuns) could not last since these people have fully given up occupational and family duties in order to search for nibbana, relying on others to feed them. For a Buddhist economy to survive, there must be both monks and laypeople. This economic dialectic between the monks and laity has a strong influence on capital formation. If a Buddhist government wishes to encourage the achieving of nibbana, it makes good sense to encourage capital formation so that in the long run a higher share of the population can become monks and engage in the necessary contemplation.

What should be the policy goals of a ruler in such Buddhist societies? If achievement of nibbana of as many people as possible were the goal, then policy should be aimed for increasing material prosperity so that more monks could be supported (since they have a higher probability of achieving nibbana) and of encouraging as many of the laity as possible to join the monasteries in order to achieve this goal.

The Problem of Needs and Wants

Underlying much of the discussion in the canonical works is a distinction between needs and wants which provides a focus for the doctrinal treatment of consumption. Needs, for instance, are embodied in the Four Requisites (food, clothing, shelter, and medicine). Although asceticism is condemned, the doctrine of nonattachment has been interpreted by many to mean that we should lead a life of simplicity and consume little more than our needs.

The reduction of consumption to the level of needs — never very clearly defined — has a certain appeal among modern Buddhists and is supported by some interesting arguments. For instance, the Thai monk Buddhadasa Bhikkhu argues that the multiplication of individual wants is always at the expense of society since if people consumed only according to their needs, there would be enough for all and in all times.[54]

On a local level, the uses of Buddhism are elastic, and doctrinal sources can be used either to justify the building of yet another temple or to provide religious support for village development work. On a national level, a similar doctrinal flexibility is found. In bygone years some Buddhist social commentators took a very passive view toward economic policy, arguing that it is even useless to try to correct some obvious shortcomings of the economy. For instance, in Burma the Buddhist Shway Yoe, writing at the end of the nineteenth century, says that the rich and powerful man has a right to govern because in a previous life he was pious and good; the poor man must be content with his lot because he must have been bad before he entered this existence.

In more recent times this appears to be changing and a considerable number of Buddhist intellectuals start their analysis of economic systems with a critique of the obvious defects of both capitalism and communism, then argue that since Buddhism is a doctrine of the Middle Way, it is possible to draw upon the positive aspects of both types of systems while, at the same time, arranging matters so as to avoid the general materialism and spiritual sickness which is found in both systems. The real question, of course, is what must the economy look like and what must the State do to avoid the various specified evils, while increasing virtue.

Buddhists both to the right and the left favor a certain minimal redistribution of income so that the basic consumption needs of all are covered. There is little agreement, however, on how to define the limits of intervention with regard to governmental activism in the economy. On the right, Buddhadasa Bhikkhu has drawn those limits rather widely: He called his ideal system "dictatorial dhammic socialism" which, among other things, means that moral governmental policies should be carried out "expeditiously"; this differs from tyranny, he argues, since in the latter the policies carried out do not serve the general interest. In any case he is not shy in urging governmental coercion to force people to contribute their labor to public works construction.

The Buddhists on the left have urged considerable governmental intervention as well, and both the Burmese governments of U Nu and Ne Win (which ruled before the present military regime) carried out a variety of direct and indirect measures to guide the economy. It also seems possible, however, for a Buddhist to draw upon the canon to urge relatively little intervention, not only on the grounds that "each must find refuge in himself" to achieve virtue but also on the grounds of the effect of such a concentration of political and economic power in the government upon the personnel in the government itself.

In short, the vagueness of the Buddhist canon on economic matters combined with its complexity and length allows room for quite different interpretations of an ideal economic system in modern times, especially since conditions are very much different than they were more than two thousand years ago when the Buddha lived.

Boomer Buddhism

by Stephen Prothero

ROUGHLY A CENTURY AGO, an American businessman named Dwight Goddard went to China as a Baptist missionary. Yet China changed him more than he changed the Chinese. After wandering into a Buddhist monastery, he embraced Buddhism. Back in the United States, he founded a monastic community called "Followers of Buddha." His dream was undeniably American: a bicoastal community of itinerant monks who would spend part of the year in Vermont, part in California, and the rest motoring across America's midsection (and spreading the Dharma along the way).

Goddard's strict monastic rules, which included celibacy and 4:30 A.M. wake up calls, scared away potential recruits, so "Followers of the Buddha" never got on track. But Goddard's *Buddhist Bible,* an anthology of Buddhist scriptures published in 1932, motored on. In the early 1950s, Jack Kerouac checked that book out of his local library, and Beat Buddhism was born. Soon Kerouac and other Beat *"bhikkhus"* were playing the roles Goddard had assigned to his "Followers of Buddha." They hit the holy road with *Buddhist Bibles* in their rucksacks, and the Zen boom of the 1950s was on. It goes without saying that the Beats did not subject themselves to the strict monastic discipline envisioned by Goddard. In fact, Kerouac did not even seek out a Buddhist teacher. He got his do-it-yourself Buddhism from books.

Today Buddhism is booming once again. The 1990s saw three Buddhist movies and a gaggle of celebrity Buddhist pitchmen, including Adam Yauch and Richard Gere. The United States is now home to at least a million not-so-famous Buddhists, many of them new immigrants from Asia. But Buddhism is also popular among hip Americans who have never set foot in a Zen center or visualized a Tibetan mandala. Often these sympathizers get their Buddhism, Kerouac-style, from books.

Buddhist bestsellers used to come along once a decade: Kerouac's *Dharma Bums* in the fifties, Philip Kapleau's *Three Pillars of Zen* in the sixties, and Robert Pirsig's *Zen and the Art of Motorcycle Maintenance* in the seventies. Today they seem to materialize monthly, along with more evanescent titles like *Zen and the Art of Stand-Up Comedy* and *Zen and the Art of Changing Diapers*. Demand for Buddhist books has turned many teachers into stand-alone brands with remarkable marketing muscle.

Of course, not all American Buddhists are eager readers of these Buddhist bestsellers. Many immigrant Buddhists do not even read English. And those who do are often far more concerned about repairing their local temples or supporting their neighborhood monks than they are about reading the latest Buddhist bestseller.

Because of the many differences between immigrant Buddhists, on the one hand, and the U.S.-born converts, on the other, scholars typically divide U.S. Buddhism into two camps. Academics continue to argue, with a sincerity only academics can muster, about what to call those two groups. I don't think it much matters, though I typically refer to immigrants and their descendants as *birthright Buddhists* and American-born converts and sympathizers as *countercultural Buddhists*. By most accounts, roughly three-quarters of all American Buddhists fall into the birthright camp. Countercultural Buddhists are far more vocal, however, so many have come to associate their Buddhism with American Buddhism writ large.

Inside the countercultural camp, Baby Boomers hold sway. To be sure, a rising generation of young Buddhists is beginning to find its voice, but Baby Boomers dominate the Zen centers, Tibetan Buddhist centers, and Vipassana centers favored by the countercultural crowd. Over the last quarter century, Boomers have quietly yet persistently refashioned American Buddhism in their own image. They have made the Buddhist tradition more egalitarian, more feminist, and more socially active. Perhaps most important, they have made it less dogmatic. Some have even given up on Buddhist staples such as karma and rebirth.

Sociologist James Coleman has lauded this Boomer Buddhism as "a profoundly subversive force" in contemporary American society. Yet what exactly is this Buddhism subverting? Is *Zen and the Art of Poker* subverting American obsessions with money? Is *Zen Sex* subverting American obsessions with the body?

Recently critics have begun to suggest that Boomer Buddhism may be subverting Buddhism itself. In *Time* magazine's 1997 cover story on "America's

Fascination With Buddhism," Robert Thurman (friend of the Dalai Lama, father of Uma, and Buddhist Studies professor at Columbia) derided ardent Americanizers of Buddhism as "non-Buddhists" preaching humanism masquerading as Buddhism.

I teach religious studies because I believe that studying religion is a truly liberal art. All of the world's great religions provide profound challenges to the unexamined life. At their best, they offer devastating diagnoses of human sickness and radical remedies for it. They make insane demands—that we love our enemies, that we deny ourselves, that we vow to liberate all sentient beings. At their best, religions are difficult, confusing, mysterious. They don't pat us on the back, assuring us that it's "easier than you think." In fact, they remind us that it's harder than we think, much harder. Like a Zen master stalking his zendo with stick, they whack us back to attention when we fall asleep. Boomer Buddhism, by contrast, is all too often shallow and small. It soothes rather than upsets, smoothing out the palpable friction between Buddhist practice and the banalities of contemporary American life, cajoling even the Dalai Lama to direct his great mind to smaller American preoccupations like conversing about money and politics.

Almost four centuries ago the Puritans came to New England intent on uplifting and improving Protestantism. By stripping Protestantism of all the last vestiges of Catholic superstition, by relying on the authority of the Biblical book alone, they would craft a new and improved Christianity. Boomer Buddhists are modern-day Puritans. They too are suspicious of priests and rituals and other traditional religious trappings. They too believe that America is a sacred place destined to perfect the religious tradition they hold dear.

What seems to be lost on most countercultural Buddhists is the possibility that it may be America's destiny to not make Buddhism perfect but to make it banal. It is, of course, far too early to determine what America's effects on Buddhism will be. Buddhism has been in Asia for two and a half millennia; it has been a force in the United States for only a century or so. So far, however, there are mixed reviews.

Philosopher George Santayana once observed that "American life is a powerful solvent. It seems to neutralize every intellectual element, however tough and alien it may be, and to fuse it in the native goodwill, complacency, thoughtlessness, and optimism."[55] Instead of preserving the Dharma, Americans seem intent on co-opting and commercializing it, dissolving a religion deeply suspicious of the Self into an engine of self-identity and self-absorption.

A year or two ago I visited the headquarters of a Buddhist church in San Francisco. In their gift shop (yes, almost all American Buddhist centers have gift shops), I saw a rock carved with the words, "What Would Buddha Do?" If the Buddha were alive today, would he be a Boomer Buddhist? Would he write Buddhist bestsellers? Direct films? Deny the reality of karma and rebirth?

Call me old-fashioned, but I think the Buddha would sprint (mindfully of course) to an American Buddhist monastery. Countercultural Buddhists have elevated the laity to heights previously unknown in Buddhism, but they have not yet obliterated monasticism. In fact, monks are now dug in all across America, doing decidedly old Buddhist things like wearing robes, conducting rituals, and even chanting. At places from the Dharma Realm Buddhist Association and Shasta Abbey in California to Zen Mountain Monastery and Dai Bosatsu Monastery in New York, ordained monks devote themselves full-time not to improving Buddhism but to preserving it. Some of these monasteries focus on translating and publishing ancient Buddhist texts. Most host laypeople for intensive retreats. Many also shutter their doors for long periods to allow monks to pursue the hard work of what the Buddha described as waking up from a long, bad dream.

Monks at these monasteries are often foreign-born. A surprising number, however, are white Americans who have, for some reason or another, decided to scuttle the easy answers of Boomer Buddhism for something closer to the real thing.

During the 1970s, a U.S.-born monk from Gold Mountain Monastery in San Francisco set out on a bowing pilgrimage up the West Coast. Beginning on the Golden Gate Bridge, Timothy Testu (a.k.a. Bhikshu Hung Ju) took three steps. Then he performed one bow—a full-body prostration, complete with forehead on pavement. Then he got up and took three more steps and one more bow until (ten months and over a thousand miles later) he found himself in Marblemount, Washington.

Thanissaro Bhikkhu is another hard-core Buddhist. Born Geoffrey DeGraff, he went to Thailand after graduating from Oberlin. There he studied in the Thai Forest Tradition under a Thai teacher for more than a decade. In 1991, he joined with another Thai teacher to found Metta Forest Monastery in the mountains north of San Diego. Thanissaro, who became abbot of that monastery in 1993, describes Boomer Buddhism as a grand game of telephone in which "a thing gets passed on from person to person, from one generation of teachers to the next, until the message gets garbled beyond recognition."

One of the key Buddhist ideas lost in that grand game of telephone is sacrifice, which he calls the "huge blind spot in American Buddhism."[56]

Thanks to Thanissaro Bhikkhu and hundreds of monks like him, Dwight Goddard's dream of an authentically Buddhist form of American monasticism is alive and well. These monks have typically not understood the Buddha's admonition to "have no abiding place" as a commandment to take to the road in a Winnebago (as Goddard did), but they are not above adapting Buddhism to American circumstances. They struggle with questions such as whether to wear winter coats instead of cotton robes in Chicago, or whether to drive cars in Los Angeles. Sometimes they hold fast to tradition. Sometimes they innovate. But they adopt American ways grudgingly rather than gleefully.

At least for now, however, Boomer Buddhists have the stage. They sell their books by the gross. Thanissaro Bhikkhu sells his by the unit. Only he doesn't actually sell them. They are available for free on the Web—a gracious gift from old Buddhism to the new.

Zen and Money

by Ming Zhen Shakya

Z EN IS AN EXTREMELY practical religion. Aside from providing efficient methods and techniques for achieving exalted spiritual states, it offers some very common sense guidelines for living in the world.

Zen first requires that we have the courage to confront ourselves. Before we commit to a course of action we have to examine our motives. We have to be like Method School actors who can't do a scene until they understand the psychology of an action. "What's my motivation?" they demand to know. Before we buy, invest, borrow, lend, cosign, or enter into any kind of contract, we have to scrutinize our desires.

Let's recall Buddhism's Four Noble Truths: One, the ego's world is bitter and painful; Two, the cause of this bitterness and pain is craving; Three, there is a cure for this malady; and Four, the cure is to follow the Eightfold Path. And the essence of the Eightfold Path is simple self-awareness.

Craving, whether obsession or whim, is the desire for something; and that's what gets us into trouble. Why do we want what we want? We have to be ruthless in our analysis. We can't disguise desire with rationalization or sentimentality in order to convince ourselves that we are acting prudently or altruistically.

Before buying anything we need to ask, "Is this something I need or just something I want?" We should give desire a time test. "When did I decide I wanted to make the purchase? Was it something I planned to buy and then went looking for, or did I decide I needed the item right after I saw it or its advertisement?" Impulsively made purchases are seldom appreciated beyond their period of novelty. So, especially with "big ticket" items, we need to take time to get beyond the impulse, to free ourselves from being pressured into acting quickly. Professional marketers are adept at creating a sense of urgency that we easily succumb to. They know that the irrational fear of losing out on a good deal will obstruct our good judgment. Also, we ask ourselves, "How much of the purchase price will go to satisfy my need and how much of it will go to satisfy my ego?"

If we need a watch, we can buy an excellent timepiece for fifty dollars. We can also buy one for five thousand dollars. The difference in price doesn't have anything to do with knowing the correct time. It has to do with ego gratification or with maintaining an image, the persona of success.

If we need a new car to provide reliable transportation, we can buy one for fifteen thousand dollars. We can also pay fifty thousand. If we can't easily afford the model we want, we should sit down and calculate its total cost. . . insurance premiums, registration fees, maintenance, repair. And if we intend to borrow money to make the purchase, we add in the interest charges to see how much the item is really going to cost. The world is filled with dejected guys who bought flashy cars because they wanted to attract girls only to discover that after they met all the expenses they didn't have any money to date any of the girls they had attracted.

Always we need to look ahead to the long-term care of a purchase. Silk shirts are nice, but they'll probably require dry cleaning every time they're worn. Aside from the expense, there's the inconvenience. That cute little puppy with the impressive pedigree is going to grow up. He needs to be taken out for walks. There'll be vet bills and license fees and food costs and grooming bills and pet insurance. . . and damage to rugs, furniture, and landscaping. . . and some chewed shoes and complaining neighbors.

We also have to resist the tendency we all have to be "penny wise and pound foolish." It's said that it's easier to get a Congressional Appropriations' Committee to approve the expenditure of billions for an atom-smashing cyclotron than it is to get them to approve ten thousand dollars for a public restroom in a park. The committee members don't know anything about nuclear physics and they don't have experience funding such one-of-a-kind projects; and, having no way to challenge an expenditure, they quickly vote yes. But when it comes to the public restroom, one Congressman says, "Two thousand dollars for a roof! What is this, the Taj Mahal? I'm from Vermont and you could get Vermont slate for less than two thousand dollars." And another Congressman says, "A thousand dollars for landscaping? You could plant Texas bluebonnets in there for ten dollars and it would look one heck of a lot better." And they can go on like this for days. Especially when making a big-ticket purchase or investment, we should ask ourselves, "Am I competent to make such a purchase?" If we're not experts, we should consult them.

Let me tell you about a businessman and his business—a small franchise company—that he successfully operated in Las Vegas some years ago. This man, the owner, was a very pleasant sort of fellow. He was trying to establish a nationwide chain of confectionary outlets. . . the kind of shops you'd find in malls. He had a pilot franchise, a kiosk, in one of the major Las Vegas resort hotels. It sold nuts and candy and had a fancy machine that made fresh nut butters like almond, peanut, and cashew. On the walls of his office were photographs of his various franchisees posing proudly outside their shops in different cities. The franchise operation had its distinctive logo and color scheme—tan, green, and orange—that identified the shops as members of the same chain.

Every few weeks, this businessman would go to a distant city—one preferably near a military base where there'd be a concentration of men who were near service retirement, and who would likely have the ten thousand dollars needed to buy a franchise. This was a lot of money at the time. You could buy a nice house for less than twenty-five thousand dollars in those days. Also, a military base gave the added advantage of providing a concentration of men who would be dispersing to various parts of the country. Since a franchise outlet has exclusive rights to a specific territory, he naturally didn't want all his prospective clients to come from the same area.

This businessman, the franchise operator, would rent a suite in a hotel and place an ad in the local papers; and then interested people would come and meet with him. He had brochures and photographs of his various franchise outlets—especially the Las Vegas outlet—and copies of beautiful display ads that had appeared in magazines; and he'd explain the operation, how really it required no business skill at all—you didn't have to be a rocket scientist to sell candy and nuts—how the company would supply everything needed to get started, including initial advertising, and how he'd always be available for consultation.

He'd explain that the company would get 10 percent of the gross sales— which was more or less standard in franchise operations—and so, this being the Company's source of income, it was to the Company's advantage to see to it that its franchisees were successful. It was the kind of "nuts and bolts" logic that anyone could understand. The plan was that the new franchisee would

find a business location in his selected city and the Company would dispatch
an interior decorator to come and apply the distinctive paint scheme, logo sign,
and get him "all set up to go."

Also, if a franchisee wanted the exclusive rights to a large area, let's say the
entire Cincinnati area, there was a price-break incentive. The potential franchisee could immediately see the advantage of having exclusive rights to a large
area. He could exploit the cheap labor market, hire high school kids or folks
on social security, and all he'd have to do was go around to his groups of outlets, supervise, and collect the money.

People liked the deal. Invariably they were enthusiastic and wanted to invest
right on the spot. But this businessman said he didn't want anyone to buy anything sight unseen. So he'd refuse to accept any money or deposits until the
potential franchisee was better informed and had firsthand knowledge of the
operation. He wanted all questions answered before any contracts were signed.
He insisted that good business sense demanded that the buyer see an actual
franchise operation, that he talk directly to another franchisee. This would pay
off in better relations down the line. There would be no misunderstandings.
This businessman was so sure of the quality of his operation that he'd offer to
fly a potential client and one other person—friend, wife, girlfriend, whomever
he wanted—to Las Vegas for the weekend. He'd pay for two roundtrip airplane tickets and two nights in a motel. The client and friend would have to
supply their own meals. The businessman would pick them up at the airport
and take them back, too. He'd also take the client to the Strip hotel that had the
operating franchise, and then he'd purposely walk away so that the client could
speak privately with the operator and satisfy himself that everything was on the
"'up and up" and that this businessman was, in fact, a decent and responsible
guy to work with.

Who could ask for a better deal or a more honest approach? If the client
was satisfied, then and only then would any money change hands. He'd go
back to the office, sign the contract and write the check. And if the client was
not satisfied with what he saw and heard, no harm done. He'd have gotten a
free trip to Las Vegas. But everybody was impressed and nobody ever just took
advantage of the free trip. They all bought franchises. And then the client—
the new franchisee—would go home and scout out a location for his operation. After he found one he'd, of course, sign a lease and would have to come
up with the necessary first and last month's rent and security deposits, and get
a phone installed, and then the decorator would come and paint the place tan

and green and orange and hang the sign outside where he'd take the photograph of the proud franchisee for the main office to hang on the wall. And then the plumbing fixtures and the expensive display cases would arrive. . . COD; and the eight hundred-fifty dollar industrial-grade nut-grinding machine would arrive. . . COD; and the expensive cash register and commercial scale would arrive. . . COD; and the paper bags and other stationery items would come. . . COD; and the product would arrive—ordinary hard candies and nuts of ordinary quality but all wildly overpriced and all. . . COD.

This wasn't what the client had expected. This wasn't "getting him started" in anything but the long slide into bankruptcy. What had he purchased for his ten thousand dollars? Good question. He had been led to believe that he'd be a "franchise operator," whatever that meant. He had had the idea that the company would own the equipment and that he'd just operate the outlet. Sure, he expected to have to buy the product and pay the company 10 percent of the gross sales of it, but not the furniture, fixtures, and supplies, or certainly not to pay so exorbitantly for them.

What about the newspaper display ads that the new franchisee had ordered to announce his grand opening? Well, as verbally requested, he had turned the bills in to the office for reimbursement or direct payment, but the office never paid a dime to the newspapers and radio stations and they were coming after him for payment. Whenever the client, who was frantic by then, would call, he'd be told that everything was clearly spelled out in the contract. And it *was* in perfect legal language.

When the new franchisee discovered that the public wasn't beating a path to his door to buy these candies and nuts that they could buy at any supermarket for a fraction of the price, he'd get the idea that he had been defrauded and he'd go to see a lawyer and the lawyer would say, "Why are you seeing me now? It's too late! Look, you signed this contract in the State of Nevada, not in the State of Ohio. If you want to sue this fellow you'll have to go to Nevada and get a lawyer." The client would mentally add up the cost of doing that, and he'd soon see the folly of his ways. His "free trip" to Las Vegas had been a trick to get him into the State of Nevada to sign the contract. Had he looked more carefully he'd have seen that that reassuring franchisee he had spoken to at the Las Vegas hotel outlet just happened to be the wife of that nice guy who sold him the franchise. But it never occurred to him to check the business license. He never checked anything.

In the office there was a locked file drawer filled with lawyers' correspondence from everybody who ever purchased a franchise from this company. In fact, in all the U.S.A. there was only one operating franchise. . . in Las Vegas. The others had all failed miserably. And the "interior decorator" who came to apply the tan and green and orange paint? He was an unemployed relative of the owner. The clients didn't get a nickel back. How could they? The owner owned nothing. Even the Cadillac he drove to the airport to pick up the potential clients was rented.

Sad to say, this scheme, though clearly unethical, was still more or less legal, and he knew it. Once, when asked if he felt at all guilty about taking the life savings of these men, he sneered, "Why should I feel guilty when I can see the greed and lust in their eyes, especially when I tell them how they can tap the cheap labor market." And he bragged and explained, "The randy guys I tell to be sure to hire only pretty high school girls since they make the best sales personnel, and I can see them salivate thinking about the girls they'll be able to dominate. Why, some of them will actually ask their wife's parents to lend them the money to buy exclusive rights to an area so they'll have more girls to play with! And the greedy guys I tell to hire people on social security who are struggling to make ends meet, who'd be willing to work for peanuts. I'd joke and say, 'You really will be paying them in peanuts.' And they'd laugh. Oh, you can't cheat an honest man!"

But that's not true. You surely can cheat an honest man. But whenever I've been shortchanged or overcharged or cheated in some way, I wonder what the person who cheated me had mentally accused me of in order to justify the theft.

So what can we learn from all this? Investigate before we invest? Sure. But we already knew that. See a lawyer before we sign a contract? Of course. But we already knew that, too.

So why, when we already know what we should do, do we allow ourselves to be swindled? It's simple. All an ego has to do is crave something, and it will sacrifice anything or anyone to get it.

Egotistical desires confuse our judgment. The images in our mind superimpose themselves, one on top of the other, a double or triple exposure. The desire for one thing colors or contaminates the desire for something else. The desire to go to Las Vegas infects the desire to be a small business owner. The ego wants to brag and gorge itself on notions of self-importance. Where's the swaggering potential in saying "I'm flying to Davenport for the weekend"? No. The ego wants to be A Player! It wants us to be able to say "I'm flying to

Vegas for the weekend." If any one of those franchise buyers had picked up a phone and called any of the other franchisees whose photographs had been shown to him, he'd have uncovered the scam. But nobody was interested in Davenport or Rockford or Boise. Egos prefer Las Vegas.

To do the Zen thing is to inspect our motives, to look ahead to the subsequent costs, and to realistically appraise our own competency. It's so clever to say, "You don't have to be a rocket scientist to sell nuts and candy." But what is the difference between marketing nuts and candy and marketing artichokes or surgical supplies? The market is the market. The laws of supply and demand apply to any market. In the particular scam I've just related most of the franchisees were career military men. How much did they really know about private enterprise? They never had to think about profit and loss. We know how government operates. Is this not the land of the free and the home of the six hundred dollar hammer? Why did these men desire to start a business at all? Other men welcomed retirement because it gave them time for reflection, spiritual development, recreation, study, or travel. Did these franchisees scoff at those other men? What did they think they knew that those other fellows didn't know? Why, so late in life, were they still so adventurously motivated by money? Why didn't they choose more conservative investments?

Why were they so incredibly trusting? What in their personalities made them respond to this con man's appeal? Was it because he was so friendly and they needed a friend—especially a friend who had such a big Cadillac. Did that car influence them? The con man must have thought so. The only time he ever got it washed was when he went to the airport to pick up potential clients. If we look deep enough we'll no doubt discover that these victims were all vulnerable because their egos craved admiration, respect, power, status. Egos crave glory and excitement and are therefore seduced by the promise of it, by glamour, which by definition is that "deceptive charm," that "spell that confuses" and destroys all common sense! Self-control can be attained only after self-scrutiny. If we can't be honest with ourselves, we lose the moral right to expect other people to be honest with us.

Examine. Scale down. Simplify. Peace is purchased by vigilance.

A Meditation on Money

by Lewis Richmond

Buddhism includes many different kind of meditations—meditation on the breath, meditation on compassion, even meditation on colored wheels and sacred paintings. It lacks a meditation on money—probably because Buddhist monks were prohibited from handling it—but it does have many meditation practices dealing with greed. Greed is a psychological state, whereas money is physical, palpable, and measurable. That is one reason why it is so powerful. It can function as a universal measure of value, and be transferred from one person to another. While our own greed remains within us, money can go anywhere. It seems to have an independent reality, a life of its own.

But does it really? How much do our own mental attitudes, our own desires and projections, affect and even create the reality of money? How does it influence our perceptions and actions in the workplace? These are the questions this chapter will explore.

Let us begin our meditation on money by examining the physical object. From your wallet or purse, take out the highest denomination of currency you have. Probably it will be a twenty-dollar bill. That is fine, but a hundred-dollar bill works even better. One hundred dollars is a lot of money. It gets your attention. So let's imagine we have the hundred-dollar bill before us.

We look at it. Peering back at us is the kindly face of Benjamin Franklin. In each corner are the large numerals indicating that this piece of green paper is one hundred times more valuable than a nearly identical one that has only the numeral "1" on it. Of course the hundred-dollar bill has no more intrinsic value than a one-dollar bill; they both cost the U.S. Treasury exactly the same number of pennies to manufacture. The greater worth of the bill with the Ben Franklin picture is determined by social agreement, convention, and law. It is a root agreement, like our understanding that the week shall have seven days, or that the hours of the day shall be twenty-four. These matters were all, at one time, up for grabs. It is only with the passage of centuries that these originally arbitrary arrangements have come to have the force of law, of inevitability, of reality itself.

Money is one more such manufactured reality. We can, with some effort, trace back the history of money to its roots. But having done that, what more can be said? One cannot go into a bank and complain that the crisp new hundred is a fiction, and you would like something of "real" value, say a gold coin. Our right to do that vanished in the 1930s, and to ask for silver coins became obsolete in the 1970s. Besides, what makes the gold or silver coin any more "real" than the paper except its weight and shine?

Let's continue our meditation with a thought experiment. In ancient times, Buddhist monks would stare for long periods of time at a disk of yellow clay, until they could perfectly visualize the object with their eyes closed. So let's try something similar here. Put the bill in front of you—say on the kitchen table —and stare at it for a while.

If I ask you, "What is it?"—what would you say?

If you say, "Well, it's a greenish piece of paper with a picture of Ben Franklin on it," I would challenge you by replying, "If that were so, you could drop it on a busy sidewalk and it would stay there for more than a few seconds."

If you say, "It's a hundred-dollar bill. I could buy a week's worth of food with it," I might reply, "No it's not. It's just a green piece of paper. Besides, how do you know it is a real hundred-dollar bill? Maybe it is a counterfeit."

In fact, counterfeit technology is so good these days that only experts, with advanced technological equipment, can identify the best ones.

As a practical matter, what makes a hundred-dollar bill real versus counterfeit is everyone's belief that it is. When you go to spend the hundred dollars, your belief in its reality and the belief of the department store clerk who accepts it conspire to produce a shopping bag in your hand. It is all a choreographed game in which we are trained from childhood.

When we read that an ordinary hair dryer once owned by Jacqueline Onassis sold at auction for $5,000, or that a desiccated piece of seventy-year-old cake from the wedding of the Duke of Windsor went for $25,000, we are reminded that money, ultimately, represents a thought or idea that may have little to do with real value or worth. Money can represent real needs, like food or shelter, but more often it measures the strength of an abstract desire. Money represents our image of ourselves, our public self. In some way we barely understand, it *is* the self.

Now let's perform another meditation experiment. Next to the hundred-dollar bill, place a one-dollar bill.

Look at the one-dollar bill.

Now look at the hundred-dollar bill.

What changes within you when you shift your gaze from one to the other?

You may not be able to sense it right away, but suppose you were to drop first one, then the other, through a grate in the sidewalk, losing it forever. Do you think your heart would beat the same in both cases, or that you might not, in the second case, curse vigorously?

The greater value you assign to the hundred-dollar bill does not reside in the physical object itself. It is something you have been taught, something you have accepted and internalized because it is fundamental to the social fabric. You give it value because everybody else does. The value is a kind of collective visualization, a made-up creation that has become real because we have all agreed to make it real.

It is difficult to step outside of this framework. When we perform this meditation in workshops, there is first a fascination with the physical object. People are surprised to find that they have used money their whole lives without ever having looked closely at it. They notice that the piece of currency they are holding is among other things a work of art, an artist's engraving with trees, buildings, and abstract designs, not to mention cryptic notations such as "C3." But when I ask people to imagine their workplace apart from money, no one has much to say. Money is too deeply a part of who we all are.

None of us can avoid money, but we can be much more conscious of how it functions in our lives. And in the workplace, one of the main uses of money is to measure time, and to be traded for time.

Time and Money

The phrase "time is money" originated, no doubt, during the heyday of "time management studies," when it was an original insight about the relationship of efficiency to profit. No other phrase so succinctly describes how money alters our perceptions of ourselves and others once we step into the workplace. In this sense, work is an exchange of time for money. You give time, and your employer gives you money.

This implies that time is something that belongs to you, a possession of value that you can exchange for money by "spending" time at work. Employers define certain activities—such as making personal calls—that should be done on your "own" time, versus the company's time. Perhaps that was what was so striking about my own transition from the monastery to the office. In the monastery time doesn't belong to anyone. It is something to be shared.

Now it may be clearer why the religious teachers of old all agreed that there was something corrosive about money. St. Paul didn't say, "Money is the root of all evil," although that is how the biblical passage is often misquoted. He said, "The love of money." It is the way that money alters our own state of mind, our sense of time, our own sense of who we are and who others are that is the problem. It is the love, the attachment to money, that drains our soul.

Time is life. We have time because we are alive, because we exist in this world. When we die, we are out of time. Time ceases for us. Time, like life itself, is a gift. It comes to us freely, simply because we are here. Time is central to the spiritual inquiry, to the fundamental questions: Who am I? Why am I here? Time embraces these questions. It gives them depth and breadth.

One of the effects of formal meditation practice is the way that it expands our sense of time. Particularly during long meditation retreats, time becomes much more vivid, more palpable, more liquid. I often use the phrase "thick time" to describe this phenomenon. At work we experience time as thin— rushed, hurried, noisy, distracted. Following our breathing, minute by minute, hour by hour, time becomes neither slow or fast. Time reverts to just what it is—breath, heartbeat, bird song, sunlight imperceptibly traveling across the rug. Time simply holds and contains us.

It may be helpful to add to our meditation on money an awareness of the breath. As we stare at the one- and the hundred-dollar bills, feel the breath going in and out. This is time, and the bills are money. Are they the same or different? Which one is a more accurate measure of your true worth?

Value

At one time I studied with Harry Roberts, a part Irish, part Native American, who gained spiritual knowledge from his uncle, a traditional medicine man. When Harry was a small boy, he watched his uncle sew feathers into a headdress used for a traditional dance ceremony. He was puzzled as he saw his uncle pull apart a whole section he had already sewn and prepared to do it over again.

"Why are you taking it apart?" the young Harry asked. "The dance is at night. Nobody will see it. Who will know?"

"I will know," his teacher replied.

This story is full of important truths about time, money, and value. Its context is a traditional, premodern society, one governed by ritual, custom, and the importance of character and personal relationships.

Robert was doing important work, but he was not getting paid for it. What's more, no one, except his young nephew Harry, was watching him do it. He could have done the task in the most expeditious way, thus saving time. But that would imply that time had some kind of quantifiable value, and that saving time was somehow important.

But saving time was not important to Robert at all. Nor was producing a headdress that was only adequate. The important thing was his own internal sense of quality, and his own state of mind. To Robert, the gift that he was going to bring to the ceremonial dance was not the headdress at all. The headdress hardly mattered. It was what he had crafted inside himself, a standard of excellence, sincerity, and quality known only to him, that was the true gift. If he were to have gone to the ceremony with a headdress that to everyone else looked fine, but which he knew was not the best he could do, he would be ashamed. He would not want anyone at the ceremony to see him like that.

Robert lived in a culture where it was clearly understood, not only that our state of mind is important, but that it is real and tangible. That was what Robert meant when he said, "I will notice." He meant that because he would notice, everyone would notice.

This way of looking at the world is very different from our modern notions of value, money, and time.

Suppose a tourist had happened by Robert's house, and had seen the headdress hanging outside on the front porch. And suppose the tourist encountered Robert and offered to buy the headdress.

Robert would have replied, "This headdress is not for sale. It's a ceremonial headdress."

But the tourist might have insisted. "Tell me how many hours you worked on it. I don't want to cheat you. I'll pay you fair value for the hours you put in. After all, time is money."

It would have been difficult for Robert to explain to the tourist that the value of the headdress didn't translate into hours or money. The value of the headdress was connected to the bonding together of the whole community, of Robert's place as an honored elder in that community, to the mutual trust that the tribe's ceremonies helped to cement.

Now let's contrast this story with one from the modern workplace. Jean was a departmental manager in a large investment firm. For the last two years, ever since a merger had forced many layoffs, Jean's job had been quite stressful. Where before the merger she had a staff of forty-five, now she had less than thirty, and the workload was if anything greater than before. It seemed to Jean that her job these days consisted mainly of listening to her subordinates' endless complaints. Though their frustration was legitimate, there was little Jean could do.

One day Charles, Jean's boss, called her into his office. "Jean, I know how frustrating the last year has been for you and your team, and I want you to know what a good job you've done, and how much the firm appreciates your effort. I found some money in the budget and I'm going to give you a $5,000 year-end bonus."

For the next few weeks, Jean felt as though she were walking on air. At last her hard work had been recognized. The fiscal year end was only a few weeks away. Jean spent the remaining weeks planning how she was going to use the money.

When she opened her year-end check she was surprised to see that the bonus was only $3,200. "Oh, yes," Charles said when she asked him about it, "They cut my budget at the last minute. You know how it is. I did the best I could."

Jean had a friend in the accounting department, and she couldn't resist. She asked her friend to check the departmental budget. "No cuts that I can see," her friend reported back. "Charles must have used the money for something else."

Jean's earlier euphoria now turned to anger. It was not the shortfall that disturbed her. The difference was only $1,800, after all, and she hadn't been expecting any bonus at all. It was what the shortfall implied about Charles's praise. It felt to Jean that Charles's acknowledgment wasn't wholehearted, but calculated. Jean now wondered if the bonus was really in recognition of her effort, or only to take the edge off her frustration.

She almost wished Charles hadn't given her any bonus at all. In the end, she didn't feel more valued, but devalued.

Who knows if her assumptions about Charles were valid? Maybe he did sincerely wish to reward her, and had a good reason for using some of the money elsewhere. Jean would never know, because she could not confront Charles about the matter without compromising her friend's confidence. So instead of feeling incentivized and rewarded, Jean felt bitter. Instead of becoming closer to her boss, she felt more distant.

The lesson of this story is that even in the most money-oriented workplace, money is not the reward that counts the most. In this case it was supposed to represent acknowledgment, but because of a subtle shift in the way it was tendered, it failed in that mission. Just as the tourist could not give Robert enough money to compensate him for the headdress, Charles's lack of straightforwardness and sincerity sapped the bonus of its intended meaning. I know of more than one company where the bonuses went up from year to year and the employees, cynical, complained to each other, "The boss doesn't really appreciate us. He's just trying to buy our loyalty." The boss couldn't understand it. "I gave them more this year than last!" He didn't understand that, in the end, it isn't just the money, but the intention, that counts.

PART FOUR

Market As Nature

The profit made by the employer is the central concern today:
both the producer and the consumer are subservient to the profit
motive. Therefore right livelihood would opt for small-scale industries
that would satisfy the creative instinct of man and the basic needs of
many more people, and would also ensure a more equitable distribution
of wealth in society. It is better to have a large number of skilled
cobblers than a well-equipped mechanized shoe factory.

—Dr. Lily DeSilva

Down to Business: Paul Hawken on Reshaping the Economy

Interview by Renee Lertzman

Lertzman: We hear a lot about "green business" these days, but it's hard to know how deep the reform goes. Is it for real or just "greenwashing," where businesses give the appearance of being environmentally responsible?

Hawken: Some businesses think that if they stop polluting so much, buy recycled paper, plant some trees, reduce overall waste, and use native plants to landscape their corporate campuses, they become green. These practices are laudable, but they don't get down to the fundamental issues of how industrial output in our society is out of control—and, more fundamentally, how the thinking that informs economic growth is both absurd and astonishingly ineffective. They also don't get to the key problems of how worldwide growth is marginalizing the environment and leading to wholesale deracination of cultures, villages, and families. When you see the underlying problems, it leads to issues that aren't on the corporate radar screen: population, women's rights, workers' rights, sovereignty, social justice, community rights, international trade rules, the corporate corruption of governments. These issues reveal a world that is in real chaos with respect to its values, priorities, and principles.

Lertzman: The reality you describe is overwhelming and rather dismal.

Hawken: It may sound hopeless on the face of it, but it's not. It *will* be hopeless, though, if we aren't willing to look at problems directly. We are like the man who goes to the doctor because he is a little short of breath and finds that his unhealthy diet and lack of exercise has led to diabetes, kidney problems, high blood pressure, arteriosclerosis, bad breath, indigestion, poor sleep, anxiety, and psoriasis. This industrial world can be saved, but it means listening to the doctor's orders and making real changes. A pill won't work, and many in business are just looking for a pill. Of course, some aren't even admitting that there's a problem.

The way to overcome people's resistance to seeing the problem is by talking about possibilities and solutions. From that vantage point, people can adjust their focus and see the damage we have done and are doing. Human beings need to create; we are born that way. Most of the damage being done is a result of misdirected creative impulses badly applied and greatly abetted by ignorance.

Lertzman: Are we at a point where our concept of business is being reinvented, re-imagined?

Hawken: We are in a period of re-imagining *big* business precisely because it has so little imagination. Look at what happened at the Hague meetings on climate change in 2000. Four countries whose governments are dominated by corporate interests—the U.S., Australia, Canada, and Japan—managed to reduce a conversation about the fate of the world and the future of energy into concepts like "restrictions" and "protecting our way of life." These four countries, which were acting as surrogates for mining, oil, gas, and car companies, managed to stop a worldwide environmental agreement dead in its tracks. The meeting brought into clear focus the incapacity of business to deal with the exigencies of global life.

Business, in its optimal state, can do extraordinary things. The world is full of small miracles brought to us by designers, engineers, and even salespeople. But the aggregate activity of commerce is destroying life on Earth. We are all to blame, to be sure, but we are hugely abetted by the scale and structure of modern business, which has more power than it can possibly handle.

Lertzman: The title of your last book, *Natural Capitalism*, written with Amory and Hunter Lovins, seems an oxymoron. What does it mean?

Hawken: Those who haven't read the book often assume the title refers to a variant of capitalism, when in fact, it doesn't refer to capitalism at all, but to the concept of "natural capital." It's a very important distinction.

The term "natural capital" was coined by economist E.F. Schumacher in

Small Is Beautiful to represent the natural resources that economists, governments, and corporations leave off the balance sheets. Natural capital includes the vital, life-supporting services that flow from living ecosystems: pollination, flood prevention, topsoil formation, oxygen production, waste metabolism, and so on. Capitalism is a profoundly *un*natural system that obliterates natural *and* human capital because it is focused on capital in the traditional sense: money and the means of production.

Lertzman: If capitalism cannot be "natural," then how can businesses be sustainable?

Hawken: Business and capitalism are not the same thing. When you talk about capitalism, you are on a whole other level. Business and enterprise preceded capitalism by a few thousand years.

Is capitalism necessarily exploitative? As it is defined and practiced, absolutely. Is it possible to restructure and redefine it such that it wouldn't be? Yes, but then it wouldn't be capitalism anymore. There is a notion that an economic system in line with ecology and human needs will suppress innovation, create unemployment, be too costly, and so forth. That is what the unimaginative declare because they have no idea what they would do in a system that wasn't based on acquisitiveness, aversion, and delusion. People have to change their values in order for the system to change.

Lertzman: Does the fate of our planet rest upon business's capacity to become "imaginative," or does it depend more upon community and individual efforts to enforce regulations and encourage healthy, ecologically sensitive practices?

Hawken: The answer is not "either/or" or even "both," but "all." Every node in the system will have to change. Human society is a subsystem of Mother Earth. As the Earth changes, every aspect of society is transformed. It is happening before our eyes. Most of the changes cause suffering. This is the problem, but also the starting point for intervention: How do we relieve suffering?

Another way to look at the population issue is to ask ourselves: How do we make a planet that truly welcomes every new being? How do we create a world where children do not suffer? If we take that as a starting point, then obvious answers arise. Of course business must change, but if we start from that point of view, then we will fall into a morass of arguments, compromises, rules, and rationalizations, because business is not the purpose of society, and it's certainly not our purpose on Earth. Businesses can serve humanity, alleviate suffering, and nurture life, but those that do are far too rare.

Lertzman: Can you provide examples of businesses that are nurturing? Is it a matter of what kind of businesses they are, or rather how they are run?

Hawken: It is both. There is Judy Wicks's White Dog Cafe in Philadelphia, and then there is McDonald's. Both are restaurants, but one helps the community, while the other extracts resources from it, paying pitiful wages in return. Discerning which is which is not rocket science. In our heart of hearts, we all know a good business when we see one.

We might ask ourselves whether fast food should even exist. It is an inherently unsustainable and destructive industry because it organizes food chains into low-cost monocultures, while eroding human health at the same time. "Slow food," the resurgence of local cuisine and biological agriculture are the other side of the spectrum.

In general, smaller is better. It is possible for a business to be sustainable on a large scale, but few will ever accomplish it, because the underlying assumptions that inform large corporations are based on dominance and power over markets and others. Sustainable businesses can be run in any number of ways, but they all involve a level of transparency and authenticity that contrasts sharply with the image put out by corporate public-relations departments. Giant institutions are very strong, but also inherently vulnerable because of their size. They create elaborate methods of deceiving themselves and others as a means of protection. Most small enterprises, on the other hand, perish without direct and unstinting honesty.

Lertzman: To many environmentalists, working with corporations is too much of a compromise.

Hawken: Working with corporations is not a compromise if you stay true to your values and principles. If you are in their thrall, that's different. David Brower, the founder of Friends of the Earth, was never opposed to working with corporations or negotiating, as long as the other party ended up doing the right thing, which David defined very clearly. What cannot be compromised are nature—wilderness, biodiversity, climatic integrity—and justice.

There are 100 million businesses in the world; ten thousand of them are big companies, and about a thousand are huge corporations that control the destiny of humankind. Those thousand need to be dealt with in every possible way. You can't speak truth to power if you are sitting in Starbucks fulminating about what's wrong. And you certainly can't educate people that way.

It is also critical to make a distinction between corporations and the people inside them. Those people are us: our sisters, uncles, daughters, fathers, and neighbors. The corporation is a strange hybrid organism—neither human nor institution—that we don't fully understand, because it's very different than anything seen before on Earth.

Lertzman: When you work with people coming from traditional corporate backgrounds, what concepts of sustainability do they find hardest to grasp?

Hawken: The key to sustainability is the capacity to see the relationship between human beings and nature as a whole system, within which are subsystems, such as commerce. In essence, it's systems thinking. Most businesses make money because they are narrowly focused. Generalist businesses do not last. Businesses "thrive" by having narrow definitions of responsibility as well. But that narrowness is what is killing us.

For example, we are burning down tropical forests and displacing and destroying traditional indigenous cultures in order to provide feedstock for cattle to make foodstuffs that cause heart disease. The rise in heart disease has led a growing biotech industry to prospect in the still-standing rainforests to find new compounds, which they will produce using recombinant organisms, to treat blocked arteries. The pharmaceutical industry uses golf-course-lined resorts in Arizona to wine and dine physicians as part of its marketing process. These junkets add to global warming because of increased use of carbon-based fuels for air travel, limousines, and golf carts. The air-conditioners that cool the buildings are fed by coal-fired power plants such as Black Mesa, which foul and pollute the air, causing increases in asthma.

This is what happens when business is narrowly focused: it causes damage every step of the way. And this is how most everything in our economy works.

Lertzman: In a recent *Boston Globe* editorial on the energy crisis, you suggested that we have a shortage not of energy, but of wisdom.

Hawken: Sustainability is a matter of seeing the world with heart and recognizing its parts as inseparably complex. Most people are worried, anxious, tense, and insecure. They have a hard time seeing far into the future or deeply into the present because they feel threatened. This is what it has come to. Until sustainability connects with the depth of people's suffering, it will remain a white person's movement from the North.

Lertzman: How does a sustainable approach "connect with the depth of people's suffering"?

Hawken: The fragmentation of experience and knowledge is a hallmark of modernity and the primary cause of unsustainability. What do people know of their place? Their survival does not depend on local science or intimacy with their bioregion.

An example may help: There were a people in Patagonia called the Yamana (Yahgán) who were first spotted by Ferdinand Magellan. (He called them "bestial.") Hunter-gatherers in one of the world's more difficult climates, the Yamana were hunted down to near extinction by bounty hunters, until there were only a few hundred left of their tribe. In the 1870s, an Anglican priest and amateur lexicographer started making a dictionary of their language. His dictionary, which lives on in the British Museum, contains 32,000 words. Japanese, by comparison, has about 40,000 words, and it's a written language. The Yamana language has more verbs than English. It is a language of place. It contains exquisite words to describe how humans interact with local living systems.

Their language is, even to this day, some of the world's best observational science. From it, we can learn about a people who spoke a language in which science, self, place, the sacred, survival, and nature were not separate. This does not mean that these concepts were "integrated," but that the Yamana never disaggregated the world into these concepts in the first place.

Today, people's survival depends on abstractions contained in stock-market data, on professional skills that are independent of place, on monetary flows, and on kinships that are scattered geographically. By discussing sustainability in the abstract, we miss a key point: the exploitation of the environment is carried out by human beings in order to dominate other human beings. So at the heart of our ecological loss are the efforts of people, as a part of corporations, to form dominant relationships to other cultures and peoples.

The sciences of ecology and biology are critical, but the source of hope is justice and a sense of not needing to harm or have power over another. It starts with gender roles and extends through the family to the community and eventually the boardroom, governments, and international politics.

Lertzman: The hierarchical structures of our institutions can be oppressive and exploiting. Do our organizational structures need to change to collectives and co-ops?

Hawken: I think one needs to be careful about taking what works in one culture and extending it to the world, as if it were a cure or panacea. Perhaps a better way to come to this is through the idea of the commons. The commons is usually defined as an open tract of public land in a city or town, but we need to use the word in the broadest sense: from the village greens, to the culture, to the sky. Generally, people who organize around the commons have been able to create more just systems than those who organize around private property.

Recognizing that a resource is common to us all does not mean it needs to be collectivized. It does mean that the dynamics of the commons will shape the culture. We see this most readily in indigenous cultures. A culture that creates material wealth outside its commons — as do the industrial nations — will be hard pressed to recognize limits or boundaries. Slowly here in the U.S., a number of issues — from sprawl, to factory farming, to overfishing, to toxic-waste dumps — have begun to bring communities back together through the recognition that people's jobs, livelihood, children, and sense of place are threatened.

Lertzman: It sounds as if you are suggesting that, as human health and the health of our ecosystem worsen, we are being forced to consider the commons as the only viable means of resolving the complex issues we face. Yet most people refuse or are unable to acknowledge the problems. Look at the rise in SUV ownership, for example, which poses a serious threat to the commons.

Hawken: I would never suggest any solution is the "only" means of solving a problem. If we are dwelling within a system that is degrading life on Earth, then every node of the system requires attention. This is heartening because it means that farmers, teachers, mechanics, parents, architects, and people in every other vocation have a role to play. We are not talking about change from on high. We are not talking about charismatic white males leading a sustainability revolution. This is change from the margins, from the understory.

Embedded in your question is the idea that there is some omega point from whence large-scale change will occur, but this concept of change is emblematic of the thinking that created the system we are living in. And if we think of SUV owners as careless, non-thinking despoilers of the commons, we are further in the hole, because then we are marginalizing—if not demonizing—our fellow human beings. Not a strong basis for change. This world is riddled with ignorance. You can blame people who knock things over in the dark, or you can begin to light candles. You're only at fault if you know about the problem and choose to do nothing.

Lertzman: It's very easy to fall into the demonizing trap. The progressive movement is rife with such good-bad thinking: companies are bad, capitalism is bad, globalization is bad. How can we *not* fall into this trap?

Hawken: We can look at ourselves. Is my heart good or bad? It is a question of self-knowledge and acceptance. Nothing is black and white, so buying into polemics, be it left or right, is a kind of indulgence. Real grassroots change is messy, because it is necessarily inclusive. It has grit.

Real change is like Buddhist practice; it's a matter of attending to what is in front of you: your house, your community, your clothing, your food, your speech, your way of life, your livelihood. It can be stimulated and enhanced by changes in power, regulations, and leadership, and I strongly support political engagement and citizen activism. But leading a life within biological and ecological constraints is first a personal choice, not a collective or political one. I have never known any other effective way to change what is around you other than to start small and, in the Gandhian sense, *be* the change you want to see. When I and many others started what is now the organic-food movement in the sixties, we didn't ask permission, do a marketing survey, or obtain definitions from the USDA. We grew food, ground it, bagged it, and ate it. The real changes occurring worldwide largely go unnoticed.

Lertzman: Can we train people to actually perceive the systems you describe?

Hawken: I don't believe you can train anybody, especially people in business.

You can only present and embody ideas. I try to help people understand the idea that valuing and conserving our stock of natural capital can lead to astonishing breakthroughs in processes, products, and design. Again, people move toward possibility. Once they see that we can actually improve the quality of life for everyone on Earth by using radically less "life," they get excited. Not just businesspeople, but students, especially, are keen on it, as are cities, government ministries, and other institutions. When *Natural Capitalism* came out in China last July, the mayor of Shanghai bought 700 copies for every administrative department in the city.

Lertzman: You say we need new "mental models" and maps. Why?

Hawken: Changed mental maps or models allow us to find the point of greatest leverage. The late Dana Meadows was great at identifying where to intervene in a system in order to have the most leverage. Downstream is obviously the least effective.

People generally don't even know they have mental models. In the U.S., we assume that twentieth-century capitalism is ordained, part of the natural order, an act of God questioned only by subversives and fools. What we don't see is that the present economic system is upside down and backward. We participate in a system that serves the few and oppresses, deadens, and exploits the many. We live in a world where decent work, peacefulness, and frugality are punished, while greed, vanity, and violence are honored. We point to pharmaceuticals, the Internet, and sanitation as proof positive that Western civilization is on the right track, all the while ignoring that we are witnessing a global holocaust of life.

One way you can tell people have a strong ideological bias based on an old mental model is when they casually accept labels as a way of demeaning or lessening others. "Left" is such a label. "Green" is another, and "socialist" is yet another. I believe the prevailing economic model usurps language and meaning, nullifying vision, reason, and perception. As Eduardo Galleano says, you would think that Darwin wrote his books in order to honor predatory capitalism. We see Darwin's writings through a lens that is passed on and enforced by the dominant institutions. We are in the process of clear-cutting human nature and strip-mining culture for the sake of money, because we are blind. The corporate capitalist system is a fabrication, an invention of the human mind, a thin veil some think is solid.

Lertzman: In your book *The Next Economy*, written in 1983, you wrote that we did not have an economic problem or an environmental problem, but a design problem. Why "design"?

Hawken: I use the word *design* because it's a concept that slips through corporate defenses. The Ojibway tribe made "dream catchers," devices that allowed the good dreams to pass through and the bad to be caught. Businesses have an opposite device, something that excludes the good dreams and lets the bad ones in. Good design is about letting imagination, delight, and innovation stream through. Most people, if given the choice, move toward good design and new possibilities. Design knows no ideology, so it is not seen as threatening.

Saying we have a design problem was my way of saying that there is a problem of seeing—that if we as a society could change the way we perceive the world, then solutions would cascade forth. And so they have. There are some extraordinary people out there with some radical and elegant solutions. The question is why, with the solutions so abundantly arrayed, are we even more destructive now than we were a decade ago?

Lertzman: That seems not only tragic, but ironic.

Hawken: The irony is that we have the means to completely transform every sector of the economy, from agriculture, to health care, to energy, but our efforts are being blocked by a corporate oligarchy that holds the power in this country and around the world. We are so numb in this country, so anesthetized, that most Americans don't realize that, in the last presidential election, we witnessed a palace coup complete with puppet dictator backed by a rich cabal.

Lertzman: Are you concerned that corporations latch on to the word *sustainability* and let it lull them into thinking they are ecologically sensitive?

Hawken: First, let me say something about the word *sustainability*: it is not a great term. And even if it were, it is a boring concept. What we need to do is restore the world, not maintain equilibrium. But yes, many corporations are doing as you suggest, using the concept of sustainability as a means to maintain a sense of legitimacy. For those corporations, being "green" is a way of *not* changing. I remember hearing a spokesperson for DuPont describe how they were embracing radical resource productivity by introducing powder coatings for SUVs. Apparently, there was a 75 percent reduction in material and energy costs. It's times like that when I sense how deep the malaise in our thinking is.

Recently, a prominent environmental organization asked me to address its funders. When introducing me, the head of the organization said I would tell them the "good news" about corporate sustainability. I was taken aback and, unfortunately, had to somewhat embarrass my host by saying that, when it comes to large multinational corporations, there is not much good news.

The real good news is that there are some seventy thousand small businesses in this country whose whole raison d'être is to create a humane and ecological economy. Some big NGOs get excited when William Clay Ford talks about making Ford Motor Company green, but the real work is occurring in the margins, where undercapitalized businesses really do make a difference. I have thought of writing a book, a thin volume, called *Corporate Sustainability*. Like "natural capitalism," the title is an oxymoron on its face. The purpose of the book would be to describe what *real* corporate sustainability would look like. It would be radically different than what passes for "green" corporations. I don't know if any multinational company would pursue real sustainability, but at least we could reclaim the language.

Lertzman: If the term "sustainability" doesn't have meaning anymore, why not get rid of the term altogether?

Hawken: Language is created by the culture. To wrest it away isn't possible.

Today, the fluency with which we describe our relationship to life has been debased. The environmental and social-justice movements are attempting to enlarge the vocabulary, to create a vastly expanded sense of the possibilities for humankind. Milan Kundera said that "the struggle of man against power is the struggle of memory against forgetting."[57] It is also the struggle of language against efforts to silence it, of intelligence against the confinement of the sound bite, of human decency against the convoluted lies of corporate public-relations offices.

Lertzman: Do you see the recent anti-globalization protests as part of this struggle?

Hawken: The protests are called "anti-globalization," but, in my mind, they are about something broader than the term conveys. For the past decade, culminating most visibly with the protests against the World Trade Organization in Seattle, a global uprising has been emerging. Little noticed and largely discounted by the media, it has been portrayed by pundits as a simpleminded rejection of progress and globalization. It is far more. It is an argument against the corporatization of the world's commons, a resistance to the growing loss of sovereignty, dignity, and self-determination. These are not minor complaints raised by marginal segments of society but central issues that will determine our future. What we are witnessing may be no less than the first global revolution, a nascent worldwide movement that will force every international institution and national government to either change or perish.

The words *uprising* and *revolution* seem threatening, with their similarity to the Marxist cant of the past. But what distinguishes this revolution from Marxist-Leninism and other proto-fascist movements of the past is the absence of a centralized leadership, a singular ideology, or a hierarchical form of organization. It is an absolutely new and different social movement. No institution or government is prepared for it. It is broad, deep, and growing rapidly. It is composed of families in India, mothers in the U.S., farmers in France, the landless in Brazil, the poor in Bolivia, the Zapatistas in Chiapas, tribes in Central America, housewives in Japan, and tree-sitters in northern California. The movement requires little money and grows in remote locations as well as major population centers. Its heroes are farmers, shoemakers, and poets. Its best-known spokespeople are people of color from the global South.

Lertzman: When did you start to realize that corporatization was becoming the key political issue of our era? Did it become clear to you at the WTO protests in Seattle, or had it begun long before that?

Hawken: Corporatization was evident during the Vietnam War, a conflict in which our foreign policy was controlled by the military-industrial complex, just as Eisenhower had foretold. I believe corporatization has been the key political issue since the conquistadors. Corporations were created to enable the exploitation of the New World by profit-seeking commercial entities who needed to limit their liability in order to protect their families. Bear in mind that the American colonies rose up not against the tyranny of a crazed King George, but against the rule of his chartered corporations.

In essence, America was created to end corporate abuse. That we have become what we feared is ironic, and would be merely of historical interest were it not for the fact that corporate activity today threatens life itself. The WTO demonstrations have a long historical lineage. They only seemed surprising because the media today are ahistorical, as is our culture. Marx was wrong. Religion is not the opiate of the masses. The drug of choice is the materialism flowing from corporations.

Lertzman: How did participating in the Seattle protests affect you personally?

Hawken: Before that, I saw business and corporations as something that could be reformed within a framework that was at least consonant with the worldview of commerce. I no longer believe that to be true. The movement brought to light that business cannot continue in anything akin to its present form without causing a breakdown in civil society and ecological integrity.

Lertzman: Did the magnitude of the protests surprise you?

Hawken: Seattle *was* surprising in terms of magnitude, but not in terms of police violence. I had been a part of the civil-rights and antiwar movements and had seen out-of-control police and facile political explanations before. What struck me most about Seattle were the extraordinary distortions in the media coverage. I wrote a piece about the protests that was published in *The Sun* and twelve other magazines, but I wrote it originally as a long e-mail to counter the propaganda in the mainstream media. I had never fully understood Noam Chomsky's theory about "manufacturing consent" until I read the Sunday paper following the protests.

Lertzman: Do you see this "uprising" as indicative of major shifts to come in how we practice and perceive business?

Hawken: I've spent a decade observing and speaking to corporations that profess a desire to use more sustainable practices. So far, the people within these companies have been unable to fundamentally change their corporate policies to support true ecological or social justice. The only exceptions have been people like Ray Anderson, the CEO and founder of Interface, and Anita

Roddick, founder of the Body Shop, both of whom own controlling interest in their companies. Otherwise, the corporation has a "life" of its own, and that life is not about human or ecological integrity. The collective behavior of the world's corporations is destroying life on Earth.

That last phrase sounds like a teaser for a "B movie," but either you say it and do something, or you begin to ponder what the requiem should be. I prefer the former.

Lertzman: How can you not become depressed in the face of such enormous problems?

Hawken: What makes this work so fascinating is its scope, and how all roads eventually lead to heart and spirit. Why get depressed? Why not get depressed? Either way works. The human condition is as it was described twenty-five hundred years ago. The question is not how to save the Earth, but how to alleviate suffering.

Lertzman: You address dozens of audiences a year. What are the most urgent questions that people pose? Are there common themes, no matter where you go in the world?

Hawken: If there is an underlying thread, it would be the need for hope: a hope that has its feet on the ground, that is credible. People want to know: Is there enough time? Will we make it? I'm sure those questions have been asked endlessly in history, but I don't think they have ever been asked so persistently by such diverse groups. And the number of people who are willing to give voice to this common fear is growing.

Lertzman: What is a hope that "has its feet on the ground"?

Hawken: What I mean is a hope that is plausible, given a thorough understanding of the world's problems. I am not comfortable with mere desire or expectation; rather, I prefer something closer to the idea of faith.

Wendell Berry wrote in his poem "Mad Farmer" to "be joyful though you know all the facts." When I speak to business and government audiences, they rarely, if ever, know all the facts. They usually think the problem is how to keep their nest clean. So it's a matter of providing them with some framework, a biological and social survey of the state of the world. From there, you can point to new ways of seeing and doing.

Audiences that are literate with respect to the issues tend to cleave into three categories. The first are people who have worked a long time on a problem and have become hardened, if not cynical. They are the most difficult to reach. The second are people who are in despair about what they know and need some sense of hope in order to inform and impel their life and activities.

The third are those who are profoundly committed to justice and restoration and need little encouragement. They need only food, housing, and a few good friends. These are the people, young and old, who form the picket lines, do the direct actions, chain themselves to trees and bulldozers, and speak truth to power on our streets and to our leaders. They are my idea of heroes and heroines. They give me hope.

Lertzman: How do you respond to the other question: Is there enough time for us to correct our destructive trends?

Hawken: I usually respond that time is irrelevant. We are all in this together, six billion of us and growing, and we have enough time to do what we need to do, even if we can't discern the future. This doesn't mean that, in the coming years, there won't be grievous losses of people and place. There probably will be an increase in human suffering, and it will be tough to witness. We cannot know the future, not even a minute from now. What is critical is to be engaged in something that is worthy, to live a life that you will feel good about when you die, even if you die tomorrow. When you are engaged in this way, the issues of life and death and time becomes less important than the care and grace with which you serve.

David Whyte, the poet, tells corporate audiences a story about a spectral ghost that, as in Dickens's *Christmas Carol*, takes a corporate manager to his future grave, scrapes off the moss, and reads the epitaph: "He made his mortgage payments." Sooner or later, everyone on Earth has to answer the question of mortality—which is always a question of whether we live a life of fear or a life of service.

Lertzman: I think having hope is particularly salient for young people today. How can we educate young people about what is happening in the world and not rob them of hope?

Hawken: You can't rob people of hope if they've never had it. Many young people were immersed in an environmental cold shower when they were little and had no context for the troubling information they received. They were told about dying whales, global warming, polluted rivers, and clear-cut forests. The last place to start to educate a child about the environment is with the problems. You want to start with the mystery. You want them to know and love nature even though they lack rudimentary knowledge of ecology. They'll learn about the problems soon enough, but in early schooling, they should play, have fun, and honor nature.

Children feel loss keenly, and they can see how absurd the present system is. Kevin Danaher of Global Exchange told an audience in Seattle during the WTO meetings that if they were confused about their priorities, ask a nine-year-old whether corporations should maximize profits or save the environment, increase CEO stock options or stop child starvation.

Children need the literacy of wonder to provide a firmament for what is happening in the world. Such children will not be hopeless, because they won't relent, never give up, never stop working at what may appear to be the impossible task of restoring the Earth.

Is There Slavery in Your Chocolate?

by John Robbins

CHOCOLATE. The very word conjures feelings of pleasure, sensuality, and the richness of life. The scientific name of the tree from whose beans we make chocolate likewise bespeaks the depth of feeling human beings have always had for chocolate. It is *Theobroma cacao L.* The name of the genus, *Theobroma,* comes from two Greek words: *theos,* meaning gods, and *broma,* meaning foods. Thus, literally, "food of the gods."

Chocolate has a remarkable history. When Cortez and his conquistadors first encountered the Aztecs and met the last Aztec emperor, Montezuma, they were amazed to find a thriving metropolis with more than one million residents, making it several times larger than the biggest city in Europe at the time. Cortez and his band were confronting a culture and an ecosystem that were wildly strange to them. Yet what they found most astonishing, according to their reports, was the fact that Montezuma's royal coffers were overflowing not with gold but with cocoa beans. Here, gold was used primarily for architectural and artistic beauty and had only secondary monetary value. The coin of the realm in pre-conquest Mexico was not gold, it was cocoa beans.

When Cortez arrived in the Aztec capital, Montezuma's coffers held more than nine thousand tons of cocoa beans. Since these beans were money, they were roasted and eaten only by the wealthiest of citizens, only by those who, literally, had "money to burn." According to the reports of the conquistadors, Montezuma himself drank only cocoa potions, and this from golden goblets which were given to the poor after a single use. This may have been one of the most extreme examples of conspicuous consumption in history—the eating of money itself.

Today we know that cacao, cocoa, and chocolate are the richest known sources of a little-known substance called theobromine, a close chemical relative of caffeine. Theobromine, like caffeine, and also like the asthma drug theophylline, belong to the chemical group known as xanthine alkaloids. Chocolate products contain some caffeine, but not nearly enough to explain the attractions, fascinations, addictions, and effects of chocolate. Chocolate addiction may really be theobromine addiction.

Slavery Lurking behind the Sweetness

Most of us, though, aren't all that concerned with the history or chemistry of chocolate. When it comes down to it, frankly, we are content so long as the market shelves remain well-stocked with affordable tins of cocoa and bars of chocolate candy.

Or at least that's how it was in the United States until the summer of 2001. For then the Knight Ridder, Inc. newspapers across the country ran a series of investigative articles that revealed a very dark side to our chocolate consumption. In riveting detail, the series profiled young boys who were tricked into slavery, or sold as slaves, to Ivory Coast cocoa farmers.

Ivory Coast, located on the southern coast of West Africa, is by far the world's largest supplier of cocoa beans, providing 43 percent of the world's supply. There are 600,000 cocoa farms in Ivory Coast which together account for one-third of the nation's entire economy. An investigative report by the British Broadcasting Company (BBC) in 2000 indicated the size of the problem. According to the BBC, hundreds of thousands of children are being purchased from their parents for a pittance, or in some cases outright stolen, and then shipped to the Ivory Coast, where they are sold as slaves to cocoa farms. These children typically come from countries such as Mali, Burkina Faso, and Togo. Destitute parents in these poverty-stricken lands sell their children to traffickers believing that they will find honest work once they arrive in Ivory Coast and then send some of their earnings home.

But that's not what happens. These children, usually twelve to fourteen years old but sometimes younger, are forced to do hard manual labor eighty to one hundred hours a week. They are paid nothing, are barely fed, are beaten regularly, and are often viciously beaten if they try to escape. Most will never see their families again.

"The beatings were a part of my life," Aly Diabate, a freed slave, told reporters. "Anytime they loaded you with bags [of cocoa beans] and you fell while carrying them, nobody helped you. Instead they beat you and beat you until you picked it up again."[58]

Brian Woods and Kate Blewett are groundbreaking filmmakers who made history when they went undercover in China eight years ago to make a documentary which shook the world, *The Dying Rooms*, about the hideous conditions in Chinese state orphanages. Recently, they made a film about the use of child slaves in African cocoa fields. "It isn't the slavery we are all familiar with and which most of us imagine was abolished decades ago," says Brian Woods. "Back then, a slave owner could produce documents to prove ownership. Now, it's a secretive trade which leaves behind little evidence. Modern slaves are cheap and disposable. They have three things in common with their ancestors. They aren't paid, they are kept working by violence or the threat of it, and they are not free to leave."

Blewett and Woods tell of meeting Drissa, a young man from Mali who had been tricked into working on an Ivory Coast cocoa farm. "When Drissa took his shirt off, I had never seen anything like it. I had seen some pretty nasty things in my time but this was appalling. There wasn't an inch of his body which wasn't scarred."[59]

Slavery Past and Present

The ownership of one human being by another is illegal in Ivory Coast, as it is in every other country in the world today. But that doesn't mean slavery has ceased to exist. Rather, it has simply changed its form. In times past, we had slave owners. Now we have slaveholders. In both cases, the slave is forced to work by violence or the threat of violence, paid nothing, given only that which keeps him or her able to continue to work, is not free to leave, and can be killed without significant legal consequence. In many cases, non-ownership turns out to be in the financial interest of slaveholders, who now reap all the benefits of ownership without the obligations and legal responsibilities.

Kevin Bales is author of *Disposable People: New Slavery in the Global Economy*, and director of Free the Slaves, an American branch of Anti-Slavery International. He points out that one of the economic drawbacks of the old slavery was the cost of maintaining slaves who were too young or too old to work. Children rarely brought in more than they cost until the age of ten or twelve, though they were put to work as early as possible. Slavery was profitable, but the profitability was diminished by the cost of keeping infants, small children, and unproductive old people. The new slavery avoids this extra cost and so increases its profits.

In the United States, the old slavery consisted primarily of bringing people against their will from Africa. This represented a significant financial investment. Bales says that before the Civil War, the cost to purchase the average slave amounted to the equivalent of $50,000 (in today's dollars). Currently, though, enslaved people are bought and sold in the world's most destitute nations for only $50 or $100. The result is that they tend to be treated as disposable. Slaves today are so cheap that they're not even seen as a capital investment anymore. Unlike slave owners, slaveholders don't have to take care of their slaves. They can just use them up, in the cocoa fields for example, and then throw them away.

Pressure for Change

As publicity about the use of child slaves in the chocolate industry mounted in the summer and fall of 2001, so did pressure on the chocolate manufacturers. Chocolate is a symbol of sweetness and innocence, but Western chocolate consumers know there is nothing sweet and nothing innocent about slavery.

On June 28, 2001, the U.S. House of Representatives voted 291–115 to look into setting up a labeling system so consumers could be assured no slave labor was used in the production of their chocolate. Unhappy with this turn of events, the U.S. chocolate industry and its allies mounted an intense lobbying effort to fight off legislation that would require "slave free" labels for their products. The Chocolate Manufacturers Association, a trade group that represents U.S. chocolate producers, hired two former Senate majority leaders — Bob Dole, a Republican, and George Mitchell, a Democrat — to lobby lawmakers on its behalf.

"A 'slave free' label would hurt the people it is intended to help" because it would lead to a boycott of all Ivory Coast cocoa, said Susan Smith, a spokeswoman for the Chocolate Manufacturers Association. She pointed out that no producer using Ivory Coast cocoa could possibly state that none of its chocolate was produced by child slavery. Slave-picked beans are mixed together with others harvested by free field hands.

For a long time, many major chocolate makers have insisted that they bear no responsibility for the problem, since they don't own the cocoa farms. But pressure on the industry was mounting. The legislation to address child slavery in West Africa that had passed in the House (sponsored by Representative Eliot Engel) was by now almost certain to pass in the Senate (where it was sponsored by Senator Tom Harkin). On October 1, 2001, the chocolate industry announced a four-year plan to eventually eliminate child slavery in cocoa-producing nations, and particularly West Africa, where most of the world's chocolate is grown. If all went according to the plan, called the "Harkin-Engel Protocol," the "worst forms of child labor"—including slavery—would no longer be used to produce chocolate and cocoa by 2005.

Larry Graham, president of the Chocolate Manufacturers Association, said that "the industry has changed, permanently and forever."[60] The agreement was signed by the manufacturers association and the World Cocoa Foundation; as well as chocolate producers Hershey's, M&M Mars, Nestle, and World's Finest Chocolate; and the cocoa processors Blommer Chocolate, Guittard Chocolate, Barry Callebaut, and Archer Daniels Midland. It was endorsed by a wide variety of groups including the government of Ivory Coast, the International Labor Organization's child labor office, the anti-slavery group Free the Slaves, the Child Labor Coalition, the International Cocoa Organization (which represents cocoa growing countries), and the National Consumer League.

The six-point protocol commits the chocolate industry to work with non-governmental organizations (NGOs) and the International Labor Organization in monitoring and remedying abusive forms of child labor used in growing and processing cocoa beans. A series of deadlines is part of the plan. For example, an independent monitoring and public reporting system was in place in May, 2002. Industry-wide voluntary standards of public certification are due to be in place by July 1, 2005. In addition, the chocolate companies agreed to fund a joint international foundation, run by a board comprised of industry and NGO representatives, to oversee and sustain efforts to eliminate the worst forms of child labor in the industry. Plus, the agreement provides for a formal advisory group to investigate child labor practices in West Africa, and a commitment by the chocolate companies to "identify positive development alternatives for the children" who might be affected.

It is clear that the recent public and political awareness of slavery in cocoa production has moved both the government and chocolate industry to action. We still have a long way to go, but progress is being made for the first time in years.

Whose Chocolate Is Made with Slavery, and Whose Is Made Without?

Even with the progress represented by the chocolate industry's plan, however, it will nevertheless take years for chocolate products to be "slave free." Is there any way for chocolate consumers to know today that they are not consuming products made with child slavery? A 2001 inquiry into the cocoa sources used by 200 major chocolate manufacturers found significant differences between companies. The $13 billion U.S. chocolate industry is heavily dominated by just two firms—Hershey's and M&M Mars—who between them control two-thirds of the market. Unfortunately, both of these companies fall into the category of those companies who use large amounts of Ivory Coast cocoa, and whose products are almost certainly produced in part by slavery. Hershey Foods Corp., the nation's largest chocolate-maker, says it is "shocked" and "deeply concerned" that its products, such as Hershey's Kisses, Nuggets, Hershey chocolate bars, and Reese's Peanut Butter Cups, may be made with cocoa produced by child slaves.[61] The company, which has a long history of involvement with children, says it is deeply embarrassed by revelations of indirect involvement with child slavery. (Hershey Foods, which has a market capitalization on Wall Street of $8.4 billion, is affiliated with a school for orphaned and disadvantaged children, established in 1909 by company founder Milton S. Hershey and his wife Catherine.)

M&M Mars and Hershey Foods Corp. are not alone. Other companies whose chocolate is almost certainly tainted with child slavery include: ADM Cocoa, Ben & Jerry's, Cadbury Ltd., Chocolates by Bernard Callebaut, Fowler's Chocolate, Godiva, Guittard Chocolate Company, Kraft, Nestle, See's Candies, The Chocolate Vault, and Toblerone. While most of these companies have issued condemnations of slavery, and expressed a great deal of moral outrage that it exists in the industry, they each have acknowledged that they use Ivory Coast cocoa and so have no grounds to ensure consumers that their products are slavery-free. Companies like Mars, Hershey, and Nestle often say that there is no way they can control the labor practices of their suppliers. But there are other chocolate companies who manage to do so, and it would seem that if the bigger companies really wanted to reform problems in the supply chain, they have the power and ability to do so.

There are in fact many chocolate companies who only use cocoa that has definitively not been produced with slave labor. These companies include Clif Bar, Cloud Nine, Dagoba Organic Chocolate Company, Denman Island

Chocolate, Gardners Candies, Green and Black's, Kailua Candy Company, Koppers Chocolate, L.A. Burdick Chocolates, Montezuma's Chocolates, Newman's Own Organics, Omanhene Cocoa Bean Company, Rapunzel Pure Organics, and The Endangered Species Chocolate Company. At present, no organic cocoa beans are coming from Ivory Coast, so organic chocolate is unlikely to be tainted by slavery. Newman's Own Organics is one of the largest of the slavery-free companies. The company's chocolate is purchased through the Organic Commodity Project in Cambridge, Massachusetts. It comes from Costa Rica where the farms are closely monitored.

Some companies go further and buy only Fair Trade chocolate. In the early 1990s, Rapunzel initiated a "Hand in Hand" program called Eco-Trade — Fair Trade and Ecology. Strict guidelines and commitments must be maintained by all Rapunzel's partners in buying, selling, trading, growing, and processing commodities in developing countries. Guaranteed fair pricing, long-term trade relationships, living wages, and no child labor are just a few of the criteria. The company's cocoa comes from cooperatives in Bolivia and the Dominican Republic. Rapunzel's program is one of the most effective means of positive change for the lives of farmers and their families worldwide. The company's donations have built a school in the Dominican Republic, an orphanage in Brazil, and provided major support for organic farmers in Bolivia. Similarly, Cloud Nine has organized 150 grower families into a certified organic cooperative, and has committed to purchasing cocoa from them year-round at over-market organic prices.

Likewise, The Endangered Species Chocolate Company only purchases cocoa through the Fair Trade Initiative. In supporting smaller farm cooperatives, the company says "we encourage the indigenous people to harvest what is naturally grown in the area rather than clear-cutting the rainforest to make way for more destructive uses of land."[62] According to Frederick Schilling of the Dagoba Organic Chocolate Company, "By being paid a premium price, these farming communities can and are developing their communities by their own means and terms, oftentimes building schools for their children."[63]

Coffee

Although it is chocolate that has gotten the most publicity of late, chocolate isn't the only American staple produced by slaves. Some coffee beans are also tainted by slavery. In addition to producing nearly half of the world's cocoa, Ivory Coast is the world's fourth-largest grower of Robusta coffee. Robusta beans are used for espresso and instant coffees. They are also blended with milder Arabica beans to make ground coffees. Often, coffee and cocoa are grown together on the same farm. The tall cacao trees shade the shorter coffee bushes. On some Ivory Coast farms, child slaves harvest coffee beans as well as the cacao pods that yield cocoa beans. More than 7,000 tons of Ivory Coast coffee arrives in the U.S. each year.

As with chocolate, coffee beans picked by slaves are mixed together with those picked by paid workers. Some coffee industry executives acknowledge the use of slaves, but say the labor issue isn't their concern. "This industry isn't responsible for what happens in a foreign country," said Gary Goldstein of the National Coffee Association, which represents the companies that make Folgers, Maxwell House, Nescafe and other brands. Neither Folgers nor Maxwell House responded to inquiries about the origins of their coffee. Shipping records, though, showed that on Sunday, March 18, 2001, 337 tons of Ivory Coast coffee beans were sent to Folgers through Houston, Texas.

The U.S. is the world's largest consumer of both chocolate and coffee. In fact, coffee is the second largest legal U.S. import—after oil. Fortunately, there is considerable momentum developing in this country and elsewhere behind the emergence of Fair Trade coffee. According to the San Francisco-based Global Exchange,

> The best way to prevent child labor in the fields is to pay work-
> ers a living wage. . . . Most people in this country would rather
> buy a cup of coffee picked under fair trade conditions than
> sweatshop labor conditions. . . . Fair Trade Certified coffee is the
> first product being introduced in the United States with an inde-
> pendently monitored system to ensure that it was produced
> under fair labor conditions. . . . To become Fair Trade certified,
> an importer must meet stringent international criteria [includ-
> ing] paying a minimum price per pound of $1.26.[64]

Paying a minimum price of $1.26 to growers is a major step, because coffee prices on the world market currently run between sixty to ninety-five cents a pound, trapping many coffee farmers in an inescapable cycle of poverty, debt, and hunger. Ten years ago, the world coffee economy was worth $30 billion—

and producers received $12 billion, or 40 percent. But today, the world market has grown to be worth $50 billion — and producers receive just $8 billion, or 16 percent. Though they have not lowered consumer prices, coffee companies are paying far less for the beans they use. This creates, at best, sweatshops in the field, and at worst, the conditions that breed human slavery.

Fair Trade, whether it's coffee or chocolate, means an equitable partnership between consumers in North America and producers in Asia, Africa, Latin America, and the Caribbean. It means that farmers' cooperatives around the world can count on a stable and reliable living wage. When consumers purchase Fair Trade coffee or chocolate, they know that their money is going to local farmers where it is then invested in health care, education, environmental stewardship, community development, and economic independence. They know it's not going to enrich CEOs making tens of millions of dollars annually. This is important because destitute farmers are struggling to survive and even resorting to child slavery, while:

1) Chicago-based Sara Lee Corp. supplies more than 200 million pounds of coffee annually to more than 100,000 restaurants in the United States. In 2000, the most recent year for which public records exist, Sara Lee CEO John H. Bryan took home $45,512,113 in compensation.

2) In 2000, Starbucks CEO Orin C. Smith received $13,873,575 in compensation from the coffee company, plus $12,847,925 in stock option exercises. He still holds more than $33,000,000 in unexercised stock options.

3) Neither of these gentlemen, however, matched the pay received by the CEO of the company that owns Northfield, Illinois-based Maxwell House. In 2000, the CEO of Philip Morris, Geoffrey C. Bible, received $45,794,705 in compensation for his services, not including the more than $71,000,000 he holds in unexercised stock options.

4) Others in the coffee industry also did well. Folgers is owned by Procter and Gamble, whose CEO, Durk I. Jager, received $32,828,276 in compensation in 2000, not including the more than $10,000,000 he holds in unexercised stock options.

5) On the chocolate side, things are a little less posh, but top management seems to be able to get by. In 2000, Kenneth L. Wolfe, CEO of Hershey Foods, took home $7,877,554 in compensation from Hershey Foods, plus $2,615,838 in stock option exercises from prior grants. He still holds more than $4,000,000 in unexercised stock options.

6) In 2000, G. Allen Andreas, CEO of Archer Daniels Midland, owner of ADM Cocoa, received $8,381,371 in compensation for his services to the company.

It is not easy for most consumers to stomach the contrast between exorbitant salaries such as these, and the gruesome reality of slave labor. Nor is it easy to swallow the reality of such excess when millions of coffee and cocoa farmers around the world who depend on their harvests to provide for their families are facing debt and starvation. There seems to be something particularly hideous about making this kind of money on the backs of the world's poorest people.

Fair Trade on the Rise

Fair trade is a growing trend. On October 4, 2000, Starbucks introduced whole bean Fair Trade coffee to 2,300 stores. A year later, the company announced it would brew Fair Trade coffee once a month. Across the country, there are now over eighty companies that have licensing agreements to offer Fair Trade certified coffee. These companies include Starbucks, Tully's, Peet's, Equal Exchange, Diedrich, and Green Mountain. Kevin Bales, director of Free the Slaves, says that consumers

> . . . can make a significant impact on world slavery just by stopping for a moment and asking themselves how that particular item got to be so cheap. The low cost of many items defies belief. Part of the reason things are so cheap is that the big chain stores buy huge quantities at huge discounts, and have designed their distribution systems to reduce overhead all along the product chain. But I suspect that these efficiencies and economies of scale don't account for all of the cheapness. You see a lot of

cheap items made in China, for example, and there are serious questions about what happens in Chinese factories. The bottom line is: oftentimes things are cheap because slaves helped produce them.[65]

Most Western consumers, if they can identify slave-produced goods, would avoid them despite their lower price. But consumers do look for bargains, and don't usually stop to ask why a product is so cheap. It is certainly sobering to realize that by always looking for the best deal, we may be choosing slave-made products without knowing what we are buying.

We have reason for hope, though, based on how well most consumers respond to the challenge of slavery—when they know about it. Once people understand that slavery still exists, they are nearly unanimous in their desire to see it stopped. Fortunately, there are people who have taken on the task of informing people about the grim reality, and providing them with empowering alternatives.

One such activist is Deborah James, the Fair Trade Director of Global Exchange. She is currently coordinating a campaign against child slavery, and for Fair Trade, in the cocoa industry in West Africa. For the last two years, Deborah has spearheaded efforts to promote Fair Trade Certified coffee among campuses, community groups, and city councils around the nation. She led the successful campaign to pressure Starbucks to carry Fair Trade coffee in their stores, and is now campaigning to get industry giant Folgers to buy Fair Trade. (To learn about the Folgers campaign, see <http://globalexchange.org/economy/coffee/folgers.html>.)

Other heroic activists have focused on the carpet industry. Not that many years ago, many Oriental carpets were handwoven by children who were forced to work in the most miserable of conditions for little or no pay. Many were made by child slaves. If you have an Oriental rug on your floor right now, there is a good chance that it was woven by slave children. But then, a few years ago, a handful of European activists working from a tiny office with minimal funds started the Rugmark Campaign. In order to earn the "Rugmark," carpet producers had to agree to cooperate with independent monitors, not to exploit children, and to turn over 1 percent of their carpet wholesale price to child-welfare organizations. A sophisticated monitoring team was built up that can detect fake labels, knows carpet making inside and out, and can't be corrupted.

Today, the German, U.S., and Canadian governments recognize the

Rugmark label, as does the largest mail-order company in the world, the Otto Versand Group. Major retailers in the United States, Germany, and Holland now import only Rugmarked carpets. In Europe, the market share possessed by Rugmarked carpets stands at 30 percent, and is growing. The 1 percent from the producers has now built and staffed two Rugmark schools in the part of India where uneducated children were formerly fodder for the slave trade. The campaign has drawn the attention of other organizations, with the result that the German government and the United Nations Children's Fund (UNICEF) now fund other schools in the areas that used to be recruiting grounds for the carpet belt.

It is clear that, once aware, most people do not want to buy chocolate, coffee, rugs, or any other product made with slave labor. On the contrary, the success of Rugmark carpets, like the dramatic rise of Fair Trade chocolate and coffee, is a heartening example that, given a chance, most consumers want to be in an equitable relationship with the people who make the products they consume.

Seven Things You Can Do

1) Educate yourself further. Good sources of information include:
   Global Exchange (www.globalexchange.org)
   The Child Labor Coalition (www.stopchildlabor.org)
   Anti-Slavery (www.antislavery.org)
   Unfair Trade (www.unfairtrade.co.uk)
   Fair Trade (www.fairtrade.org/html/english.html)
   Abolish: The Anti-Slavery Portal (www.iabolish.com)
   For information on specific chocolate companies, see
      <www.radicalthought.org>
   Kevin Bales's book *Disposable People* (University of California Press,
      2000) is a thoroughly researched exposé of modern day slavery.

2) Write a letter to the editor or an article in your local newspaper.

3) Buy Fair Trade chocolate and/or coffee for gifts and show that you care about fairness for everyone. Or sell Fair Trade chocolate and/or coffee as a fundraiser for your church, school, or community group.

Fair Trade chocolate is available at
http://store.globalexchange.org/chocolate.html
Fair Trade coffee is available at
http://store.globalexchange.org/peace.html

4) Get stores in your community to carry Fair Trade chocolate and coffee. For support, email fairtrade@globalexchange.org.

5) Contact the big chocolate companies, and ask them to buy Fair Trade cocoa. Hershey Foods Corp. can be reached at 100 Crystal A Drive, Hershey, PA 17033; (717) 534-6799. Mars, Inc. can be reached at 6885 Elm Street, McLean, VA 22101; (703) 821-4900. Tell them that you expect something to be done immediately to ensure that cocoa imported into the U.S. is not harvested by enslaved children.

6) Support the Fair Trade campaign by joining organizations such as Global Exchange. They can be reached at 2017 Mission Street, #303, San Francisco, California 94110; (415) 255-7296; info@globalexchange.org.

7) Support the anti-slavery movement by joining organizations such as Anti-Slavery International. They can be reached in the U.S. at Suite 312-CIP, 1755 Massachusetts Avenue, N.W., Washington, D.C. 20036-2102. The main office is Anti-Slavery International, Thomas Clarkson House, The Stableyard, Broomgrove Road, London SW99TL, England.

Sarvodaya

by Joanna Macy

"We Build the Road and the Road Builds Us."
—Sarvodaya slogan

"REAL DEVELOPMENT is not free trade zones and mammoth hydroelectric dams," the young trainer told us. "It's waking up to our own needs and our own power."

I was sitting in an open-walled classroom with two dozen Sri Lankan village workers, absorbing the principles of a movement that promised to revolutionize Third World development. "This awakening happens on different levels. It's personal and spiritual as well as economic and cultural. These aspects of our lives are all interdependent." I wished planners at the World Bank could hear him.

A Buddhist-inspired people's self-help movement, Sarvodaya Shramadana Sangamaya was the largest nongovernmental organization in Sri Lanka, active in several thousand villages. It modeled a different kind of development than that preached and promoted by the industrialized countries. I had encountered it three years earlier on a trip to South Asia while I was still at Syracuse University. Throughout my graduate studies, I had sustained a strong interest in the potential for social change to be found in Asian religions, especially Buddhism. "Go talk to Ari," a community organizer in Bodh Gaya had advised me. He was referring to Sarvodaya's founder and president, A.T. Ariyaratne, a former high school teacher. "Some call him the Gandhi of Sri Lanka."

I did as I was told, and on that same trip in 1976, flew to Sri Lanka. When I walked into Ariyaratne's crowded little office in the Sarvodaya complex outside Colombo, it took me no more than two minutes to know that I wanted to stay and learn from his movement. For in this voluble, diminutive dynamo I found a scholar-activist who took the social teachings of the Buddha seriously and dared to believe that they could inspire change in the modern world. He had banked his life on that conviction, drawing from ancient traditions to empower what he called "the poorest of the poor."

When I completed my dissertation two years later in 1978, Ari invited me to come live with Sarvodaya for a year and study how it worked. And so, as soon as Peggy, my daughter, graduated from high school, I took off. I came equipped with a typewriter, a modest grant from the Ford Foundation, and half a year's instruction in Sinhalese from the kind monks at the Washington Buddhist Vihara.

Gandhi had taken the term *sarvodaya* from the Sanskrit word which means the "upliftment of all." Ari brought it to Buddhist Sri Lanka and recast it in terms of awakening. He explained that that's what the Buddha did under the Bodhi tree. He woke up. And that is what we all can do — awaken to our innate wisdom and power to act. Ari added the word *shramadana,* "gift of labor," so the movement's full name means, in effect, "everyone wakes up by working together." I listened with growing excitement. Here was the "liberation Buddhism" that I had imagined might be realized some day, with luck and the blessings of all the bodhisattvas.

My fascination with the shramadanas grew. From the start, these village work camps had constituted the movement's central organizing strategy. When Ari was still teaching high school, he heard about church-sponsored work camps in postwar Europe. He immediately saw how that kind of service could fit with the Buddha Dharma and how it could generate self-reliance and solidarity. But he didn't say, "Here's a great idea from the West, let's adopt it and imitate it." He said, "Let's draw from our own traditions and our own strengths." Using the word Gandhi had coined for the maintenance of his ashram and the cleaning of its latrines — "shramadana," gift of labor — Ari took the concept much further.

Sarvodaya's slogan was "We build the road and the road builds us." The process started early. A movement organizer would invite villagers to gather, perhaps in their temple's preaching hall, to discuss their needs and to deliberate on the choice of a project. Should they first dig some public latrines, or clear the weed-choked irrigation canal, or open a shortcut to the nearest by route? Then they considered where tools would be found and who would do what. This process was slow, involving more and more people, from elders to children. By the time the actual shramadana began, a good part of its purpose —to get the community working together—had already been achieved.

Teenagers were lugging out car batteries and hanging loudspeakers from the trees when I arrived at my first road-building shramadana. "You can't work without music!" they informed me. Huge cooking pots appeared as well, along with baskets of food that the children had collected from every household. Older women scolded and laughed as they cleaned rice, chopped pumpkin, and scraped coconut for curries. I joined one of the eight work teams, and we counted off to see who would be our leader for the first shift. The lot fell to a thirteen-year-old who made sure we each got a *mamoty*—a heavy Dutch hoe —and led us to our work site.

Much of my research entailed interviewing Sarvodaya monks, for the more progressive ones offered vivid examples of the role that clergy can play in social change. They opened their temple precincts to Sarvodaya preschools and literacy and sewing classes for adults. They drew from old Dharma stories to teach courage and self-respect. They used their status to draw villagers together in "family gatherings," recruited school dropouts to help organize shramadanas, and encouraged the young women and girls to take part. By their very presence they stilled any disapproving gossip about village daughters mixing with boys.

As I called on these monks and we spoke of village plans and scripture passages, what I loved most was the scent of courage. I never heard a word of complaint from Sarvodaya monks, but I began to realize the price they paid for engaging in community development work. It was more than the time it took, added on to hours of *puja* (rituals), temple care, and pastoral duties. It was more than the physical exertions involved: leaving the tranquil comforts of the temple for the wattle and daub shacks of the poorest families, or suffering the brain-addling sun of a shramadana, or trying to navigate the daunting bureaucratic labyrinths of government. The harshest cost was in reputation and prestige. One was not applauded by the larger, traditional Sangha, nor by the larger, conservative laity. On the contrary. The forest-dwelling monks in meditative retreat and the scholarly ones in their libraries received the most reverence. Their kind of renunciation did not rock the boat. When I had the nerve to raise the topic outright, the Sarvodaya monks responded with a calm yes. "Yes, that is true, by a lesser kind of monk. But it doesn't matter. It makes no difference."

Ethnic conflict between Hindu Tamils, residing largely in the North and

East, and the majority Buddhist Sinhalese erupted into civil war in 1983: blood-letting that continues to this day. Sick at heart, I wondered for years how the violence and polarization was affecting Sarvodaya. Returning for short visits, I found the movement heavily engaged in relief and rehabilitation work, along with occasional marches for peace. Its most distinctive contribution to easing hostilities lay, I soon realized, in the way it embodies the tolerance and nonvi-olence the Buddha taught, and his rejection of dogmatism. This stands in sharp contrast to the nationalism and anti-Tamil chauvinism displayed by the pow-erful Buddhist clergy.

Today in Sri Lanka Sarvodaya plays a critical role in modeling an under-standing of the Dharma that is consonant with a pluralistic society. At a time when the Buddhist majority finds itself in a narrowly defensive posture, acting as if Sri Lanka were by right a Buddhist Sinhalese state, Sarvodaya demon-strates the tolerance and respect for diversity that is integral to the Buddha's teachings. To Gautama, the notion of possessing an absolute truth or exclusive historical privileges was a dangerous delusion, leading to attachment, aversion, and suffering. Hence, the inclusivity he taught, which Sarvodaya exemplified from its outset by engaging with people of all faiths, showed a way of being true to the Dharma while working actively for the needs and rights of all, and not falling prey to Buddhist nationalism.

Rebuilding the Movement to Win

by Peter Montague, Ph.D.

THE PROGRESSIVE ecological movement is a huge, powerful political force that would appear to be unstoppable. In thirty short years it has passed a dozen pieces of national legislation, creating a government regulatory system that its adversaries dubbed "command and control," forced corporations to reveal each year that they routinely dump millions of tons of cancer-causing chemicals into our common property (our air and water), launched a very fundamental critique of the entire industrial enterprise, that it is not "sustainable," and even challenged the bedrock idea that all human activities add up to "progress."

Furthermore, by publicizing evidence of environmental damage, the environmental movement has gained the support of most of the public. Large majorities of the public—at least two-thirds—when asked, say they want the environment protected, even at considerable expense. Yet despite these phenomenal successes and the political power of these issues, in recent years anti-environmental forces have gained the upper hand. Progress toward environmental protection has stalled and in some instances slid backward. In Washington, the environmental movement has been on the defensive, really, since Ronald Reagan took office in 1980. Things improved only marginally during the Clinton/Gore years, and have taken a decided turn for the worse with George Bush, Jr.

How did anti-environmental forces become so powerful? During thirty years of hard work, self-styled "conservatives" have mobilized a huge constituency that accepts a corporate-driven anti-environment agenda. Most such "conservatives" tend to hold traditional European beliefs: that nature was created in a primitive and unfinished state by a Christian God who also put humans on Earth, separate from nature and superior to it, with a sacred duty to improve the environment by dominating and controlling it. In this view, humans are entitled—even obliged—to exploit nature because God put them on Earth for that purpose. (The alternate view clearly stated in the book of Genesis, that humans are the appointed stewards of God's creation, is a distinctly minor strain in Christian and secular European thinking.) This "conservative" constituency includes various groups that share one or more of the following goals:

(a) to reduce taxes to make government smaller (and as a consequence, intended or not, to reduce the number of government jobs, which tend to be union jobs and which tend to be available to nonwhite people);

(b) to increase U.S. military power, and to avoid entangling alliances (such as the UN) so that the U.S. can remain free to pressure any country, as needed, to protect access to foreign supplies of cheap labor and raw materials;

(c) through "free trade" agreements, to give U.S. corporations freedom and power to maneuver abroad, to evade taxes, to bribe public officials, to support private armies, to exploit indigenous labor, to extract natural resources, and to dump toxicants, as needed to improve profitability;

(d) to stamp out abortion and homosexuality, to return women to their early twentieth-century roles, and to enforce overt allegiance to selected Christian slogans in our public institutions;

(e) to keep the economic "playing field" tilted to the advantage of white people by denying the existence of white privilege, which gives unearned advantages to whites from birth;

(f) to imprison nonwhites in numbers far out of proportion to their rates of involvement in various criminal behaviors, applying a different standard of justice to whites;

(g) to punish the poor by making their lives difficult;

(h) to routinely violate international human rights agreements and standards by making it difficult or impossible for U.S. workers to form unions, bargain collectively and, if all else fails, to strike;

(i) to create and sustain an enormous industry devoted to distorting, ignoring, and, in some cases, fabricating scientific "facts" without any basis, as needed to retain political advantage;

(j) to retain and expand the influence of private wealth in public elections;

(k) to slowly replace popular democracy with control by corporate elites.

Naturally few or no "conservatives" hold every one of these views, and some "conservatives" find some of these ideas utterly repugnant. Still the "conservative" movement is a huge tent holding many different people, some of whom hold each of these views, and because they work together they create a potent political force that promotes the corporate anti-environment agenda in return for support on other "conservative" agenda items.

Today the traditional environmental movement is not well-positioned to prevail against these pro-corporate anti-environmental forces because the traditional environmental movement was founded on the assumption that legal and scientific expertise, and rational debate, would suffice to protect the environment. Without detracting from the very substantial legislative accomplishments of the traditional environmental movement — achieved through years of dedication, personal sacrifice, and extraordinary effort — it nevertheless remains true that the "traditional strategies and policy solutions being employed are proving to be increasingly limited," notes Professor Daniel Faber at Northeastern University.[66] This is something of an understatement. Traditional approaches have relied on lawsuits and on lobbying, and neither tactic is presently very effective. Legislatures and the courts are dominated by "conservative" activists who see the environment as something God intended us to exploit and who tend to believe that, since the corporate agenda works for them, it's good for us all.

In sum, to build on the successes of the traditional environmental movement and overcome the anti-environmental forces now arrayed in Washington and in statehouses across the country, some new approaches will be needed. Since 1980, an alternative to the traditional environmental movement has been slowly forming in the U.S., though so far it has gained little national visibility. It is called the "environmental justice" movement, and though it has some problems of its own, it represents a different approach to environmental protection, one that speaks to people about protecting the places where they live, work, and play.

As Daniel Faber has documented,[67] the fabric of the environmental justice movement is woven from six strands:

(1) The civil rights movement. Apartheid officially ended in the U.S. in 1964, but environmental racism is still all too common. The environmental regulatory system created during the 1970s and 1980s had the unintended effect of funneling pollutants into communities of color. Well-off white people can usually buy their way out of polluted neighborhoods, but people of color and the poor often cannot. Pollution trading schemes, being promoted by some traditional environmentalists, may be economically efficient but they tend to heap additional burdens and injustices on the poor and people of color.

(2) The occupational safety and health movement. The U.S. passed its first national job safety law in 1970, but since then enforcement has been lax or nonexistent. Furthermore, the law excludes tens of millions of workers, such as farmworkers. At least 60,000 workers die each year as a result of injuries and illnesses related to dangerous working conditions. Another 850,000 are made sick. At least 35 million nonunion workers say they would join a union if they could, to protect themselves, but U.S. laws violate international human rights standards by making unionization an uphill battle. Added to existing unions, those 35 million would create the largest union movement the U.S. has ever known, effectively shifting the balance of power between the corporate elite and wage earners.

(3) The indigenous peoples' and native land rights movements, made up of Native Americans, Chicanos, and other marginalized indigenous communities struggling to retain and protect their traditional lands. Partly these groups are fighting to control land resources, and partly they are trying to retain cultural lifeways that are threatened with extinction by the dominant society.

(4) The toxics movement (also known as the environmental health movement) has been fighting for the cleanup of thousands of contaminated waste sites across the country since 1978. The toxics movement has also taken the initiative in discouraging toxic technologies such as municipal garbage incinerators, pesticides,

so-called low level radioactive waste dumps, coal-burning power plants, buried gasoline tanks, toxicants dumped by the military, and more.

(5) Solidarity movements, human rights movements, and environmental activists in the Third World are providing powerful allies and examples of extraordinary, fearless activism. In South Africa, Mexico, Burma, Indonesia, Nigeria, Central America, the former Soviet Union, and elsewhere, local groups are fighting the same fights being fought in the U.S. but with fewer resources and against greater odds — sometimes sacrificing their lives in their persistent demand for environmental protection, sustainability, self-determination, and justice.

(6) Community-based activists working for social and economic justice have traditionally focused on issues of housing, public transportation, crime and police conduct, access to jobs, a living wage, redlining and lender practices, affordable daycare, deteriorating schools, and dozens of other neighborhood issues. They have not traditionally viewed their work as "environmental" but now when they work on lead poisoning, cleaning up abandoned toxic sites ("brownfields"), poor air quality, childhood asthma, and other issues with an environmental component, they are indisputably a part of the "environmental justice" movement.

In addition to these six strands, we see a powerful, burgeoning seventh — people whose health has been affected by multiple chemical sensitivities, birth defects, breast cancer, endometriosis, lymphoma, diabetes, chronic fatigue, veterans affected by Agent Orange and Gulf War Syndrome, and many others.

An eighth strand includes the international "zero waste" and "clean production" movements, which are quietly revolutionizing the material basis of the industrial enterprise. This powerful environmental justice movement — which clearly has the potential to become a new political mass movement — is still in its infancy. To grow to its potential it will need to be fed, nurtured, cared for. It will need resources. In their report, *Green of Another Color,* Daniel Faber and Deborah McCarthy show that, of all funds available for environmental work during the period 1996 to 1999, some 96 percent went to the lawyers and scientists of the traditional environmental movement, and only 4 percent went to all the thousands of groups working to build the "environ-mental justice" movement. To really protect the environment (and overcome the political power of the anti-environment "conservatives"), these funding priorities would have to change substantially.

Where Does It Come From?
Where Does It Go?

by Tyrone Cashman

WHEN I WAS GROWING UP in a small Midwestern town, my mother almost always knew which farms the meat, the potatoes, and the corn on our table were raised on. From our upstairs window we could see the water tower where our water came from. We played by the wells that fed the tower. We kids had learned about the workings of the local sewage plant, and we knew what the water looked like that flowed from it into the river and on down to the next town. We had visited the dump and knew how the garbage got there, and what was done to it then. It is true that we didn't know where the cloth in our clothes came from, or which trees had been felled to make the paper in our school pads. But we did understand how most of our world was connected.

Over the four decades since my childhood, the supply lines for most of us have become much longer. Few Americans have any idea where their food and fuel comes from, or which river or bay is flavored by their flush water. It is a rare person who knows where the garbage she produces comes to rest.

All of our supplies still connect us to the world. An environmental price was paid for the rubber in the soles of my shoes, for the paper towel I use and throw away, for the packaging around my new computer, for a hamburger, for each gallon of gas I buy and burn. Sometimes the price is small; sometimes it is great. But I don't know, anymore, what the environmental cost is for the objects that fuel my life.

As this development occurred, television entered our lives. Like an electronic telescope it allows us to see at a distance. By showing pictures from around the world, the "telescope" has the ability to track the longer lines of supply for us. Once again we have the power to learn what ecological price is paid at both the supply and effluent ends of our life-support systems. If we want to know the costs, they can be shown.

But an odd thing happened once people got used to not knowing what was at the end of their umbilical cords. We began pretending the world was not designed in an interconnected way. We've come to pretend that each of our "goods" somehow originates from money rather than from a particular farm field, forest hillside, or cranny in a local ecosystem. Children now think that milk comes from cartons.

Manufacturers think that wheat, tin, and gypsum come from the commodities market. And we all pretend we can get away with thinking the world exists in this fragmented way because it helps us avoid responsibility. Our unawareness gives us permission to be lavish. Instead of showing us reality, the media aid and abet us in our daily efforts to pretend the world isn't interconnected.

Any real awareness of the web of life has to begin with an unfragmented perception of our immediate surroundings. By keeping our eyes on the television set (like having a telescope strapped to the face), we can ignore our immediate surroundings for hours, weeks, years.

Events on the evening news are far away. The actors and commentators who appear on it are not in my environment. They require no commitment and they offer me no way to connect to them. Yet they visit my living room every night.

As I sit watching, the scene shifts quickly from five dead Kurdish mothers and children poisoned by nerve gas at the hands of their own government, to a Washington politician denying sexual and/or financial improprieties, to a convincing actor telling me that I will be more successful coping with stress in the office if I take two pain-killing pills of the brand he assures me is better than all others. The only connective links between these disparate events are the anchorpersons offering me a mixture of distant ruined lives and happy talk in order to keep me watching commercial lies.

Staying Speedy

Our long-term focus on such images fragments our thinking and blunts our feelings. Because my daily life does not intersect with the people I see and hear in any natural way, I seem to have no stake in their lives. Thus, news becomes gossip, and I as viewer become a mere curious onlooker, a kind of busybody. Our real mutual connections as human beings and co-inhabitors of the same planet become lost.

Electronic media insulate us from the environment in another way. Their instant scene switching helps us stay speedy. We could not endure a lifestyle in the fast lane with its tight deadlines, constant interruptions, decisions made too quickly on insufficient data, and frequent unpredictable emergencies if we were used to living attuned to the rhythms of the Earth.

After a hectic day, an evening in front of the television set allows me to physically stop, to let my body down into a chair, but still maintain my mental, stomach, and muscle tension in sync with the pace and violence of the nightly news or the suspense of a murder mystery followed by a couple of 90 mph car chases. Viewing allows me to "relax" without losing the special adrenaline high that accompanies a successful, competitive life.

Once at that high cruising speed, it is painful to come down. Its intensity makes us feel alive, but the feeling is an illusion. Our attempts to stay at that speed flatten the real world down to the two dimensions of the TV screen. Our judgments are limited to our reading of the constricted patterns within those few inches of the screen.

The comfort of the speeding images is seductive. But only when we slow down enough for the peripheral world to come into focus do we begin to hear and see and feel the detail of our lives and the truth and sadness of our own hearts. Only when we begin to replace the tube's images of reality with our own experience will we regain awareness of our place in nature and relearn the immense debt we owe to the natural world for the clothes in our closets, the gas in our gas tanks, and the food on our tables.

How We Connect

It takes only one summer for a child of the right age to bond with the natural world, to know in her bones that the world is alive and wild and kin to her. There is a kind of imprinting that either takes place, or doesn't, in a girl or boy before the age of ten or eleven.

As long as the wilderness survives, there is a place for this bonding to occur. As long as there are unspoiled natural places near enough for us to reach them and spend enough time in them, our children can have that inner awakening and sense of connection.

But it can never happen through media. Television's nature programs are wonderful. They must continue. They are probably the most important programming in our time. But we humans cannot form that essential bond through the tube.

The majesty, the power, the presence of a world uncreated by humans and uncorrupted by them cannot be reduced to the size of a TV screen, or glossy photographs in beautiful magazines, not even to the wraparound screen of an Omni theater. Something essential is stripped from nature when it comes as a mediated image instead of a direct encounter.

When, for the first time, a nine-year-old barefoot boy and a wild crawfish encounter each other by surprise in a cold spring creek, there is nothing like it in the world. The boy's life is changed. And if he explores this watery world and the woods that surround it for the length of a long summer, he will have taken the whole ancient biosphere into his soul, never to be forgotten. The imprint is for a lifetime.

But if those imprintable years are allowed to pass for a boy or a girl with only vicarious, mediated experience of nature, it is likely that as adults they will never be able to understand why a mountain forest is anything more than a pretty scene for a postcard or potential pulpwood for the commodities market.

Right Livelihood, Spirituality, and Business

by Duncan Williams

Right Livelihood

ZEN MASTER DOGEN, the founder of the Japanese Soto Zen Buddhist tradition, upon reaching China by ship in 1223, found that he had to remain on board for some time before he could disembark to pursue his studies at some of the Chinese Zen monasteries. An elderly monk, who was the head cook at Mt. Ayuwang, had walked the great distance from the monastery to the ship to buy *shiitake* mushrooms so that he could offer a special noodle soup to the monks. Dogen asked the elderly cook to stay for a while as he thought there must be other monks who could prepare the meal at Ayuwang, but the cook refused to be sidetracked from his duties as the head cook. When Dogen asked the cook why such a venerable monk was still cooking for others when he could be meditating or studying *koans,* the cook laughed and told the young Japanese monk that he did not yet understand the true meaning of Zen practice.

This experience remained vividly in Dogen's memory and is recorded in his text, the *Tenzo Kyokun* (Instructions to the Cook), which was completed in 1237. He wrote this manual for monastery cooks on the proper way to serve meals to the other trainees. But the text is also concerned with the attitudes required of a head cook who, through his cooking, was responsible not only for nourishing the physical but also the spiritual well-being of others. According to the *Tenzo Kyokun,* it is the duty of the cook to ensure that the best possible meal be prepared for the monks with whatever ingredients were available.

Buddhist spirituality includes both the inner discipline of meditation and the ability to engage the world with the qualities of insight and compassion discovered in this practice of awareness. Learning to become a "Zen cook," therefore, means to shed light on the "ingredients" that exist in one's life, which includes everything from one's personal character traits to the social environment in which one lives. This attention to the "ingredients" is the starting point from which one can skillfully use these raw materials to serve the meal of life itself, that is, to engage the world in a spiritual manner.

This engagement with the world, in a process of discovering oneself, leads to what might be understood as the Buddhist equivalent of the Christian notion of vocation or calling, namely, the Buddhist concept of "right livelihood." Right livelihood is the fifth spoke of the traditional Buddhist Eightfold Path outlined by the Buddha as the proper way to conduct oneself in the world, especially in regards to how one ought to make a living. Buddhist practice requires the practitioner to reflect on one's economic livelihood as necessarily being work or a career path that is guided by the Buddhist precepts as a whole.

Traditionally, right livelihood has been defined in Buddhist texts negatively, such as the avoidance of occupations such as executioner or butcher, because of their violation of the first Buddhist precept against the taking of life. Put in positive terms, since the Buddhist path is ultimately concerned with the alleviation of suffering, it means to choose a career that provides for the betterment of the lives of all beings. This path is not some kind of abstract ideal to strive toward, but rather, a way of life born from "cooking" the ingredients one has been endowed with. Whatever one's talents and gifts are, knowing how to appropriately express them in one's engagement with the world is the first step on the path of right livelihood.

Mañjusri's Sword of Wisdom

Zen Master Dogen, in his *Shobogenzo,* exhorts those who wish to follow the Buddhist path, "To study the Buddha way is to study the self." Buddhism starts with studying the self, whether in meditation or other practices, because it is thought that without knowing who one really is, it is impossible to free oneself or others from a world full of suffering. Before one can engage compassionately with the world, if one cannot see the true nature of oneself or the world, it is thought likely that one might cause more suffering, however good one's intentions are.

This practice of "studying the self" is the practice of cultivating wisdom (Sanskrit: *prajña*). In Zen monasteries, the central altar is occupied by the bodhisattva of wisdom, Mañjusri, who holds a sword in his hand to cut away preconceptions and delusions. The practice of meditation is to use the sword of wisdom within ourselves to allow our self to appear as it is — that is, to reveal the ingredients that we have available to us. This notion of wisdom might be Buddhism's closest equivalent to the Christian doctrine of discernment.

And just as discernment in the Christian tradition leads to action, it is said in Buddhism that wisdom leads to compassionate action. Indeed, wisdom without compassionate action is not living Buddhism, but a sterile type of insight. Conversely, compassionate action without wisdom, however well-intentioned, can be dangerous and cause even more suffering. Likened to two wings of a bird, a Buddhist practitioner needs both wisdom and compassion to fly freely.

For Buddhists, nurturing compassionate action is based on the fundamental insight that one's own freedom from suffering is none other than the freedom from suffering for all beings. This is because Buddhist teachings emphasize the nonexistence of the self (Sanskrit: *anatman*), either as an eternal soul or as an autonomous unit. Instead, the self is understood as constantly changing and developing in relation to other beings, both human and non-human. To care only about one's present body and mind is to misunderstand the true nature of the self, which in a Chinese Buddhist text, is likened to a jewel which exists in the node of an infinite net. This net, being infinite, contains infinite jewels (selves) which are shaped in such a way that each jewel reflects all the other jewels as if it were a mirror. Each jewel, then, contains all the other jewels. The self, seen in this way as existing only interdependently with all other beings, cannot but act compassionately. The authentic self, rather than being defined as essentially selfish, if seen in its true nature, naturally engages the world in a compassionate manner. The Zen Master Dogen suggests this in *Shobogenzo* when he writes, "To study the self is to forget the self."

This compassionate approach to the world, particularly in thinking about one's career or the world of economics, provides an alternative model to the dominant capitalistic economic system, based on a view that the world is constituted of discrete "selves," capable of acting only in narrow, self-interested ways. Just as the Christian notion of vocation is tied to the community, the path of Buddhist right livelihood necessarily dismisses the accumulation of personal profit or the alleviation of one's privatized suffering, and involves the alleviation of the suffering of, in Buddhist parlance, "all sentient beings."

Buddhist Economics: Self-Benefit, Other-Benefit, One Big Circle

Buddhism has traditionally been a religion of merchants. Spread along the Silk Road by traveling merchants and supported by those in the middle classes, it has been a religion that has neither denigrated moneymaking nor promoted laissez faire economics. Known as the "Middle Way," the tradition has always avoided extremes. The Buddha in his quest for enlightenment found that neither the self-indulgent life of his early life as a spoiled prince nor the extreme self-denial of his days as a forest-wandering ascetic led to wisdom and compassion.

If what we conventionally call "happiness," assuming that is the goal of economic activity, is defined in a formula, it might be happiness equals money divided by desire. In this equation, greater happiness can be achieved in two ways: either increase money or decrease desire. While the Buddhist approach doesn't deny moneymaking, it emphasizes the increase of happiness by reducing desire. Buddhist alternatives to the dominant capitalistic system predicated on "self-benefit" above all are based instead on the Buddhist notion of "increase wisdom, decrease desire."

Simultaneous to decreasing desire, Buddhist teachings are not inherently against making money. Making money just cannot be value-free or based on self-benefit alone. Instead, as the medieval Buddhist priest Shinran suggests in his text the *Jodo Wasan,* "self-benefit, other-benefit, one big circle." In other words, because the self is inextricably interconnected with all beings, we must act in a way that acknowledges the fact that true self-benefit exists in a continuum with the benefit of others. Whether on the level of making products that benefit society and the environment as a whole or in a managing style that benefits everyone in the company, the Buddhist approach to business needs to be both profitable to the company as well as beneficial to everyone associated with the company. This is so for the stockholders, workers, consumers, as well as those affected positively or adversely by its product (including non-human beings in the ecosystem).

In the past twenty years, Buddhists, especially in Thailand, Japan, and the West, have taken a lead in thinking about and acting on these principles of Buddhist economics. In Thailand, Buddhist monks and lay activists, such as Payutto Bhikkhu and Sulak Sivaraksa, have emphasized the role of Buddhism in creating an alternative model of economic development that is sustainable and compassionate, rather than oppressive to workers and destructive to the environment. In Japan, CEOs of major corporations, such as Inamori Kazuo of KDDI and Kyocera, have incorporated Buddhist practice and philosophy into their corporate culture, management philosophy, and company training. Institutes such as the Bukkyo Keizei Kenkyujo (Institute for Buddhist Economics) and the Bukkyo Keizai Forum (Buddhist Economics Forum), regularly publish academic journals on Buddhist economics as well as invite leading CEOs to share testimonials about how they incorporated Buddhism into their businesses.

Even in the West, a number of "socially responsible" businesses such as England's Windhorse Trading, a distributor of Balinese handicrafts and other trinkets from the Third World, is run by members of the Friends of the Western Buddhist Order (FWBO). In the United States, Bernard Tetsugen Glassman, the cofounder of the Zen Community of New York, has been a leading advocate of "socially conscious" businesses that not only support the livelihood of Zen centers, but also the communities located around the temples. He argues that the need for Buddhists to run such enterprises comes from the spiritual recognition of the interconnectedness of all life (including one's neighbors, the homeless, or the rainforests). The community's main business, Greyston Bakery, is a gourmet bakery that has served major clients such as Bloomingdale's. As a "Zen business," the bakery has combined the principles of engaging in work that minimizes suffering, making the workplace a spiritual environment (a meditation hall exists in the same building), and tackling social problems. Because the Zen community is located in New York, the problem of homelessness was particularly obvious. Glassman provided jobs for the homeless in the Greyston Bakery. This expanded into the Greyston Family Inn project to help the homeless build their own homes. Glassman recognized the interconnectedness of the need for job training, housing, childcare, and counseling in basic life skills.

Glassman's enterprises reflect a middle way of conducting business that steers a course between moneymaking which has only profit as the bottom line and a nonprofit organization which doesn't seek to accumulate wealth at all. He distinguishes this kind of "sustainable" business which benefits both the company and the community from a corporate philanthropy which doesn't have social action built into the company structure. At the same time, these businesses represent a particularly Buddhist orientation toward money and government. On the one hand, Glassman worked with entrepreneurs, state bureaucrats, Republicans, and Democrats, viewing them as necessary "ingredients" to cook the meal of social betterment. And on the other hand, Glassman was deeply sensitive to the power of the spiritual and the need to reach out to the most needy and rejected parts of society.

Buddhist economics, then, represents a spirituality that is based on a world-view that the world is full of suffering and that our mission in life as Buddhists is to alleviate this suffering based on a path of wisdom and compassion. In the Zen Buddhist tradition, the path of meditation is sometimes spoken of as a discipline of "seven times fall down, eight times get up." This phrase refers to the practice of bringing one's attention back to the present moment when the inevitable nature of human mind to wander and fall off the path occurs. In the same way, it is to be expected that one will inevitably stray from the path of see-ing clearly (wisdom) and acting for the benefit of oneself and others (com-passion). Yet the path beckons us again and again, as we engage in our work in the world, choosing a path of right livelihood. A hundred times fall down, a hundred and one times get up.

PART FIVE

The Path of Mindful Consumption

When the consumer finally begins to exercise the virtually untapped power of citizen action, consumers will take their logical place at the head of the economic process.

— Ralph Nader

Diet for a Mindful Society

by Thich Nhat Hanh

MINDFULNESS is the blood of our psyche. It is exactly like the blood in our body—it has the power to wash away the toxins and heal our pain, the pain in our consciousness.

When we are not mindful, we ingest many poisons into our consciousness. In fact, we water the seeds of suffering every day, and the people around us water these seeds also. As a result, our suffering increases. When we spend four days together in a retreat, we water the seeds of happiness inside us and around us, and we refrain from watering negative seeds, like anger, hatred, and fear. At the end of four days of practicing like this, we feel much better. We need an intelligent policy concerning our cultural environment so that we do not allow ourselves to indiscriminately ingest TV, movies, magazines, advertising, and other so-called "cultural products." Many of these things poison us every day with their frantic energy, noisiness, sexual exploitation, and violence. We need a diet for our consciousness to avoid ingesting so many of these poisons.

When we ingest toxic substances into our body, we get sick. When we ingest toxic "cultural products" into our consciousness, we also get sick. Our society has so many kinds of spiritual and cultural foods that are toxic. Television is poisoning us and our children, as are many magazines, news images, and so on. We practice watering the seeds of anger, fear, and violence every day. We have to learn to live our daily lives in a way that can help us refrain from taking in more poisons. When these poisons enter our store consciousness, they weaken our power of mindfulness. Without some kind of diet for our consciousness, it is very difficult to practice mindfulness. There are already so many toxins in our store consciousness; we should stop ingesting more.

Many unwholesome seeds have been transmitted to us since our childhood. Practicing mindfulness, we become aware of that pain. But we are not yet strong enough to transform it, so it is important that we stay in touch with the many wonderful, refreshing things that are inside us and all around us — the blue sky, the eyes of a child, the evening sunset. When our mindfulness becomes strong, we will be able to touch our pain with it, and the pain will be transformed. I often talk about the mother as the symbol of tenderness, love, and care. When a baby is crying, the mother comes and takes the baby into her arms. Her tenderness penetrates into the baby, and the baby stops crying. When we practice mindfulness of breathing and touch our pain with that energy, our pain will be calmed and will begin to be transformed.

But our seeds of suffering are always trying to emerge, and we try to suppress them. By doing so, we create a lack of circulation in our psyche, and we get sick. As the blood of our psyche, mindfulness can loosen our pain and help dissolve it. Every time our pain is embraced by mindfulness, it loses some of its strength and returns to our store consciousness a little bit weaker. When it arises again, if our mindfulness is there, our pain will be even less. In that way, we create good circulation in our psyche. If the blood in our body circulates well, we feel much better. If our mindfulness circulates in our consciousness, we also begin to have a feeling of well-being. We needn't be afraid of our pain when we know that our mindfulness is there, ready to embrace and transform it.

If we have not been practicing for some time, our mindfulness may be of poor quality. It may only be a fifteen-watt light bulb. But if we practice for a few weeks, it will become a one-hundred-watt bulb. For mindfulness of good quality, conscious breathing should be practiced. Conscious breathing is the kind of fuel that can keep the light of mindfulness alive. If you practice five minutes of conscious breathing, you will keep mindfulness alive for five minutes. When contemplating a beautiful tree, if you stay in touch with your breathing for five minutes, you also stay in touch with the tree — for five minutes. If you lose awareness of your breathing, thinking may settle in, and the tree will vanish. Breathing is a wonderful way to sustain the seed of mindfulness in your consciousness.

In Asia, since early times, we have known that there is no boundary between food and medicine. When we eat and breathe properly, we nourish our blood. Our blood has the power to rinse away the toxins in our bodies and heal our pain. If we have good circulation, we will have a feeling of peace and joy, because the blood can go anywhere in our body and wash away the debris eliminated by our cells. We know that if we ingest a lot of toxic food into our intestines, our blood will receive many of these toxins and its power of cleansing and healing will be diminished. So we need to practice a kind of diet to help our blood stay clean.

Following a diet does not mean to suffer. There are many delicious foods that have great nutritional value. And we don't have to eat a lot. Sometimes, when we are too sad and don't know what to do, we take refuge in eating. One woman who came to Plum Village told me, "Thây, every time I feel anxious, I just open the refrigerator door and eat. I cannot control myself." By taking refuge in eating, we stuff a lot of poisons into our stomachs that we know are not good for our blood. Sometimes we also take refuge in studying, social work, protecting the environment, or watching television. We have many refuges that we use in order to run away from ourselves, from our own unhappiness.

We should select the things we eat carefully, and chew our food very well, at least fifty times. If you do so, after eating just half the usual quantity, you will feel satisfied. And chewing every mouthful carefully and slowly, your food will reveal itself to you, and it will already be partially digested by your saliva even before it enters your digestive system. Its passage will not be slowed down, and putrefaction will not take place in your intestines. Eating in this way prevents poisons from entering your blood.

Massage is also very important. When there is a spot in the body where the blood cannot circulate freely, we feel some pain. The oxygen in the blood isn't able to go there and flush out the toxins. Massage is a technique to revitalize circulation. If I practice massage on the spot that is sore, fresh blood will come there to nourish the cells and create a feeling of peace and joy in that spot. For healing to take place, we need the blood to circulate into the zone of pain.

Blood is the agent of healing. We know that to improve the quality of our blood, breathing is important. Our lungs have a three-and-a-half quart capacity, but usually we breathe in and out only one-tenth of a quart. And if we don't breathe good air, the amount of oxygen we take in will be even less, and the quality of our blood will be poor. Therefore, we practice breathing in and out consciously, and as our breathing becomes deeper, we exhale more carbon dioxide and inhale more fresh, clean air. We have to learn to breathe more deeply, from our abdomens, and to breathe air that is of good quality. Diet, massage, and conscious breathing improve the quality of our blood. They also increase the quality of our mindfulness.

Please write down three things: First, what kind of toxins do you already have in your body, and what kind of toxins do you already have in your psyche?

"Breathing in and breathing out, I recognize that these toxins are already in my body." What kind of toxins do you have in your consciousness? A guilt complex is a toxin, anger is a toxin, despair is a toxin, jealousy is a toxin. If you need to practice walking meditation or sitting meditation in order to look, please do so. Look and see for yourself what kind of toxins you have in your body, and what kind of toxins you have in your mind. What makes you suffer now? What blocks of suffering do you have right now? When you have done that, you will know what you have in your body and in your consciousness. Then, please go further, and look into the bodies and souls of your children and your spouse, since all of you are practicing together as a Sangha. (Practicing as a community or a family is always easier. Not only will you refrain from watering the seeds of your own suffering, but your spouse and children will also practice not watering the seeds of your irritation, anger, and so on. That is why we take refuge in the Sangha, the community that practices together.) When you recognize these toxins and list them on a sheet of paper, that is also meditation —looking deeply, recognizing, and calling things by their true names.

Next one should ask, "What kind of poisons am I putting into my body and my consciousness every day?" We do this as individuals, as a family, as a city, and as a nation. We need administrators, legislators, and politicians to practice with us. If you are a psychotherapist, a writer, an artist, a filmmaker, a lawyer, a businessperson, or a social worker, you have to practice in this way for all of us. What am I ingesting every day that is toxic to my body and my consciousness? What is my family ingesting? What are my city and my nation ingesting every day concerning violence, hatred, and fear? The beating of Rodney King, the young driver in Los Angeles, by the five policemen is a good example of how much hatred, fear, and violence are in our society. What kinds of poisons do we ingest every day in our families, our city, and our nation? This is a collective meditation. We need everyone to participate.

Third, write down the prescription that arises out of that insight. For example, "I vow from today on not to ingest more of this, this, and this. I vow only to use this, this, and this to nourish my body and my consciousness." This is the ground of the practice—the practice of loving kindness to yourself. You cannot love someone else unless you love and take care of yourself. Practicing in this way is to practice love, peace, and enlightenment. Enlightenment is insight. When you look deeply, you have insight, and your insight brings about compassion. Before you begin to eat, breathe in and out and look at the table to see what is good for your body and what is not. This is to practice the precept of protecting your body. When you want to watch television or go to the movies, first look deeply in order to determine what should be viewed and what should not be viewed by you and your children. Think about the books and magazines you read, and decide what should be read and what should not be read by you and your children. Practicing together as a community, we don't need to take refuge in eating or entertaining ourselves with any more poisons. Practicing the precepts in this way helps all of us. Buddhist precepts are not imposed from the outside. From our own insight, we decide what to ingest and what not to ingest into our bodies and our souls.

For example, if all of us practice looking deeply into war, we will see into the true nature of our society and we will know what to do and how to live in order to prevent the next war. If we prescribe a healthy diet to ourselves, our families, our cities, and our nation, and practice that kind of diet, another war will not take place. If we do not practice, a war like the one in the Middle East will happen again in one, two, or five years. If we continue to live forgetfully, we will be overwhelmed again when we have to confront such a war. The true nature of war and the true nature of our collective consciousness are the same. For war not to come, we need to begin now to prevent it. The best way to prevent a war is to change our collective consciousness. As long as people believe that the war in the Middle East was a war of liberation, a clean and just war, they will be tempted to do it again as soon as there is another conflict somewhere in this world. To change that kind of mentality, we have to practice looking deeply in order to understand the true nature of the war, which was not liberating, moral, or clean. If we don't practice mindfulness, the amount of hatred, illusion, anger, and violence in our society will lead our leaders to adopt such means again. Without an intelligent diet, we cannot reduce the amount of delusion, hatred, and violence in our society. When we practice well, we will stop bringing poisons into our blood, our soul, and our society.

Insight meditation, looking deeply, is a practice of massage. You practice in order to push the energy of mindfulness into your pain. As it penetrates more and more deeply, your pain will dissolve. I offer you an example: There are those who do not get along with their fathers (or their mothers), because their fathers have made them so unhappy, and have created in their store consciousness so many seeds of unhappiness that they don't want to look at him, they don't even want to hear his name. They may have been abused as children. For these people I offer the meditation on the five-year-old child, which is a mindfulness massage. "Breathing in, I see myself as a five-year-old child.

Breathing out, I smile to the five-year-old child in me." During the meditation you try to see yourself as a five-year-old child. If you can look deeply at that child, you can see that he or she is so vulnerable and fragile, can be hurt easily by anything that is not kind, can be wounded very easily. A stern look from his father can cause internal formations in his store consciousness. A shout from his father can cause another wound within his store consciousness. When his father makes his mother suffer, when his parents fight and scream at each other, the five-year-old receives a lot of seeds of suffering in him. I have heard young people say, "The most precious gift my parents can give is their own happiness." If parents live happily with each other, that is the greatest gift they can offer their children. This is true, and I hope all parents can understand it.

By living unhappily, by making his wife suffer, the father is making his son suffer a lot. He may have brutalized him so severely that the young man has not been able to smile or think of his father. But now he is sitting and visualizing himself as a five-year-old child, very vulnerable, easily hurt. When he smiles at that child, he smiles with compassion. "I was so young and tender, and I received so much pain."

The next day, I would advise him to practice this: "Breathing in, I see my father as a five-year-old child. Breathing out, I smile to that child with compassion." We are not used to seeing our father as a five-year-old child. We think of him as always being a big person, stern, with a lot of authority. But we have not taken the time to see our father as a tender, young boy who can be easily wounded by other people. The practice is to visualize your father as a five-year-old boy—fragile, vulnerable, easily hurt. If it helps, you can look in the family album to study the image of your father as a boy. When you are able to visualize him as vulnerable and easily hurt, you will realize that he too may have been the victim of his father. If he received many seeds of suffering from his father, of course he will not know how to treat his son well. So he makes you suffer, and the circle of *samsara* continues. Grandfather makes father unhappy, father makes son unhappy, and so on. If you don't practice mindfulness, you will do exactly the same to your own children.

The moment you see your father as a victim of brutality, compassion will be born in your heart. When you smile to him with compassion, you will begin to bring blood into your pain. With mindfulness touching the pain, insight will also begin to touch your pain. If you practice like that for several hours or several days, your anger toward your father will dissolve. This is to massage the pain by way of mindfulness. It works in exactly the same way as the blood does in your body. One day, you will smile at your father in person and hug him, saying, "I understand you, Dad. You suffered very much during your childhood."

Therefore, mindfulness is the blood. Whatever it touches, it transforms. When it touches something beautiful, it makes it more beautiful. When it touches something painful, it begins the work of transformation.

Please discuss among yourselves a diet for your body, a diet for your consciousness, and also a diet for the collective consciousness of our society. This is the basic practice. It is true peace work. Peace begins with each of us taking care of our bodies and our minds every day.

Voluntary Simplicity

by Duane Elgin

AT THE HEART of the simple life is an emphasis on harmonious and purposeful living. There is no special virtue to the phrase "voluntary simplicity"—it is merely a label and a somewhat awkward label at that. Still, it does acknowledge explicitly that simpler living integrates both inner and outer aspects of life into an organic and purposeful whole.

To live more voluntarily is to live more deliberately, intentionally, and purposefully—in short, it is to live more consciously. We cannot be deliberate when we are distracted from life. We cannot be intentional when we are not paying attention. We cannot be purposeful when we are not being present. Therefore, to act in a voluntary manner is to be aware of ourselves as we move through life. This requires that we not only pay attention to the actions we take in the outer world, but also that we pay attention to ourselves acting—our inner world. To the extent that we do not notice both inner and outer aspects of our passage through life, then our capacity for voluntary, deliberate, and purposeful action is commensurately diminished.

To live more simply is to live more purposefully and with a minimum of needless distraction. The particular expression of simplicity is a personal matter. We each know where our lives are unnecessarily complicated. We are all painfully aware of the clutter and pretense that weigh upon our lives and make our passage through the world more cumbersome and awkward. To live more simply is to unburden our lives—to live more lightly, cleanly, aerodynamically. It is to establish a more direct, unpretentious, and unencumbered relationship with all aspects of our lives: the things that we consume, the work that we do, our relationships with others, our connections with nature and the cosmos, and more. Simplicity of living means meeting life face-to-face. It means confronting life clearly, without unnecessary distractions. It means being direct and honest in relationships of all kinds. It means taking life as it is—straight and unadulterated.

When we combine these two ideas for integrating the inner and outer aspects of our lives, we can describe "voluntary simplicity" as a manner of living that is outwardly more simple and inwardly more rich, a way of being in which our most authentic and alive self is brought into direct and conscious contact with living. This way of life is not a static condition to be achieved, but an ever-changing balance that must be continuously and consciously made real. Simplicity in this sense is not simple. To maintain a skillful balance between the inner and outer aspects of our lives is an enormously challenging and continuously changing process. The objective is not to dogmatically live with less, but is a more demanding intention of living with balance in order to find a life of greater purpose, fulfillment and satisfaction.

While simpler living has unprecedented relevance for coping with the current ecological crisis, this way of living has a long history with deep roots in the human experience. As is the case with every spiritual tradition, including the American transcendentalists, Eastern spiritual traditions such as Buddhism, Hinduism, and Taoism have encouraged a life of material moderation and spiritual abundance. From the Taoist tradition, we have this saying from Lao Tzu, "He who knows he has enough is rich." From the Hindu tradition, we have these thoughts from Mahatma Gandhi, the spiritual and political leader for India's independence, "Civilization, in the real sense of the term, consists not in the multiplication, but in the deliberate and voluntary reduction of wants. This alone promotes real happiness and contentment. . . ."[68] Gandhi felt the moderation of our wants increases our capacity to be of service to others and, in being of loving service to others, true civilization emerges.

Perhaps the most developed expression of a middle way between material excess and deprivation comes from the Buddhist tradition. While Buddhism recognizes that basic material needs must be met in order to realize our potentials, it does not consider our material welfare as an end in itself; rather, it is a means to the end of awakening to our deeper nature as spiritual beings. Self-control and a simple life are valued highly as is the practice of charity and generosity without attachment to one's wealth and property. A modern expression of this view is given by Sulak Sivaraksa, who describes the necessity for a more compassionate and simple way of living: "We can only save ourselves when all humanity recognizes that every problem on earth is our own personal problem and our personal responsibility. . . . Unless the rich change their lifestyle considerably, there is no hope of solving the problem of famine in the world."[69]

E.F. Schumacher, author of the classic book *Small Is Beautiful,* described Buddhism as a middle path that emphasizes simplicity and nonviolence. Applying the middle way to economics, Schumacher described a Buddhist economy as one that provides an adequate range of material goods, and whose production processes are in harmony with both the environment and available resources. The middle way of Buddhist economics moves between mindless materialism, on the one hand, and needless poverty on the other. The result is a balanced approach to living that harmonizes both inner and outer development.

Misconceptions about the Simple Life

Some people tend to equate ecological living with a life characterized by poverty, antagonism to progress, rural living, and the denial of beauty. It is important to acknowledge these misconceptions so we can move beyond them. Although some spiritual traditions have advocated a life of extreme renunciation, it is inaccurate to equate simplicity with poverty. Poverty has a very human face—one that is very different from "simplicity." Poverty is involuntary and debilitating while simplicity is voluntary and enabling. Poverty is mean and degrading to the human spirit whereas a life of conscious simplicity can have both a beauty and functional integrity that elevates the human spirit. Involuntary poverty generates a sense of helplessness, passivity, and despair, whereas choiceful simplicity fosters a sense of personal empowerment, creative engagement, and opportunity. Historically, those choosing a simpler life have sought the golden mean—a creative and aesthetic balance between poverty and excess. Instead of placing primary emphasis on material riches, they have sought to develop, with balance, the invisible wealth of experiential riches.

If the human family sets a goal for itself of achieving a moderate standard of living for everyone, computer projections suggest that the world could reach a sustainable level of economic activity that is roughly "equivalent in material comforts to the average level in Europe in 1990."[70] If we do not delay but act with decision and determination, then humanity need not face a future of poverty and sacrifice. The Earth can sustain a moderate and satisfying material standard of living for the entire human family.

Turning Away from Progress

Ecological living does not imply turning away from economic progress; rather, it seeks to discover which technologies are most appropriate and helpful in moving towards a sustainable future. Ecological living is not a path of "no growth" but a path of "new growth" that includes both material and spiritual dimensions of life. A simpler way of life is not a retreat from progress; in fact, it is essential to the advance of civilizations. After a lifetime of study of the rise and fall of the world's civilizations, the historian Arnold Toynbee concluded that the measure of a civilization's growth was not to be found in the conquest of other people or in the possession of land. Rather, he described the essence of growth in what he called the "Law of Progressive Simplification."[71] True growth, he said, is the ability of a society to transfer increasing amounts of energy and attention from the material side of life to the non-material side and thereby to advance its culture, capacity for compassion, sense of community, and strength of democracy. We are now being pushed by necessity to discover freshly the meaning of "true growth" by progressively simplifying the material side of our lives and enriching the non-material side.[72]

Rural Living

Although the simple life has been advocated as a way of achieving more direct contact with the infusing Life-force and, although this suffusing presence is often most evident in the natural world, this does not mean that people must move away from urban areas and live on farms. Still, in the popular imagination, there is a tendency to equate the simple life with Thoreau's cabin in the woods by Walden Pond, and to assume people must live an isolated and rural existence. Interestingly, Thoreau was not a hermit during his stay at Walden Pond—his famous cabin was roughly a mile from the town of Concord and every day or two he would walk into town. His cabin was so close to a nearby highway that he could smell the pipe smoke of passing travelers. Thoreau wrote that he had "more visitors while I lived in the woods than any other period of my life." The romanticized image of rural living does not fit the modern reality as a majority of persons choosing a life of conscious simplicity do not live in the backwoods or rural settings; they live in cities and suburbs. While ecological living brings with it a reverence for nature, this does not require moving to a rural setting. Instead of a "back to the land" movement, it is more accurate to describe this as a "make the most of wherever you are" movement.

Denial of Beauty

The simple life is sometimes viewed as a primitive approach to living that advocates a barren plainness and denies the value of beauty and aesthetics. While the Puritans, for example, were suspicious of the arts, many other advocates of simplicity have seen it as essential for revealing the natural beauty of things. Many who adopt a simpler life would surely agree with Picasso who said that "art is the elimination of the unnecessary." The influential architect Frank Lloyd Wright was an advocate of an "organic simplicity" that integrates function with beauty and eliminates the superfluous. In his architecture, a building's interior and exterior blend into an organic whole and the building, in turn, blends harmoniously with the natural environment. Rather than a denial of beauty, simplicity liberates the aesthetic sense by freeing things from artificial encumbrances. From a transcendental perspective, simplicity removes the obscuring clutter and discloses the spirit that infuses all things.

It is important to acknowledge these misleading stereotypes because they suggest a life of regress instead of progress. These misconceptions make a simpler life seem impractical and unapproachable and thereby reinforce the feeling that nothing can be done to respond to our critical world situation. To move from denial to action, we need an accurate understanding of the nature of simpler living and its relevance for the modern era.

Common Expressions of Ecological Ways of Living

There is no cookbook for defining a life of conscious simplicity. Richard Gregg, for example, was insistent that "simplicity is a relative matter depending on climate, customs, culture, and the character of the individual."[73] Henry Thoreau was also clear that no simple formula could define the worldly expression of a simpler life. He said, "I would not have anyone adopt my mode of living on my account. . . I would have each one be very careful to find out and pursue his own way. . . ."[74]

Nor did Gandhi advocate a blind denial of the material side of life. He said,

> As long as you derive inner help and comfort from anything, you should keep it. If you were to give it up in a mood of self-sacrifice or out of a stern sense of duty, you would continue to want it back, and that unsatisfied want would make trouble for you. Only give up a thing when you want some other condition so much that the thing no longer has any attraction for you. . . .[75]

Because simplicity has as much to do with each person's purpose in living as much as it does with their standard of living, and because we each have a unique purpose in living, it follows that there is no single "right and true" way to live more ecologically and compassionately.

Given that there is no dogmatic formula for simpler living, there is a general pattern of behaviors and attitudes that is often associated with this approach to living. Those choosing a simpler life:

1) Tend to invest the time and energy freed up by simpler living in activities with their partner, children, and friends (walking, making music together, sharing a meal, camping, etc.), or volunteering to help others, or getting involved in civic affairs to improve the life of the community.

2) Tend to work on developing the full spectrum of their potentials: physical (running, biking, hiking, etc.); emotional (learning the skills of intimacy and sharing feelings in important relationships); mental (engaging in lifelong learning by reading, taking classes, etc.); and spiritual (for example, learning to move through life with a quiet mind and compassionate heart).

3) Tend to feel an intimate connection with the Earth and a reverential concern for nature. In knowing that the ecology of the Earth is a part of our extended "body," people tend to act in ways that express great care for its well-being.

4) Tend to feel connected with and a compassionate concern for the world's poor. In feeling a sense of kinship with people around

the world, a simpler life fosters a concern for social justice and equity in the use of the world's resources.

5) Tend to lower their overall level of personal consumption—buy less clothing (with more attention to what is functional, durable, aesthetic, and less concern with passing fads, fashions and seasonal styles); buy less jewelry and other forms of personal ornamentation; buy fewer cosmetic products; and observe holidays in a less commercialized manner.

6) Tend to alter their patterns of consumption in favor of products that are durable, easy to repair, non-polluting in their manufacture and use, energy efficient, functional, and aesthetic.

7) Tend to shift their diet away from highly processed foods, meat, and sugar toward foods that are more natural, healthy, simple, and appropriate for sustaining the inhabitants of a small planet.

8) Tend to reduce undue clutter and complexity in their personal lives by giving away or selling those possessions that are seldom used and could be used productively by others (for example, clothing, books, furniture, appliances, and tools).

9) Tend to use their consumption politically by boycotting goods and services of companies whose actions or policies they consider unethical.

10) Tend to recycle metal, glass, and paper and to cut back on consumption of items that are wasteful of non-renewable resources.

11) Tend to pursue livelihood or work that directly contributes to the well-being of the world and enables a person to use more fully his or her creative capacities in ways that are fulfilling.

12) Tend to develop personal skills that contribute to greater self-reliance and reduce dependence upon experts to handle life's ordinary demands (for example, basic carpentry, plumbing, appliance repair, gardening, crafts, and others).

13) Tend to prefer smaller scale, more human-sized living and working environments that foster a sense of community, face-to-face contact, and mutual caring.

14) Tend to alter male/female roles in favor of nonsexist patterns of relationship.

15) Tend to appreciate the simplicity of nonverbal forms of communication—the eloquence of silence, hugging and touching, the language of the eyes.

16) Tend to participate in holistic health care practices that emphasize preventive medicine and the healing powers of the body when assisted by the mind.

17) Tend to involve themselves with compassionate causes such as protecting rainforests, saving animals from extinction, etc., and tend to use nonviolent means in their efforts.

18) Tend to change transportation modes in favor of public transit, car-pooling, smaller and more fuel-efficient autos, living closer to work, riding a bike, and walking.

Because there is a tendency to emphasize the external changes that characterize simpler living, it is important to reiterate that this approach to life is intended to integrate both inner and outer aspects of existence into a satisfying and purposeful whole.

Maintaining Ourselves and Surpassing Ourselves

An ecological approach to living invites us to continuously balance two aspects of life—maintaining ourselves (creating a workable existence) and surpassing ourselves (creating a meaningful existence). A statement by the philosopher and feminist, Simone de Beauvoir, is clarifying in this regard. She said, "Life is occupied in both perpetuating itself and in surpassing itself; if all it does is maintain itself, then living is only not dying."[76] On the one hand, if we seek only to maintain ourselves, then, no matter how grand our style of living might be, we are doing little more than "only not dying." On the other hand, if we strive only for a meaningful existence without securing the material foundation that supports our lives, then our physical existence is in jeopardy and the opportunity to surpass ourselves becomes little more than a utopian dream. Although many of the expressions of a simpler life listed above emphasize actions that promote a more sustainable existence, this should not distract from the importance of the inner dimensions of a life of conscious simplicity.

The many expressions of simpler living, both inner and outer, indicate this is much more than a superficial change in the style of life. A "style" change refers generally to an exterior change such as a new fad or fashion. Simplicity goes far deeper and involves a change in our way of life. Ecological living is a sophisticated response to the demands of deteriorating industrial civilizations. Simpler ways of living in the ecological era will result in changes as great as the transition from the agrarian era to the industrial era. In an interdependent, ecologically conscious world, every aspect of life will be touched and changed: consumption levels and patterns, living and working environments, political attitudes and processes, international ethics and relations, the uses of the mass media, education, and many more.

The Push of Necessity and the Pull of Opportunity

Two compelling reasons exist for choosing more ecological approaches to living: the push of necessity and the pull of opportunity. The combined impact of the various pushes of necessity are staggering to contemplate. The litany of problems we face are well-known but always bear repeating:

By 2025, the world's population will approach nine billion people. The vast majority of the increase in human numbers is occurring in the less developed nations. As these new billions of persons seek a decent standard of living, the world's ecosystem—already under great stress—will be further compromised.

The gap between the rich and the poor is widening. More than a thousand million people (1.2 billion) now live in absolute poverty—a condition of life so limited by malnutrition, illiteracy, disease, squalid surroundings, high infant mortality, and low life expectancy as to be beneath any reasonable definition of human decency.

Global warming will likely alter patterns of rainfall and disrupt food production, flood enormous areas of low-lying lands, displace millions of people, destroy fragile ecosystems, and alter patterns of disease in unpredictable ways.

Tropical rainforests are being cut down at an alarming rate, contributing to global warming, and destroying precious ecosystems that required millions of years to evolve (and that, among other riches, contain a treasury of undiscovered pharmaceuticals).

Cheaply available supplies of oil are being depleted rapidly and, within a generation, the world will be deprived of an energy source basic to our current form of high intensity agriculture.

Toxic wastes are being poured into the environment and pollution-induced outbreaks of cancer and genetic damage may reach massive proportions.

Overfishing and pollution of the world's oceans have led to a leveling off in annual fish catch at the same time that the demand for food from the world's oceans is increasing.

The ozone layer is thinning over populated regions of both the southern and the northern hemispheres and threatens to cause skin cancer and cataracts in humans and unknown damage to the rest of the food chain.

Thousands of plant and animal species are becoming extinct each year, representing the greatest loss of life on the planet since the massive extinction of dinosaurs and other animal and plant life roughly sixty-five million years ago.

Acid rains from coal burning are damaging forests, farmland, and fresh-water streams.

These are not isolated problems; instead, they comprise a tightly inter-twined system of problems that require us to develop new approaches to living if we are to live sustainably. To live sustainably, we must live efficiently— not misdirecting or squandering the Earth's precious resources. To live efficiently, we must live peacefully, for current military expenditures represent an enormous diversion of resources that could be applied to basic human needs. To live peacefully, we must live with a reasonable degree of equity or fairness for it is unrealistic to think that, in a communications-rich world, a billion or more persons will accept living in absolute poverty while another billion live in conspicuous excess. Only with greater fairness in the consumption of the world's resources can we live peacefully, and thereby live sustainably, as a human family. Without a revolution in fairness, the world will find itself in chronic conflict with wars over dwindling resources and this, in turn, will make it impossible to achieve the level of cooperation necessary to solve problems such as pollution and overpopulation.

If the world is profoundly divided materially, there is very little hope that it can be united socially, psychologically, and spiritually. Therefore, if we intend to live together peacefully as members of a single, human family, then each individual has a right to a reasonable share of the world's resources. Each person has a right to expect a fair share of the world's wealth sufficient to support a "decent" standard of living—one that provides enough food, shelter, education, and health care to enable them to realize their potential as a productive and respected member of the family of humanity. This does not mean that the world should adopt a single manner and standard of living; rather, it means that each person needs to feel part of the global family and, within a reasonable range of differences, valued and supported in realizing their unique human potential.

With sustainability, we can expand our experiential riches of culture, compassion, community, and self-determination. With a growing abundance of experiential riches the entire process of living will be encouraged and a self-reinforcing spiral of development will unfold. Therefore, reinforcing the powerful push of necessity is the pull of opportunity—the potential of the simple life to yield a more satisfying and soulful existence. Many persons in developed nations find life to be psychologically and spiritually hollow—living in massive urban environments of alienating scale and complexity, divorced from the natural environment, and working in jobs that are unsatisfying. Many yearn for a more authentic approach to living—one that provides a fulfilling relationship with one's self, with others, with the Earth, and with the universe.

A large fraction of the American public has experienced the limited rewards from the material riches of a consumer society and is looking for the experiential riches that can be found, for example, in satisfying relationships, living in harmony with nature, and being of service to the world. The combination of the push of necessity and the pull of opportunity working in concert creates an entirely new situation for humanity. On the one hand, a life of creative simplicity frees energy for the soulful work of spiritual discovery and loving service—tasks that all of the world's wisdom traditions say we should give our highest priority. On the other hand, a simpler way of life also responds to the urgent needs for moderating our use of the world's non-renewable resources and minimizing the damaging impact of environmental pollution. Working together, these pushes and pulls are creating an immensely powerful dynamic for transforming our ways of living, working, relating, and thinking.

Meanwhile, since World War II, we've seen the most massive experiment that's ever been undertaken in programming the psyche of a civilization. And it has worked. The advertising culture has succeeded in creating identity consumption—a sense that our meaning in life depends upon the significance of what we consume.

A retail analyst, Victor Lebow, who promoted consumption as necessary to our economy in the postwar period, was very clear about this. He said, "Our enormously productive economy demands that we make consumption our way of life, that we convert the buying and use of goods into rituals, that we seek our spiritual satisfaction and our ego satisfaction in consumption. We need things consumed, burned up, worn out, replaced, and discarded at an ever-increasing rate."[77]

People are having a very tough time separating their sense of spiritual identity from their consumer identity. And, there's a conscious blending of the two by advertisers to make it seem as though our spiritual or soulful significance is manifest in our consumption. The effects are so pervasive that we don't see them. They are just accepted — like the air we breathe. Advertising is creating a lethal addiction. Overconsumption is not a matter of taste, it's a matter of survival. We're promoting a mass psychology that will result in our own ruin. This is not good mental heath! Jung defines schizophrenia as mistaking the dream for reality. We have been so inundated with the televised-generated version of the American Dream (each person watching roughly 25,000 commercials a year) that we have mistaken it for reality. We're literally going crazy — on the one hand knowing we need to learn to live with less, and on the other hand being continuously encouraged to consume ever more. We are being divided against ourselves. Something has to give.

I feel that the future of the species will depend to a large degree on the future of communications. If the mass media presents a shallow, secular, and consumerist view of the world, then we will be more inclined to allow the destruction of the global environment. Then, a majority may not see, until it is too late, that we live within a sacred universe. In my view, our collective use of the mass media will need to be infused by a sacred sense of reality if we are to reconcile ourselves to living sustainably on the Earth. We need communication that comes from a place of compassion if we are ever going to collectively envision and then reach agreement around a common pathway into the future.

George Gerbner (professor of communications and founder of the Cultural Environment Movement) says that to control a nation, you don't have to control its laws or its military, all you have to do is control who tells the nation its stories.

Television tells most of the nation most of its stories most of the time. If television is our social brain, then American television currently has the highest level of intelligence that beer and car commercials can buy. And this dumbing down of the U.S. public is happening at the very time when we face unprecedented social upheaval and change. As people have really tried to live out the television dream, and seen how hollow it all is, they are becoming deeply cynical about it and saying, "I don't care how many more ads you show me, I don't believe them anymore. I don't know what to believe, but I just don't believe it anymore."

We're literally becoming schizophrenic—divided against ourselves. On one hand, we believe the advertiser fiction; on the other hand, we don't believe it. Here's how I'd summarize the polls: about 75 percent to 80 percent of the public say, "We're going to need to make major changes if we're going to live sustainably on Earth." I find it very significant that such a large fraction of the overall public recognizes that, like it or not, there are great changes ahead. Next, about 60 percent of U.S. adults say, "Not only do we need to change, we want to change." Still, this is largely rhetoric as most are sympathetic but disengaged—still waiting for the starting gun to go off.

Then, about 25 percent are actually doing something by changing the way they live—perhaps by not taking the job promotion that would require them to move somewhere; maybe one of the partners in the relationship will stop working or take a lower-paying job that's closer to home. These are the so-called "downshifters" who are disengaging from the rat race of our consumer society.

Finally, about 10 percent of U.S. adults are "upshifters" who have gone even further and are pioneering a new way of life that is more sustainable, satisfying, and soulful. They're making a whole-pattern shift in their lives that grows out of an ecological awareness and the sense that "I'm here as more than just a consumer to be entertained; I'm here as a soulful being who wants to grow. I want to have meaningful work, a meaningful life with my family, a meaningful connection with my community, and a meaningful sense of spiritual development."

About two-thirds of the economic activity in this country is based upon consumer purchases and even a small shift in consumer activity creates tidal-wave reverberations throughout the economy. Seemingly small lifestyle changes can accumulate into big impacts when multiplied by millions of consumers or citizens. Small changes are beautiful. Little changes can accumulate into a tidal wave of change!

Arnold Toynbee looked at the rise and fall of over twenty civilizations and summarized civilizational growth with his Law of Progressive Simplification. In accord with this law, Toynbee said that the essence of civilizational growth is not power over land, or power over people (and I think now he would also say it's not how much we consume). The essence of a civilization's growth is its ability to transfer increasing increments of energy and attention from the material side of life to the psychological, spiritual, cultural, and aesthetic sides.[78]

What is emerging is not a "new American dream" but a more conscious and purposeful "central project" for the entire human family. The central project of the human family is to somehow come into harmony with three core "ecologies"—physical, social, and spiritual. I think of these as three "Ss."

One "S" stands for a more sustainable way of life—a way of life that's in harmony with the Earth's physical ecology. The second "S" is for a more satisfying way of life—one that's in harmony with our social ecology—with other people, our work, our community, the rest of the world, members of the opposite gender, and so on. The third "S" stands for a more soulful way of life—one that is in harmony with spiritual ecology, however described.

The human family is fast approaching one of the most pivotal points in the entirety of human evolution—the point at which we consciously recognize, for the very first time, that we are inextricably a single "species-civilization," a single planetary family whose destiny is intimately intertwined. Knowing this, we then have the choice of moving toward a new central project for the human family—that of discovering and building a sustainable, satisfying, soulful way of living upon the Earth.

The Responsibility for Change

Unless dramatic changes are made in the manner of living and consuming in industrialized nations, we will soon produce a world of monumental destruction, suffering, conflict, and despair. Within this generation, we must begin a sweeping reinvention in our ways of living or invite the collapse of our biosphere and allow global civilization to veer off into a long detour and dark age.

Because we face a crisis in the interconnected global system, changes at every level are needed. At a personal level, we need a magnified global awareness and simpler lifestyles. At a neighborhood level, we need new types of communities for sustainable living. At the national level, we need to adopt new policies with regard to energy, environment, education, media, and much more. At a global level, we need new partnerships among nations. Although changes are necessary at every level, the foundation upon which success can be built is the individual and family. It is empowering to know that each person can make a difference by taking responsibility for changes in their immediate lives.

Just as we tend to wait for our problems to solve themselves, so too do we tend to wait for our traditional institutions and leaders to provide us with guidance as to what we should do. Yet, our leaders are bogged down, trying to cope with our faltering institutions. They are so enmeshed in crisis management that they have little time to exercise genuinely creative leadership. We may keep waiting for someone else, but a key message of this book is that there is no one else. You are it. We are it. Each of us is responsible. It is we who, one by one, must take charge of our lives. It is we who, one by one, must act to restore the balance. We are the ones who are responsible for making it through this time of sweeping change as we work to reconcile the human family around a sustainable future for the planet.

Toward Dematerialization

by Rolf Jucker

W̲E ALL CONSUME. Consuming is part of living. The starting point for any sensible theory or practice of consumption has to be the insight that every time you buy and/or consume something—be it a tiny battery to keep your watch going or be it a TV, a car, or a hamburger—you are making an impact on the social, economic, and ecological environment. In the words of Anwar Fazal, former president of the International Organization of Consumer Unions (IOCU), "The act of buying is a vote for an economic and social model, for a particular way of producing goods. We are concerned with the quality of goods and the satisfaction we derive from them. But we cannot ignore the environmental impact and the working conditions under which products are made."[79] Our relationship with these products or goods does not end with our enjoyment of possessing or consuming them. We are linked to them and perpetuate them and therefore share some direct responsibility for them.

We also bear some responsibility for the answers to the following questions:

1) Are the products produced in an environmentally harmful or sustainable manner?

2) Do the workers that produce them get a fair price?

3) Do they have safe and healthy working conditions?

4) Are the substances used in production and in the product itself safe or toxic?

5) Can the product be recycled at the end of its life span? If not, is it biodegradable or does it release toxic substances when landfilled or

incinerated (such as PVC, which releases Dioxin, one of the most toxic substances mankind has ever invented)?

6) Do we pay the price for all the social and environmental costs a product is creating or are these costs shifted onto other people (e.g., "Third World" countries) or the public (e.g., environmental cleanup measures, usually paid for by the taxpayer)?

7) Does the company producing the goods deal with oppressive regimes, thereby furthering human rights abuses?

8) Is the company involved in arms production, nuclear energy, animal testing, factory farming, irresponsible marketing, or suppression of workers' rights?

9) Is the production company donating money to political parties?

Once we recognize our complicity in these conditions it becomes virtually impossible to buy children's toys from China anymore (in the face of Tibetan suffering), or from other Southeast Asian countries (because of the way the factory workers are treated). Another example is the "McLibel" campaign. Triggered by the libel writs against Helen Steel and David Morris, an international cadre of supporters have exposed the worldwide business practices of McDonald's to public scrutiny which resulted in devastating condemnations of the company, particularly on ethical and environmental issues.[80]

Promoted by slogans like "consumer choice," the notion that we should approach all our decisions, whether they are political, such as voting, or personal, such as career choices, as "ideal citizens" is accepted more and more. It means that we should make an effort to fully and independently inform ourselves about all aspects and consequences of our choices. If we take seriously the ethic that we should try not to buy any products which conflict in any significant way with our own moral, political, environmental, and social beliefs, then there are important questions we should be able to answer with regard to any product we buy.

Constant propaganda suggesting that consumers are "in the driver's seat" and that consumer satisfaction is the primary concern of the corporation, has been effective. But most advertising is really designed to divert scrutiny of the product, its quality, and social and ecological impact. A clear trend in advertising is to provide less and less information about a product, but more and more seductions to build consumer loyalty through lifestyle, atmosphere, or identification with a certain culture which is supposedly represented by the product in question. Advertising is obviously less about giving consumers full and independent information about a product, as it is to sell as much of the product as possible, boost profits, and collect dividends for shareholders.

It is arguable that the success of business propaganda in persuading us, for so long, that we are free from propaganda is one of the most significant propaganda achievements of the twentieth century. A good example of how corporations, despite their claims to provide consumers with more choice, are actively limiting such choice, is the introduction of genetically modified soya in the marketplace. Only one company (Monsanto in the U.S.) was selling genetically modified seeds and only 2 percent or less of the world's soya harvest was genetically modified. But nevertheless the industry (in other words, the world's leading multinational chemical companies) claimed that it was impossible to segregate and label genetically modified soya, to make it distinguishable from non-modified soya, thus depriving the consumers of the chance to exercise choice. Independent food safety experts regard genetically modified food to be a potential health risk, while the chemical multinationals tried to present the consumer with a fait accompli. After massive consumer protests, especially in Europe, there are now moves underway to segregate and label genetically modified foods. Suddenly, it seems to be possible.

In response to industry's attempt to prevent consumers from getting relevant information and on the basis of some very successful consumer boycott movements (e.g., on CFC reduction, genetically modified soya, products made from whales, rainforest destruction, etc.), independent research is now being made available to consumers. We now have the power to buy and invest according to our ethical, political and environmental beliefs. This "ethical consumption" often involves a so-called "fully-screened approach" which checks companies against criteria such as pollution, environmental policy, involvement in nuclear power, animal testing, factory farming, oppressive regimes, workers' rights, marketing, armaments, and political donations. This allows the consumer to "vote" whenever you buy something, to cast your vote for fair trade, good social conditions for workers, for environmentally friendly production, etc.

The advantages of such a system are obvious: you can influence the market directly without waiting for government action by buying "good" products and by not buying "bad" ones (and letting them know, perhaps on their website, why you did or did not do business with them). Democracy in consumption has increased, and consumer dependence on advertising for product information is reduced. (There are also several sites on the Web offering consumers "green" products, including Gaiam, GreenMarketplace.com, and Real Goods.)

Ethical consumption is a re-orientation of consumers from passive purchasers, who willingly and uncritically accept advertising messages, to active, responsible citizens who see the dynamic connection between their purchases and their values. It is to be expected that industry will fight back. The World Trade Organization (WTO) tried to outlaw and suppress attempts to provide more consumer information (such as ecolabels etc.), on the basis that they obstruct competition. The struggle to preserve real choice is particularly difficult in a society where "free access to information" is, in principle, a right, but which in reality works rather differently. As Noam Chomsky aptly put it, "In a perfectly functioning capitalist democracy, with no illegitimate abuse of power, freedom will be in effect a kind of commodity; effectively, a person will have as much of it as he can buy."[81]

Current economic production with its worship of "growth" is simply unsustainable for the future, a view globally accepted at the Rio and Rio + 5 conferences. The easiest way to substantiate that claim is to project Western consumption levels onto the whole world (which is the "hidden" aim of the current world economy and its worship of "growth"): the biosphere can't cope. It is estimated that we would need three additional planet Earths.

Sustainable action results in effects compatible with healthy and enduring human life on Earth. Sustainable use, in other words, only spends the interest and not the capital. Since current levels of air, water, and soil contamination, and the intense exploitation of natural resources cannot persist, we must recognize that our consumer society is not sustainable. This economic technosphere of human activity is just a subsystem of the biosphere. The biosphere is the life-support system of all forms of life on Earth and all forms of economic activity inescapably depend on it (and not the other way round as some economists try to make us believe).

To return our economic systems to the fold of sustainability, only so much of a renewable resource should be used as is regenerated in the same period; only such an amount of material/waste/products should be released into the environment as nature can process and digest; and the turnover of energy and materials must be lowered to a safe level.

In order to bring that down to a practical and measurable level for consumers, Mathis Wackernagel and William Rees have developed a system called "ecological footprint" which can be used to measure the impact of one's lifestyle or even particular purchases and compare them to a level which would guarantee sustainability for the whole world. What the system essentially does is to calculate the area of land you would need in order to balance out the negative ecological impact our lifestyle has on nature. For example, you calculate the area of forest you would need to absorb the amount of carbon dioxide you produce by driving so and so many miles per annum with your car or by flying overseas. The results can then be compared. While for a sustainable level of economic activity every person on Earth would have 1.7 hectares (17,000 m²) available, the average British person uses 4.8 hectares (2.8 times too much), the average U.S. American 8.6 hectares (5 times too much), the average German 4.9 hectares (that is 2.9 times too much), whereas the average Indian uses 0.8 hectares (roughly half of what they "could"). These calculations give us an indication of the factor by which we have to reduce our ecological footprint in order to become sustainable.

One of the biggest obstacles to ecologically sound production and consumption is that the costs we pay for services and goods "lie," that is they do not involve all the costs that would accumulate if ecological damage during production and costs for recycling and/or waste management had to be accounted for. That is partly because the traditional (and still most influential) theories of economy simply forget about the resources and waste problem.

We can only ignore these aspects at our peril. That is why a team of international economists and ecologists tried to calculate the value (since the leading capitalists only understand anything if it is expressed in terms of dollars) of the world's ecosystem services and natural capital which we generally exploit without giving a thought. If we had to pay for ecosystem services such as gas, climate, and water regulation, water supply, erosion control and sediment retention, soil formation, nutrient cycling, waste treatment, pollination, biological control, food production, raw materials, genetic resources, recreation, and cultural services at market prices, it would cost us, on a conservative estimate, $33 trillion per year globally. That is 1.8 times the total global Gross National Product (the Earth would grind to a halt without the services of ecological life-support systems, so in one sense their total value to the economy is infinite).

There are two related concepts that attempt to take the entire social, environmental and other costs of a product into account. The first are so-called

Life Cycle Analyses (LCA). They try to integrate not only the amount and variety of raw material that is needed to produce certain goods, but also the energy that goes into production (gray energy), the environmental and other costs of packaging, the likely life span, and the costs for recycling or waste management. Only with an LCA can you really assess whether a product is "green." It is on the basis of LCAs that you can see the advantage of recycled paper over virgin paper, of terry diapers over disposables, of glass bottles over aluminum cans, etc.

Batteries are another example. We throw away more than 20,000 tons of mixed battery waste each year in the U.K. alone. Twenty thousand tons of batteries equal 870 semitrailer truckloads or, in other words, an eight-mile nose-to-tail queue of semitrailer trucks. We throw these batteries away, despite the fact that most materials used are non-renewable, scarce (like cadmium), or produce emissions like carbon dioxide, and cause acid rain. Additionally, zinc, manganese dioxide, alkaline, nickel, and particularly cadmium are highly toxic substances that cannot be properly recycled or safely disposed of. Wherever possible, buy products that do not run on batteries. More and more products are available which either run electrically or are mechanically driven, like watches that derive their energy from the movement of your arm, or the Freeplay radio which, wound up for twenty seconds, plays for sixty minutes, etc.

Transport, packaging, and storage are also important factors that determine whether a product is ethically and ecologically fit to consume. In Germany, 20 percent of energy and material consumption is used to put food onto the table—that includes diesel for tractors, crops for factory farming, energy for the food industry, petrol for long distance lorries, electricity for cooling in supermarkets, energy for cooking, plus infrastructure (pipelines, motorways, factories, lorry fleets etc.). A single average German yogurt is transported around 8,000 kilometers before it gets to the table. The energy it takes to get a single tomato from the Canary Islands to a kitchen in the U.K. could keep a light bulb on for almost four days. The alternative is to buy local products wherever possible, and in the case of food, only local organic products, since their production uses 50 percent less energy and materials, compared with similar quantity and quality of conventional agricultural products.

Another interesting example, particularly since it focuses on an industry that is still caught up in the frenzy of "more, faster, better," is computers. With the average life expectancy of three to four years, PCs consume more than 50 percent of their total energy during their production, and not in their use. And since a PC is manufactured out of roughly 700 different materials, and the way they are manufactured at the moment means that most of these components cannot be recycled and are thrown into landfills, the biggest problem with PCs is after you stop using them.

If the principle were taken seriously that the producer has to take responsibility for the full life cycle of a product and that prices should tell the truth about all costs involved from design, raw-material extraction, production, transport, marketing, usage to disposal, the world economy would reorganize itself overnight into regional markets. The reality is somewhat different. There are hundreds of subsidies, and most of them environmentally damaging, that distort the prices (e.g., EU agricultural subsidies, subsidies for electricity and cars in the U.S. etc.). There are even tax advantages for environmentally senseless behavior. In general, it can be said that the costs of environmental, social, and health damage caused by, say cars or industry, are externalized, meaning that neither the producer nor the user are paying the costs they created, but the state, i.e., all the taxpayers, are. Various estimates put the accumulated costs of subsidies, necessary cleanups, follow-on costs, pollution, and wasteful use of resources at roughly half of GNP.

If you attempt to calculate the social costs of private cars fueled by fossil fuels—costs which have to be shared by the whole population, not just the users who amount to less than 50 percent of it—you arrive at a figure of around 5 percent of GNP. Those costs include accidents, loss of time through traffic jams, pollution, and other environmental damage, destruction of roads, land use, etc.

Only by making those who create the costs pay for them can markets work properly and insure that you will face the full costs if you decide to buy environmentally damaging products. More importantly, it means that you would benefit financially if you care to buy environmentally sound products. In order to make mindful purchases, one should consider the following questions before making the transaction:

1) Do I really need this?

2) Can I buy it secondhand?

3) Can I borrow, rent, lease, or share it?

4) Can we own it as a group?

5) Can I build it myself?

This set of questions start from the assumption that we need a shift in perspective away from the product towards the service we require. For example, we don't want the washing machine, we want clean, dry washing; we don't want the drill, we want to have a picture hung. So we need to establish first what service we want and then try to find out how this service can be provided in a sustainable manner. In other words, we have to take a fresh and penetrating new look at our needs.

1) Where is it produced?

2) Can I buy the same product locally?

3) Can I assess the overall environmental impact of buying this product, including production, energy and materials usage, transport, advertising, packaging, and disposal?

4) Does this product last as long as possible or can I only use it once?

5) Is it upgradable, reusable, recyclable?

6) Does the producer guarantee to take the product back and recycle it at the end of its lifetime (particularly important with products that use a lot of resources in production, e.g., refrigerators, washing machines, TVs, stereos, cars, etc.)?

7) Is the product the most energy and materials efficient model on the market, using environmentally harmless substances, both during production and in the product itself (i.e., no use of toxic substances or PVC etc.)?

If it is a foreign product:

8) Are environmental standards observed in production?

9) Do the actual producers (i.e., factory workers or farmers) get a fair price?

10) Are their working conditions safe and healthy or would a Western worker under no circumstances work in such a factory?

11) Does production of these goods take away high quality farming land from food production for the local population (cash crops, cut flowers, etc.)?

Reducing our ecological footprint is an important aspect of sustainability, but improving our own environment is not good enough if we are simultaneously degrading other people's (for example through imports). In order to make progress towards a sustainable lifestyle—which we owe both to our children and to poorer countries—we need to check how products stand up against the above mentioned criteria of a "fully-screened" approach.

Ultimately we even have to go one step further. As we are just beginning to grasp the need to reduce, reuse, and recycle, if we bear in mind that around 50 percent of all materials used and moved by mankind cannot be recycled, the ultimate challenge is to work toward the dematerialization of our lifestyles.

The New Storytellers

by David Korten

THE GOAL in the New Story is to displace the corporate institutions of global capitalism with a global system of mindful market economies. The process involves gradually increasing the options the mindful market offers us as we reduce our dependence on those offered by the institutions of global corporatization. For example, I buy dry goods from the local Bainbridge Island supplier, located within walking distance from my home and run by a wonderful family who add something of their love of the Earth and our island community to every transaction. Each time I buy products from my neighbor (rather than those from large corporations), or purchase a head of lettuce at our Saturday morning farmers' market that is grown by another wonderful neighbor on her organic farm (rather than lettuce from our local Safeway corporation outlet that is grown thousands of miles away by the Del Monte corporation on a factory farm), I act to nurture the mindful market economy while withdrawing legitimacy and resources from the global corporate economy. And each time I forgo the purchase of something I don't really need, substitute a product made by my own hand, or engage in a cooperative exchange with my neighbor, I weaken my dependence on global corporate institutions. And, in most instances, I also reduce my burden on the planet.

Our task is no longer one of creating countercultures, engaging in political protest, and pursuing economic alternatives. To create a just, sustainable, and compassionate post-corporate world we must face up to the need to create a new core culture, a new political center, and a new economic mainstream. Such a bold agenda requires many kinds of expertise working at many levels of society—personal and household, community, national, and global. It requires breaking the bonds of individual isolation that leave us feeling marginalized when in fact we may already be part of a new majority. There are thousands of useful tasks to be undertaken.

Start from Where You Are

Obviously, we are not going to bring about this transformation to a mindful economy just by buying a locally grown head of organic lettuce, though it is a useful start. We must work in many ways at many levels. The best that can be done here is to offer a general framework and a few illustrative suggestions that you may find helpful in defining a personal strategy to help starve the cancer and nurture life. There are no universal blueprints. Indeed, the one universal response to the question, What can I do? is "Start from where you are." That means making use of the resources at your command, and most important, doing what allows you to become more of who you really are.

If you are a member of a church or Dharma group, you might organize discussion groups and events to examine these issues and explore how individuals can act on them as an expression of their spiritual values. Or you might initiate a study group that deepens the group's sense of connection to place by gathering and sharing information on such things as the history of the locality where you live, the foods that are produced there, the source of your water, the distinctive characteristics of your native species, and how your local ecosystem has changed over time.

If you are a parent, you might campaign to make your local schools advertising-free zones. If you are a teacher and your school requires students to watch the teen portal Channel One, you might use it as a resource for teaching students to deconstruct advertising and propaganda messages to help immunize them against media manipulation. Or you might engage your students in projects that deepen their understanding and caring about their local ecosystems. If you teach in a university, especially in a school of business, organize a course on the moral defense and critique of capitalism to engage students in a critical examination of the issues relating to the design of an economic system.

If you are a natural networker, you might work with others to develop a guide to local organizations and initiatives for people in your locality who are looking for ways to become positively engaged. Or you might compile and publicize a directory of local, stakeholder-owned businesses. Your efforts might even lead to the formation of new alliances among these groups to strengthen the newly emergent whole.

If you are the CEO of a large corporation, you could establish a policy that your corporation will not make political contributions or otherwise seek to influence elections or legislation. Better yet, organize the breakup and employee buyout of your corporation to turn it into a network of independent stakeholder-owned, community-based businesses. If you are an investment counselor or money manager, build a specialty in socially responsible investment and the financing of stakeholder buyouts. If you are a small business owner, build your identity as a values-led, community-based enterprise and engage in the formation of networks and alliances of like-minded businesses.

If you are a union member, campaign for applying a social responsibility screen to the investment of union pension funds, with special attention to investing only in companies that hire union workers and have good employee relations. Promote the use of pension funds to finance a labor buyout of selected corporations to convert them into stakeholder enterprises.

If you work with small farmers in a low-income country, encourage them to save and use local seeds and not become dependent on the seeds and chemicals of transnational corporations. Help them organize to resist the takeover of their lands by corporations and development projects such as those funded by the World Bank and other foreign development agencies. If you are a citizen of a low-income country, join the citizen resistance against IMF and World Bank structural adjustment programs.

If you are a politician, consider building your campaign on a pledge to take only small contributions and to support serious campaign reform.

If you are an economist, become active in the International Society for Ecological Economics and participate in building and popularizing a market economics for a living planet. If you are a lawyer, connect with one of the groups working on issues relating to the legal status of corporations and help develop a legal strategy to overturn the doctrine of corporate personhood.

If you are a resident of a low-income neighborhood, especially a racial minority neighborhood in the U.S., your community is likely to be a favored site for polluting industries, waste disposal, and the routing of new highway construction and will likely be underserved by public transportation. If existing groups are working to stop harmful projects, demand the cleanup of existing facilities, and promote public transportation suited to your community's needs, and consider getting involved with one of them. If an effective group does not already exist, create one.

If you have talents as a speaker, develop a presentation on the relationship of the business system to the health of the environment and make yourself available to groups interested in delving into such issues. If you are a journalist, write stories about the newly emerging culture; values-led, stakeholder-owned businesses; and the many citizen initiatives moving us toward a post-corporate world—the stories that corporate PR specialists don't want told. If the publication from which you earn your bread and butter has no taste for such stories, do them on a pro bono, freelance basis for independent publications that still believe journalism has a role beyond generating advertising dollars.

If you are inclined to political activism, you might get involved in campaigns to end corporate welfare in all its many forms, strip corporations of their rights of personhood, and get big money out of politics.

Whoever you are, you have an important role in changing the system—for change will only come from the actions of millions of people, and each of us is important.

Intervene at Multiple Levels

Although the most important changes generally begin within ourselves, they must eventually be translated into changes in community, national, and global institutions. We must be mindful of the changes needed at all these levels and contribute to their realization. The basic themes, however, remain the same. Start from where you are to starve the cancer of global corporatization and nurture life.

Let's take the levels one at a time and explore some of the possibilities. Bear in mind this is a list of possibilities focused on changing the economic system. It is neither prescriptive nor comprehensive, but only a partial answer to the question, "What can I do?"

Personal and Family

At the personal and family level our opportunities to shift the energy of the economic system center on issues of consumption, where we live, and how we obtain and use our money. The following are some specific things you might consider:

SIMPLIFY YOUR LIFE. In a capitalist economy, cutting back on consumption is a revolutionary act. Cut back on clutter and unnecessary consumption. Sort out which expenditures are really important to you and which are not. Figure out your real take-home pay after deducting taxes and the costs of transportation, clothing, and tools used in your occupation. Then calculate what you earn per hour and translate each prospective purchase into the hours of your life energy that you must devote to your job to pay for it. Each time you make a purchase, ask whether the item is worth that many hours of life energy you might be using in other ways. For greater support, form a voluntary simplicity group to share ideas and experiences.

BUY SMALL AND LOCAL. Making your purchases at small stakeholder-owned firms and buying locally produced products are also revolutionary acts against capitalism. Patronize your local farmers' market or organize a community supported agriculture (CSA) program with a local farmer. If you celebrate Thanksgiving, participate in the "Thanksgiving conspiracy," which involves planning and producing your Thanksgiving dinner based exclusively on foodstuffs produced within thirty miles of your place of residence, and encourage others in your community to do the same. In good market fashion, you are voting with your dollars. It may take some research to figure out what is produced locally and how you can adjust your consumption patterns to meet more of your needs through the market rather than through the capitalist economy, but that is part of the consciousness-raising process. Again, consider forming a support group to share your experience and information.

CHOOSE A LIFE-AFFIRMING JOB. Consider doing work that has real meaning with a values-led, community-based organization or enterprise that is contributing to the life of the community and the planet even if it is lower-paid.

KEEP INFORMED. Reach out beyond the mainstream media by becoming a regular reader of journals and books published by reliable alternative press groups that report on news and issues relating to corporate agendas.

PUT YOUR CASH IN A COMMUNITY BANK. Do your banking with an independent bank or credit union committed to serving your community. If the banks in your community are all branches of one of the large national or international banks, ask the branch manager for the figures on how the local deposits to that branch compare with the branch's total lending in your community for local businesses and home ownership. If local deposits are substantially greater than local lending, you know that local money is not supporting the local economy. Consider banking by mail with a community bank located elsewhere. At least you will know your money is supporting someone's local market economy rather than creating economic instability in the global financial casino.

VOTE WITH YOUR SAVINGS. If you participate in the stock market, choose a mutual fund that screens investments for social responsibility or make use of an investment service or advisor who specializes in socially screened stocks. Use your ownership vote to support positive shareholder initiatives. Also, avoid consumer debt. Those who maintain debt balances on their credit cards mortgage their lives to capitalism.

REDUCE YOUR AUTOMOBILE DEPENDENCE. Living without a car is no small challenge in most American localities, and auto manufacturers, oil companies, and construction contractors all benefit from keeping it that way. We serve ourselves and all life by reducing that dependence. When deciding where to live and where to work, try to choose the location that allows you to walk, bicycle, or take public transportation to work, shopping, and recreation. In many households, just eliminating the need for a second or third car is a positive step.

FUND CHANGE. Support nonprofit organizations that are challenging global corporatization and working in favor of equity, environment, and community. Whatever your level of income, reserve a portion for charitable giving to these organizations. You can even support groups doing work in which you believe by such a simple act as signing up with a long-distance phone service that offers discounted rates and donates a portion of your payment to groups working for systemic change.

Community

At the community level, action opportunities center on strengthening the local market economy, creating a healthy livable environment, and building a sense of community based on mutual trust and caring. Contributing at this level requires that we reach out and become a part of our community's public life. The following are a few ideas you might consider:

JOIN AN INDICATORS PROJECT. If your community has a sustainability or livability indicators project, get involved. If not, consider organizing some friends to initiate one. The more people involved in dialoguing on the nature of the community in which they want to live and in selecting the indicators by which they will know when they have created it, the more likely the effort will have a meaningful impact.

The Rocky Mountain Institute (RMI) offers a variety of technical and organizational resources for increasing community sustainability. See its website at www.rmi.org for current information, or contact RMI, 1739 Snowmass Creek Road, Snowmass, Colorado, 81654-9199. For those interested in organizing a program to create a strong community economy based on the use of local resources to meet local needs, see Michael J. Kinsley, *Economic Renewal Guide: A Collaborative Process for Sustainable Community Development.* Available from RMI, it is an excellent practical guide and also includes an extensive directory of additional resources.

CREATE A DIRECTORY FOR THE MINDFUL MARKET. A barrier to supporting the mindful market economy is figuring out which products come from values-led local firms. Perhaps you have created a support group and you are developing a serious information base. Your next step might be to publish, distribute, and publicize a community directory to your local mindful market.

SUPPORT OR CREATE A COMMUNITY CURRENCY. Local currencies reduce dependence on money controlled by global banking institutions, build a sense of community, strengthen the identity of local businesses and products, and make visible the distinction between money that stays in the community and money that doesn't. If your community has a local currency, give it your support. If not, consider forming a group to establish one.

ENCOURAGE GROWTH BOUNDARIES, AFFORDABLE HOUSING, AND PUBLIC TRANSPORTATION. The move to establish urban growth boundaries to limit sprawl, reverse urban decay, create pedestrian-friendly neighborhoods, and increase the viability of public transportation is an idea whose time has come. If your community has a growth management plan designed to increase livability, consider getting involved. If not, then consider organizing support to create one. Be sure affordable housing is an element of the agenda, so that people at all income levels will have access to the improved livability of your area.

WORK FOR COMMUNITY ECONOMIC SELF-RELIANCE. There is a growing divide between localities that approach economic growth by providing subsidies to attract facilities from global corporations and those that are strengthening smaller local businesses. If these issues interest you, find out who is responsible for economic development policies in your community and get involved, either by seeking a seat on the relevant local commission or by organizing a watchdog and lobbying group to mobilize support for sensible economic policies.

National

GET POLITICAL. There is no democracy without an active citizenry. The only way we are going to bring change to our corrupted political system is through greater involvement by citizens who care about their community. Run for office and bring your values into the political mainstream. Build your campaign in part on a pledge to finance your election with small contributions and avoid obligations to big-money interests. Much of the impetus for change is coming from the local level and there are important opportunities to make a difference as a local officeholder. Furthermore, to reclaim national politics we must first build a local base. If you're fed up with the pandering to big money by the major political parties, consider joining a smaller party, such as the New Party, which is engaged in building its base on a platform of citizen democracy in both political and economic life.

USE YOUR POLITICAL FRANCHISE. Study the issues, check the voting records of your legislators or parliamentarians, find out who finances their campaigns, and use your vote to favor the politicians who are trying to serve the public interest. Let the politicians who represent you know you are watching their records and that you favor serious campaign finance reform that gets big money out of politics, strong environmental regulation, a living wage, strong antitrust enforcement, small- and medium-size local business, stakeholder ownership, strong unions, and a progressive tax policy. Let them also know that you oppose international trade and investment agreements that increase the rights and reduce the accountability of global corporations and financial institutions; funding for the International Monetary Fund, the World Bank, and the World Trade Organization; corporate subsidies; the privatization of social security; capital gains tax cuts and other tax breaks for the wealthy; bank deregulation; patents on life; and corporate intellectual property rights monopolies — to name a few issues that bear directly on the balance of power between capitalism and democracy and the market economy.

If the politicians who represent you don't represent your interests, others probably feel unrepresented as well. Consider running for national office yourself. At the national level, the action agenda centers on political education and changing the rules of the game to favor democracy and not the market economy.

GET ACTIVE IN POLITICAL MOVEMENTS AND ADVOCACY GROUPS. Although the major political parties may be hopelessly captive to big-money interests, there are many political movements and advocacy groups that are not. These groups are vehicles for mobilizing broad grassroots support behind initiatives that advance the public interest on issues such as those listed in the previous paragraphs. Pick out one or two with a strong grassroots base that align with your interests, get involved, and give special attention to campaign finance reform.

International

At the international level, a positive agenda centers on people-to-people exchange and dialogue that builds a globalizing civil society as a potent force for positive change.

GLOBAL NETWORKS. There are many global citizen organizations working in solidarity on issues ranging from voluntary simplicity to opposing international trade and investment treaties that are designed to strengthen corporate rights and weaken their accountability. If the issues you are working on at community and national levels have an international dimension, you may want to link your local and national efforts to a related international network or alliance.

GLOBAL INSTITUTIONS. Global institutions are an especially appropriate concern of global networks. Citizen groups have come to realize that the most powerful of our international institutions are generally those—such as the World Bank, the International Monetary Fund, and the World Trade Organization—that have been created to serve and strengthen global corporatization. Groups of concerned citizens worldwide have responded with well-organized initiatives aimed at holding these institutions accountable to the human and environmental interest. There is much to be done to strengthen institutions dedicated to protecting the economic rights of people and communities. If this agenda interests you, find a relevant network and get involved.

MUNICIPAL FOREIGN POLICY. As national governments have pursued foreign policies largely alien to the values and interests of many of their citizens, a number of towns and cities have put forward their own positions on key foreign policy issues. For example, some have boycotted corporations that do business with repressive regimes, such as in Burma or apartheid South Africa. In many instances local governments around the world are reaching out to work directly with one another to prod and challenge their national governments on official positions relating to such issues as global warming, nuclear disarmament, and human rights. While national governments have been negotiating the Multilateral Agreement on Investment (MAI), aimed at virtually eliminating the ability of national and local governments to regulate international investors and speculators, a number of towns and cities in the United States, Canada, Britain, Australia, and other countries have passed official resolutions declaring themselves MAI-free zones to underscore their protest against this attack against democracy.

Those who define values and progress in terms of money define international cooperation primarily in terms of financial relationships. As we awaken to life as our defining value and measure of progress, we come to see that the foundation of more meaningful international cooperation centers on people-to-people communication and the free exchange of friendship, information, and technology. We are learning that international relations are too important to be left to national governments captive to corporate interests. If your municipal government has an active foreign policy, get involved. If not, learn what other local governments are doing and campaign to get yours involved. Give special support to initiatives aimed at strengthening the rights of peoples to protect their economic and environmental interests against predatory global capital.

Enchanted by their Sirens' song, we have yielded to the institutions of capitalism the power to decide our economic, social, and technological priorities. Intimidated by their power, we have been reluctant to see the naked truth that they bear the Midas curse, appropriating the life energies of whatever they touch to the end of making money. Finding our choices narrowed to the options global corporations find it profitable to offer us, we seek meaning where there is none to be found and become unwitting accomplices in fulfilling the deadly curse.

Given the seriousness of our situation, it may seem anticlimactic to suggest that our survival depends on something so obvious and undramatic as embracing the living universe story as our own and making mindful choices for democracy, markets, and healthy lifestyles. Perhaps we have been so busy searching the distant horizon for exotic answers to our deepening crisis that we have failed to notice the obvious answers that are right in front of us.

Or perhaps we have been reluctant to face the troubling truth that it is our voice that sings the Sirens' song. It is we who divert our eyes from the emperor's nakedness. It is by our hand that the Midas curse turns life into money. We can sing as well life's song, find the courage to speak of the emperor's delusion, and put our hands to life's service, discovering along the way more of who we truly are as we live a life-fulfilling future into being.

The gift of self-reflective intelligence gives our species a capability for mindful choice well beyond that of any other. Yet we have avoided the responsibility that inevitably goes with freedom by assuming it is not within our means. We have further diminished ourselves by developing elegant ideological arguments to rationalize our irresponsibility.

Thus, we have approached democracy as though it were a license for each individual to do as he or she wishes, when in truth it is about acting on the faith that each individual has the capacity for full and equal participation in making responsible choices mindful of the needs of all. We have approached the market as though it were a license to amass unlimited individual wealth without individual responsibility, when in truth it is about meeting basic needs through the mindful participation of everyone in the equitable and efficient allocation of society's resources. We have treated the good life as a process of material acquisition and consumption without limit, when in truth it is about living fully and well in service to life's continued unfolding.

Whatever the barriers to our taking the step to species maturity, our era of adolescent irresponsibility is ending for the very reason that we have reached the limits of the planet's tolerance for our recklessness. It is now our time to accept responsibility for our freedom or perish as a species that failed to find its place of service in the web of life.

Start from where you are. Do what's right for you. Give yourself permission to be the one. And together we can and shall create a positive, life-friendly future for humanity and the planet.

Nourishing Ourselves, Nourishing Others: How Mindful Food Choices Reduce Suffering

by Kate Lawrence

THE CHOICES WE MAKE regarding the foods we eat, particularly the choices of whether to consume meat and other animal foods or not, have far greater consequences than may be immediately apparent. These consequences are felt in our own bodies, in those of our children, by other people—especially the poor—by animals, plants, and by the Earth herself. What guidance can we find in Buddhist teachings to assist us in making these choices?

Among core teachings accepted by virtually all Buddhist traditions, we can begin with the Noble Eightfold Path and look at Right Action, specifically at three of the Five Precepts or Mindfulness Trainings. These statements illuminate the kinds of behaviors that cause harm to ourselves and others, and that lead to anger, violence, hatred, despair, and destruction.

The First Precept

The First Precept, as stated in the Pali Canon, is to refrain from destroying living creatures. The most immediate way that we participate every day in taking the lives of living creatures is through our diet; some life forms must be destroyed in order for us to eat. We cannot hope to follow this precept perfectly and avoid all killing for food. Even a conscientious vegetarian organic vegetable gardener cannot completely avoid killing insects and other small creatures in the soil, as well as some of the wild plants that we call weeds that compete with the vegetable plantings. Although we cannot avoid these kinds of killing, how can we eat so as to reduce to a minimum the pain we inflict?

Views on the sentience (ability to feel; in this case, to feel pain) of other beings, except for the view that neither plants nor animals are sentient, would include: (1) that plants are not sentient beings; (2) that plants and animals are both sentient, but animals suffer more than plants when injured or killed; and (3) that plants and animals are both sentient, and they suffer equally.

The first view, that plants do not count as sentient beings at all, makes our food choice clear: we can eat plants with impunity, whereas animals suffer, so we would want to eat plant foods and avoid injuring and killing animals.

The second view seems to be the most commonly held; many people have an instinctive feeling that although a plant may suffer a little, an animal suffers much more than a plant when it is killed. Picture a cutting board in front of you and a knife in one hand. In your other hand you have a fistful of sprouts—live, whole plants. Consider how you would feel if you placed the sprouts on the cutting board and began to chop them up. Now imagine that, instead of the sprouts, you have a baby chick—a live, whole animal—on the cutting board, and consider your feelings if you began to chop up the chick. Most people would have an immediate visceral reaction to the prospect of killing a live animal, very different from their reaction to the killing of live plants. Furthermore, we know that animals have a central nervous system that, as a survival mechanism, sensitizes them to pain so that they can escape from it if possible. Plants lack a central nervous system, so we can only presume that their suffering is less. If this is our view, we would want to eat plants, so as to cause less suffering.

The third possibility assumes equal sentience, that there is just as much suffering when a carrot is wrenched out of the ground as when a chicken or calf is killed. How would we choose our food in this case? We know that it is the eating of hundreds, if not thousands, of plants by an animal that enables it to grow large enough to be useful as meat. Far more plants must be killed to feed an animal in order to obtain meat than must be killed for an equal amount of food calories if we eat the grains directly. Therefore, if our interest lies in causing the least amount of suffering to living beings, we would *still* want to eat plants instead of animals. In all three views of plant and animal sentience, the conclusion if we want to cause the least suffering is to eat plant-derived food.

Furthermore, unlike meat that always requires a being to be killed, the taking of plant food suitable for us to eat does *not* always require killing the host plant. Fruits, seeds and nuts, beans, some grains, vegetables such as broccoli, cauliflower, squash, peas, tomatoes, peppers, eggplants, most kinds of greens

—all of these can be taken without killing the plant. It is primarily the root vegetables, such as onions, carrots, and beets, that require a plant to be killed when they are taken. Thus, eating plants necessitates less taking of plant life than people might assume, and fortunately, the human body tends to be healthier on a plant food diet, as we'll examine later.

Because most of us do not live near a slaughterhouse, we have no idea of the scale of the violence involved. Every year in the U.S. alone, roughly *nine billion* cattle, pigs, sheep, chickens and turkeys are killed to put meat on our tables.[82] Slaughterhouses operate around the clock every day of the week. If you do the math, you will discover that this number means that 17,000 animals are killed every minute, and about 285 each second. This amount of killing, and the fear and pain of all these animals leading up to the moment of slaughter, is nearly incomprehensible. It is more than ten times the number of animals that are killed by humans in all other ways combined: for medical research, products testing, fur, and those euthanized in animal shelters. Fish are not included in these figures, as they are counted by the pound rather than as individuals, but their numbers are legion. Some experts have said that fish suffer much longer in the process of suffocation when taken out of the water—perhaps for as long as an hour—than land animals do during standard methods of slaughter.

When I first began giving talks over a decade ago to educate people on the issues related to meat eating, that figure of annual slaughter was about six billion. It has been steadily going up because the consumption of red meat has been decreasing while the consumption of poultry has been increasing. Chickens and turkeys are much smaller than cattle and pigs, which means that many more animal lives must be taken to supply a given amount of meat. If we seek to practice the First Precept, how can we justify, much less participate in, this horror?

We've looked at animals that humans kill directly for food, but what about other animals killed in the process of bringing food animals to market? In order to protect ranchers' livelihoods, USDA Wildlife Services, formerly called Animal Damage Control, spends millions of taxpayer dollars every year to kill thousands of coyotes, wolves, and other species that prey on livestock. None of these animals would be killed if humans didn't eat meat. The male chicks of egg-laying hens are killed shortly after birth, often by suffocation, because as males, they will never lay eggs, nor are birds bred for egg-laying suitable for meat. Many thousands of sea animals are killed in drift nets in order to bring in a fish catch. Some years ago there was widespread concern about dolphins being killed in these nets, but the many other species caught and killed have not received public compassion.

The Second Precept

The Second Precept is to refrain from stealing, from taking that which is not given. Again there are several ways in which we violate this precept if we eat animal flesh. When we, by our food choices, require animals to be killed, we are taking their lives by force; no animal comes voluntarily to a slaughterhouse and offers to die. Of far greater significance are the ways in which we deprive these animals of any semblance of well-being in the time period between their birth or hatching and their slaughter. Animals are deliberately bred to be killed, and their growth is manipulated to please human palates. For example, in turkeys what is prized is white meat, the turkey's breast, so these animals are bred to have huge upper bodies. They are so top-heavy that they cannot come together normally to mate; turkeys must all be artificially inseminated, by minimum-wage workers under time pressure, who cannot take care to handle them gently.

We also "steal" animals' body parts. Animals raised for food are routinely — depending on the species — debeaked, dehorned, castrated, branded, or have their tails docked, all without anesthesia. They are confined in small cages or stalls without sunlight or exercise, fed an unnatural diet, and forced to inhale fumes from their own excrement. Infants, such as calves destined to be veal, are removed permanently from their mothers after only one day, so that humans may drink the milk. The mother cows cry out and search for the lost babies. During transport to the slaughterhouse, animals may be starved and exposed to extremes of temperature. And once at the slaughterhouse, the stunning process is not effective in every case to render animals unconscious; perhaps 10 percent are fully conscious when killed. Drawing a parallel to the Holocaust, Nobel Literature laureate Isaac Bashevis Singer wrote, "To [these animals] we are all Nazis; for them it is an eternal Treblinka."[83]

How else do we steal the well-being of animals to support flesh-eating? To grow grain and soybeans to feed to livestock so that we may eat meat, it is necessary to farm far more land — roughly seven to ten times as much — than would be necessary if we ate the grains and soybeans ourselves. This additional cultivated land is thus no longer available as wildlife habitat, and many species of birds and animals have either declined or disappeared as a result.

By feeding so much grain—about three-fourths of all the grains grown in the U.S.—to livestock animals, we steal the lives of Third World children who need that grain to survive. Approximately 40,000 children per day starve to death, while countless other children and adults remain severely malnourished. "If we use that amount of grain in order to make a piece of meat," writes Thich Nhat Hanh, "we waste a lot of food, and many people in the world are starving because of that way of eating."[84] Not only are available supplies of grain fed to animals, but large amounts of land in Third World countries, on which food could be grown to feed these starving people, are used to graze cattle for the West.

We also, in eating meat, steal resources on which the well-being, and possibly the lives, of our descendants and all other unborn beings depend. The resource-intensive nature of livestock agriculture puts at grave risk the future ability of the Earth to sustain life at all. For example, the primary reason that tropical rainforests—the planet's lungs—are being cut down is to create grazing land for livestock. If there were no demand for meat-eating, there would be much less profit in cutting down these forests, which are still, despite widespread public awareness, disappearing at an alarming rate.

Farmers and gardeners know that no food at all can be grown unless there is rich topsoil, an inch of which can take 100 years to be created. Yet because of the huge amounts of land that must be brought under cultivation in order to grow crops for livestock, that topsoil is being eroded away far faster than it can be created. Similarly, water from the great Ogallala aquifer, which underlies much of central North America, and which took millions of years to form, is being pumped out to irrigate livestock agriculture far faster than it can be replaced.

Because livestock are raised in concentrated "factory farm" facilities, massive amounts of their excrement accumulate in one place. As economic considerations make it unfeasible to spread these mountains of manure back onto the land, they are held in lagoons that may leak into rivers and streams, or overflow in times of heavy rainfall. The resulting high levels of nitrates in the water supply kill fish and other species and pose serious risks to human health. This contaminated water, as it continues through the hydrologic cycle, falls as acid rain, undermining the well-being of our remaining forests.

Livestock agriculture, the most environmentally destructive of all human activities, causes other damage as well. Overgrazing by cattle has ruined much formerly lush grassland in the western U.S. Cattle produce methane, which contributes to global warming, as does the increased amount of carbon dioxide produced due to the additional amounts of fossil fuel energy that must be used to bring meat, as compared to grains and vegetables, to market.

The Fifth Precept

The Fifth Precept is to refrain from intoxicants that lead to carelessness. These intoxicants have also been more broadly understood in recent times to include any food or idea we might take in that is toxic to our physical and mental well-being.[85] Based on current human mortality figures for Western—that is, heavily meat-eating—countries, meat qualifies as a toxic substance, and thus violates the practice of this precept. The diseases which kill the most people in Western countries, such as heart attacks, strokes, colon cancer, breast and prostate cancers, diabetes, and obesity, are all highest among populations which have high meat consumption. Conversely, vegetarians have been shown to live longer, with a better quality of life. In addition to degenerative diseases, there have been numerous cases of serious illness and death resulting from microorganisms found in meat: E.coli, salmonella, listeria, and so on. We now face something far more threatening even than these: the so-called "mad cow disease," which may take several decades to develop in humans, is always fatal, and cannot be prevented by cooking the infected meat.

The high cost of health insurance figures in here as well. Why does health care cost so much? Because so many people are sick. Why are they sick? Because to a large extent, even in Western countries in which most people could purchase the most wholesome food available, people still choose to pursue unhealthful lifestyles, to which meat-eating contributes substantially. When we eat meat, we increase our chances of contracting a disease that will be chronic and expensive to treat (for example, a heart bypass operation costs an average $45,000), and we drive up the cost of health care. High health care costs put pressure on our economy, taking funds away from other needed services, and drive the cost of health insurance so high that lower-income people cannot afford it. These people, who have no choice but to live without health insurance, are thus forced to risk being denied health care or to incur massive costs that can plunge them into debt for years. So for us to eat unhealthful foods and get sick, when we might have been healthy, is to take health care away from those who can least afford it.

Often people say that they eat only a little meat, and therefore are not at increased risk for the major killer diseases. In a similar situation concerning another toxic substance, alcohol, Thich Nhat Hanh was asked what is wrong with drinking two glasses of wine per week, since someone at this level of consumption will not incur health damage from the habit. He replied, "It's true that two glasses of wine do not harm you. But are you sure they do not harm your children?" He concluded by saying, "If you give up wine, you'll be doing it not only for yourself, but also for your children and for your society."[86] Regardless of the kind of consumption we participate in, our participation itself serves to encourage all those who observe our consumption to act likewise; in this way, we foster habits that, while we may manage them acceptably, may have painful and destructive results for others.

Right Livelihood

Meat-eating also necessitates the violation of another aspect of the Noble Eightfold Path: Right Livelihood. The five excluded livelihoods are the trading in weapons, human beings, animals for slaughter, alcohol, and poisons. Not raising animals for slaughter or trading in meat is clear; although most people who eat meat do not raise the animals, sell, or kill them. However, if these occupations are clearly specified by the Buddha to be harmful, ought we to live in a way that requires other people to engage in these livelihoods? If not, we cannot eat meat.

One type of livelihood related to providing our meat is often overlooked: that of meat packers. These workers, who have the highest injury rate of any factory workers,[87] must endure hellish conditions—they must stun, kill, and dismember mammals and birds, stand on floors covered with blood and grease, use very sharp tools at high rates of speed, and work in refrigerated environments, to give a partial description. It is usually the very poor, including recent immigrants, who must do our "dirty work" for low pay, yet we could free them all, and the animals as well, by simply changing our diets. "If slaughterhouses had glass walls," says longtime vegetarian Paul McCartney, "everyone would be vegetarian."[88]

An Animal Killed Especially for You

In addition to the Noble Eightfold Path, what other teachings of the Buddha bear on this subject? One of the most commonly cited is the Buddha's statement to his monks that it is acceptable to eat meat unless you suspect the animal was killed especially for you. First of all, we cannot be sure the Buddha actually said this, as several hundred years elapsed between his lifetime and the first written compilation of his teachings. One Buddhist author, Dr. Tony Page, asserts that the Buddha did say this, but that it has been mistranslated. Page quotes the Buddha's statement from the *Jivakasutta* as: "I, Jivaka, say that in three cases, meat may not be used: if it is seen, heard, suspected." He says the "killed especially for you" meaning is a later addition, and that what the Buddha meant is that meat may not be used if it is "seen, heard, suspected" *to be meat.* In other words, if a monk unknowingly eats food that contains meat, there is no fault in that, but if he suspects in any way that the food contains meat, he may not eat it. Immediately following the "seen, heard, suspected" teaching, the Buddha goes on to say that a monk should live with a mind filled with friendliness *(metta),* suffusing the whole world everywhere, in every way. "Would this attitude of loving kindness," asks Page, "be compatible with then supporting animal butchery?"[89]

Roshi Philip Kapleau, founder and retired director of the Rochester Zen Center, offers this comment:

> If the Buddha actually uttered the statements attributed to him, what they would mean effectively is that with the exception of a handful of persons who were offered meat from an animal killed just for them—and, of course, hunters, slaughterers, and fishermen—he freely sanctioned meat-eating for everyone, including his monks. Not only does this contention fly in the face of the first precept. . . it also implies that the Buddha approved of butchering and the horrors of the slaughterhouse. Yet slaughtering is one of the trades forbidden to Buddhists, and with good reason. To say on the one hand that the Buddha sanctioned flesh-eating in all cases except those already noted, and on the other that he condemned the bloody trades of slaughtering, hunting and trapping, not only denies the link between the two, it involves one in an absurd contradiction.[90]

On the other hand, what sense can we make of the "meat eating is OK unless the animal is killed especially for you" controversy if we assume the Buddha *did* make this statement? When taken in the context of the society and time period in which the Buddha lived, it may have actually saved the lives of animals.

Imagine a poor householder living at the time of the Buddha. He hears that the Buddha and his monks are coming to the area, and the householder wants to give them his best hospitality. His first impulse might be to have an animal killed so that he can offer meat to the monks. Because of the Buddha's rule that the monks will not eat any meat that was killed especially for them, however, the householder knows the monks would not eat such meat, and therefore does not have an animal killed. Thus the Buddha's rule has the effect of *sparing* the life of the animal that might otherwise have been killed.

Consider also how the process works in the different way we obtain meat today. If our householder, rather than going to a butcher to obtain meat for the monks, goes to a supermarket instead, he—and the monks to whom it will subsequently be served—can be assured that that animal was not killed especially for them. The animal—let's say it is a chicken—was dead long before the householder went to the supermarket, and whoever slaughtered that chicken had no idea who would ultimately eat it. Does this mean those who purchase meat at a market can have an easy conscience about being responsible for the killing of animals? Let's pursue this argument a step further.

Some hours after our householder goes to the supermarket and buys the chicken, the supermarket meat buyer is compiling an order for his supplier to restock the bin of chickens. He looks at his inventory printouts and notices that one has been sold—the one our householder bought—and so the buyer orders another one. It's that *second chicken* that *is* killed especially for our householder and his guests, because the foods we purchase determine that more of the same will appear in the market. If our householder had decided to prepare a tofu dish instead of meat, a supermarket buyer would order more tofu. So even though the chicken the householder actually bought was not killed especially for him, the *next* chicken to appear in the bin was.[91]

In modern society it is extremely difficult, in fact nearly impossible, to obtain or eat meat on a regular basis without an animal being killed especially for oneself. Perhaps if a person is walking through the forest, and just happens to be approached by a hunter who offers to give him freshly-killed meat, saying that the hunter has more meat than he could possibly eat—that might be a case in which meat not killed especially for oneself could be obtained, but how likely is that kind of scenario in our modern life? Yet thousands of Buddhist monks and laypeople justify meat-eating based on the "not killed especially for you" argument.

Other statements attributed to the Buddha are less ambiguous. In the *Surangama Sutra,* we read: "How can you eat the flesh of living beings and so pretend to be my disciple?"[92] The *Lankavatara Sutra* devotes an entire chapter to the subject of meat-eating, which includes these statements attributed to the Buddha: "For fear of causing terror to living beings, let the bodhisattva who is disciplining himself to attain compassion, refrain from eating flesh . . . ." It also contains this passionate proscription: "Meat-eating in any form, in any manner, and in any place is unconditionally and once and for all prohibited. . . . Meat-eating I have not permitted to anyone, I do not permit, I will not permit."[93]

Although by no means unanimous on the subject, Buddhist teachers today have made numerous statements against the practice of meat-eating and cruelty to animals. Robert Thurman, from the Tibetan tradition, has written, "Nonviolence against humans cannot take firm hold in a society as long as brutality and violence are practiced toward other animals."[94] The most prominent Tibetan teacher, the Dalai Lama, although not himself a vegetarian, has made pro-vegetarian statements over many years. Fully thirty-five years ago he wrote, "I do not see any reason why animals should be slaughtered to serve as human diet; there are so many substitutes. After all, man can live without meat."[95] He continues to speak out on the subject, as evidenced by this statement published in 2001: "In order to satisfy one human stomach, so many lives are taken away. We must promote vegetarianism. It is extremely important."[96] Contemporary vegetarian Buddhist teacher Thich Nhat Hanh has every monk and nun in his tradition vow "to be a vegetarian for the whole of my life."[97] Roshi Kapleau and his Dharma heir, Bodhin Kjolhede, are vegetarians as well.

Each Person Can Make a Difference

How can we move in dietary directions more in keeping with the practice of mindful consumption and compassion? Those who have not yet begun to explore vegetarian diets may feel overwhelmed at making basic changes in the foods they eat. People may feel that if they can't be completely vegetarian, there is no use in making any change at all. They might say, "I could never give up cheeseburgers" or "If I didn't eat the pot roast my mother serves when I visit, she would be terribly hurt." Even if you don't want to give up eating the occasional cheeseburger yet, or the meat that your mother prepares when you visit, it is extremely important that you do what you can. A gradual change may be best, perhaps just giving up one type of meat at first, then progressing to the next. Another approach is to have one meatless day per week, then two, and so on. Even small changes make a difference—choosing a bean burrito instead of a beef one, or a veggie pizza instead of a pepperoni one. Everyone can do something.

Many resources to support dietary change await your discovery. Find out whether your natural foods store offers vegetarian cooking classes. Learn which restaurants have vegetarian entrees. If there is a local vegetarian society where you live, attend one of their potlucks or other events. You don't have to be a vegetarian to get involved, and the more people you meet who support your compassionate diet, the more comfortable you'll feel. If you can't find people in your area to talk to about reducing meat consumption you can communicate with vegetarians online. A number of helpful books and websites may be found in the Resources list below.

When we bring mindfulness to the dinner table, it suffuses the rest of our life as well. We become more sensitive to the well-being of animals, of the environment, and of ourselves and our families. We are more aware of the choices we make in all areas of our life. We enjoy food more, knowing that, while the obtaining of even plant foods necessitates some suffering, the amount and kind of suffering is dramatically reduced when we leave meat off our shopping lists and out of our kitchens. We become more aware of how meat consumption feeds violence and anger. "We should learn to eat in such a way that compassion can remain in our hearts. Otherwise, we will suffer and we will make ourselves and all species around us suffer deeply."[98]

Those nine billion animals who are killed each year are killed because consumers demand that amount of meat. If consumers cut back their meat consumption, fewer animals will be killed. If consumers eliminate meat consumption entirely, the operation of slaughterhouses—and all the suffering and devastation of meat production and consumption—can be permanently brought to an end. The breeding and torturing of animals for slaughter will stop, forests and grasslands vibrant with wildlife will flourish, the human food supply will increase to an amount sufficient for all, the quality of air, water, and human health will improve dramatically, and with renewed life energy we can turn our attention to other ways to reduce the suffering of all sentient beings and of the Earth.

Resources to Support Dietary Change

BOOKS ON THE ISSUES

Akers, Keith, *A Vegetarian Sourcebook*. Denver, CO: Vegetarian Press, 1993.

Melina, Vesanto, R.D. and Brenda Davis, R.D., *Becoming Vegetarian*. Summertown, TN: Book Publishing, 1995.

Robbins, John, *The Food Revolution*. Berkeley, CA: Conari Press, 2001.

Singer, Peter, *Animal Liberation*. New York: Avon Books, 1977; reprinted by Ecco Press, 2001.

VEGETARIAN COOKBOOKS

McDougall, John and Mary McDougall, *The McDougall Quick and Easy Cookbook*. New York: Penguin Putnam, 1999.

Raymond, Jennifer, *The Peaceful Palate: Fine Vegetarian Cuisine*. Summertown, TN: Book Publishing, 1996.

Robertson, Laurel et al., *The New Laurel's Kitchen*. Berkeley, CA: Ten Speed Press, 1986.

Stepaniak, Joanne, *Table for Two*. Summertown, TN: Book Publishing, 1996.

Wasserman, Debra, and Charles Stahler, *Meatless Meals for Working People*. Baltimore: Vegetarian Resource Group, 2001 (3rd ed.).

WEBSITES

Society of Ethical and Religious Vegetarians <http://www.serv-online.org>

Vegetarian Resource Group <http://www.vrg.org>

VegSource <http://www.vegsource.com>

Sustainable Living

by Colin Moore

THERE ARE MANY different responses to the pressing ecological and human disasters that beset humanity in the new century. Protesters of globalization in Genoa and elsewhere, whether peaceful or violent represent only some of the most vocal. Differing perceptions of the ecological crises and the causes generate different responses. At the "shallow" end there is the short-term, superficial reformist approach such as many kinds of conservation and the "greening" of our major political parties and businesses. Some of the violent disruptions of the kind we have seen recently would also have to be considered superficial. At the "deep" end there are the long-term responses which involve a thoughtful critique of the dominant worldview and which involve changed behaviors in our daily lives that generate harmony with all that lives. Peaceful protests could fall into this category.

While reforms and short-term responses are beneficial, there is a growing awareness that they are not enough. The roots of the problem, of which the environmental crisis is but a symptom, must be understood. Without this understanding, our actions will only exacerbate the problems. This deeper understanding, once cultivated, will inform our actions (or non-actions) by putting them on the firm foundation of being motivated by universal compassion, universal responsibility, and wisdom.

Let's explore further how Buddhist teachings can shed light on the various ecological and social disasters looming ahead, and how they might aid our responses to them. The Dharma could be described as the "laws of nature" or things as they are. These teachings, according to senior Tibetan teacher Tai Situ Rinpoche, "are a coherent and detailed description of perceived reality which clearly indicates moral codes regarding our relationships with all life forms and includes a strong sense of individual and social responsibility."[99]

Prince Siddhartha took an ancient *ayurvedic* diagnostic tool usually applied to illness and then radically applied it to life itself. He was concerned, as are all modern people, with the deep existential questions such as "How can I live my life happily and beneficially in the midst of the difficulties and uncertainties of life?" He asked the essential questions: What is the sickness? What are the causes of the sickness? Is there a cure? What are the elements of the cure? The Buddha produced a startling and detailed analysis of all our ills and their causes as well as solutions to them. Like a doctor, he diagnosed the greater illness and then offered the most comprehensive remedy. His medicine was the Four Noble Truths. Dukkha (that disatisfaction which is to be known deeply), the causes of dukkha (that dissatisfaction which is to be let go of), the ending of dukkha (that which is to be realized), and the paths to the ending of dukkha (that which is to be cultivated).

Buddhism has always adapted to the particular culture into which it has traveled, but in order for it to remain a living tradition in the twenty-first century and the emergent global consumer culture, it must address the existential questions that concern us today. While much of what causes people to suffer has not changed since the time of the Buddha—there is still birth, old age, sickness, and death—new factors must be taken into account, such as the systemic ecological problems that have the potential to terminate all forms of life.

Looking closely at the First Noble Truth, the Truth of Suffering (that dissatisfaction which is to be known deeply) we see that all beings in conditioned existence, from the largest to the smallest, from the most powerful to the weakest, seek happiness, peace, comfort, and security. They do not wish to suffer and, holding their own life dear, do not wish to die. We also learn that all beings do not find permanent happiness, peace, comfort, or security and do in fact suffer and die. The First Noble Truth is a bold statement of fact: there is suffering in conditioned existence and we must face the situation squarely before we can begin to deal with it. To try to escape from it, deny it, ignore it or indulge in despair is to miss what it can teach us about ourselves and our situation. Denial of a problem is a common problem, as any doctor or psychotherapist will tell you.

This tendency to be in denial with respect to the ecological crisis is a major obstacle. Many people would rather not face the seriousness or magnitude of the situation, nor do they have much compelling exposure to it. Preferring to escape by endlessly distracting and entertaining themselves or even flatly denying the problem and their responsibility for it, they maintain a "business as usual" attitude. After the Titanic hit the iceberg people continued to dance, believing that the ship was unsinkable, despite the sensory evidence of disaster all around them! If such a dramatic example of changing circumstances can be ignored, imagine how easy it is to deny a problem when the more subtle changes—and the suffering they cause—happen at a much slower pace, often over generations!

The Buddha stressed the urgency for change saying that the human situation is like a man whose house is on fire. What was true for the individual then is becoming increasingly true for our collective existence today. Even a superficial investigation into the causes of the crisis, as called for by the Second Noble Truth, will reveal that the collective behavior of humanity and the impact it is having on living systems is the cause. The Earth is under tremendous stress, and we are clearly overstepping the limits of her life-support systems to cleanse and balance the pollution and preserve nature as we know it in all its beauty and diversity. Meanwhile the consumer society with its dire attendant social and ecological impact goes largely unquestioned and mostly unchallenged.

The Third Noble Truth reassures us that a cure is possible, that we can arrive at an awakened plenitude not only for ourselves but more importantly for all beings. As Tai Situ Rinpoche put it, we can fully awaken to the "perfect embodiment of universal wisdom, great compassionate love and personal power to help whomever is open to that help."[100] So in our analysis of the ecological crisis we need to recognize that a cure to ecological ills is possible. Indeed in some ways this has already been revealed by the Gaia Hypothesis which states that the Earth is a self-regulating organism which always tends towards balance and harmony. The problem is that Gaia may just harmonize humans right out of the picture! So from the human perspective we need to look at how we can live on the Earth in a way which will sustain and support all living systems. But by identifying ourselves more with Gaia than as individual consumers, we will be less motivated by fear of our own impermanence as a species, and able to fully respond to the situation we face from a place of deep connectivity.

Buddhism can be a big help in this regard because it trains us in a habitual attitude of reverence towards all life. The teachings counsel us that we are not really separate from all beings and that the happiness we all seek lies, ultimately, in the happiness of all beings. This is the Fourth Noble Truth in its essence: the path that must be cultivated. By training our minds in the six *paramitas*—

or perfections—our being literally becomes the path, and all our actions spontaneously shift from being part of the problem to being part of the solution.

The first of the paramitas is generosity, which can also be translated as liberality or openness. This has many aspects to it but can involve the giving of resources, shelter, comfort, space, help, and so on, at a very practical and physical level. It can also be the willingness to "hear the cries of the world" and to respond with wisdom and compassion. Ultimately it is the recognition that one is not a separate "skin enclosed ego," that there is no inherent "self" or "other," no "giver," no "gift," and "no one who receives."

The second paramita, right conduct or ethics, is not to kill, cheat or steal, to avoid unwholesome actions and to develop wholesome attitudes. Ultimately it is to practice restraining selfishness and to find positive ways in which to support the welfare of all sentient beings. Right livelihood is a key aspect of this. In his book *Small Is Beautiful,* E.F. Schumacher said that "Buddhist economics must be very different from the economics of modern materialism, since the Buddhist sees the essence of civilization not in a multiplication of wants, but in the purification of the human character."[101] Right conduct means noninvolvement with those activities that contribute to the suffering of the world. They require one "to live simply so that others might simply live!" Such a lifestyle would be, as Bill Devall said, "simple in means but rich in ends." Although we would consume less, we would be happier knowing that our lives are in harmony with all living systems.

The third paramita is forbearance, which is also described as patience—the opposite of anger. Ultimately it is to have more patience than the mountains and rivers themselves, indeed than Gaia herself. It is to have the patience of the Dharmakaya. The problems we face are vast, endless, complex, daunting. . . without patience, the game is up before it begins.

The fourth paramita counsels us to be strenuous, energetic, and persevering in our efforts. It is one thing to overcome our own denial, take responsibility for the problems, and become part of the solution. It continues to be challenging to live in a society where most people are clearly not doing this.

The fifth paramita highlights the practice of meditation so that we may attain concentration and oneness in order to serve all beings (a.k.a. our true self). It involves perfecting a stable, peaceful mind that is able to concentrate and develop penetrating insight. Thus we can begin to free ourselves from the tendency of the mind to become scattered through the push and pull of craving and aversion and take rest in equanimity. From this firm foundation of a peaceful mind we are able to investigate all the other mental states in ourselves and others so that we can free ourselves from the suffering of conditioned existence.

The *prajña* paramita, or sixth paramita is our ability to rest in this wisdom, and in so doing, give benefit to others. Just as a smile is infectious, and causes delight in others, so, much more powerfully, our wisdom and compassion shine like a warm and tender light on those around us, and our very being becomes a gift to others.

The practices in the *Vajrayana* are powerful "skillful means" which rapidly develop and mature the mind. It is said that they are particularly suitable for this time in history because the present global crisis is itself like a tantric teaching. The tremendously powerful delusions that keep us locked into a destructive way of life and produce great suffering individually and globally are supported by social structures and institutions that are based on values inimical to sustainable living. Beliefs in ideas such as the existence of value-free (objective) knowledge, unlimited progress, and growth, coupled with an attachment to individual freedom without corresponding responsibilities have eroded the moral values of our ancestral religions. Secular society gropes for values with which to deal with the maze of moral problems confronting it. Buddhism is favorably placed to offer tools for transformation to a secular society because it does not rely on belief but rather on experience gained from inquiry and insight.

I once asked Ringu Tulku Rinpoche how to deal with the enormity of what we may be facing. His simple answer impressed me deeply. If you do your best and the situation is turned around then that is good and there will be good fruits of those actions. But, he said, if you do your best and the situation is not turned around then that is still good and there will still be good fruits of those actions. We will never know if it is enough. Motivation and intention is everything. The outcome is out of our hands.

Vinaya: A Modern Buddhist's Guide to Global Consumer Culture

by Santikaro Bhikkhu

VINAYA is a term well-known in Buddhist countries as the discipline or extensive set of rules that nuns and monks follow, or are supposed to follow. In this essay, I will explore the meaning and importance of vinaya more broadly within Buddhist tradition, emphasizing its applicability today within Western consumer societies among "convert Buddhists" coping with modernity and postmodernity, and in traditional Buddhist societies among those who are struggling to come to terms with rapid modernizing change.

Understanding vinaya as merely a set of rules, some of them legalistic or out-of-date, if not downright sexist, is not quite right. While the individual trainings can be seen as rules that monastics should follow, they are always expressions of deeper principles. Blindly following "rules" can never be the Buddha's liberating way and can even put one into conflict with the Dhamma, for it is merely one of the Ten Fetters that bind us to cyclic existence.

The cultural soil in the developed West is obviously different from that of Southeast Asia, China, and Tibet when Buddhism first entered those regions. The West no longer has the village-centered cultures, agrarian economies, and feudal politics that nurtured Asian Buddhism since its inception. Educated laypeople in the West have more overt teaching and leadership roles within Buddhist groups, yet generally lack the unwritten vinaya of Asian Buddhist tradition. What they do have is often drawn more from Judeo-Christian, Greco-Roman, and modernist traditions.

Understanding what has previously occurred in Asia is necessary for Western Buddhists seeking the way through modernity. On the other hand, Asian Buddhists need to understand how vinaya has been trivialized (superficialized) so that this can be corrected in order to better adapt the ancient vinaya tradition to the complicated changes that are transforming all Asian societies and the Buddhist institutions within them, even while the monastic hierarchies try to stick their heads in the sands of the past.

In order to reappraise the meaning, purpose, and value of vinaya, especially in modern and postmodern times, it is worth recalling that the Buddha himself spoke more often of "this *Dhamma-vinaya*" than of his "message, teaching, or religion." The Buddha encouraged a way of looking into life and consequently living life that he claimed, from his own experience, leads to the quenching of suffering.

Dhamma can be compared to the flesh of a sweet, naturally ripened mango. It is very rich and succulent, delightful and delicious, refreshing and nutritious. Yet, no mango would produce its sweet inner flesh without a skin. The skin provides protection for the growing seed and flesh, and structure that helps them take shape. The role of the mango's skin is akin to the role vinaya plays in relation to Dhamma. Just as no sweet mango flesh develops without the requisite skin, the Dhamma cannot flourish without an appropriate vinaya. And just as a mango skin without flesh inside is neither appetizing nor nourishing, vinaya without Dhamma is not Buddhism.

The ultimate meaning and purpose of vinaya is to lead us out from under or remove the power of negativity and positivity, that is, the power of ignorance, craving, clinging, and their resultant greed, anger, and delusion. The fundamental operative principle that gets us to the heart of vinaya is non-harming. This principle is inseparable from the natural law of conditionality, interdependence, and interrelatedness that governs all of nature. Because our lives are fundamentally interwoven with the lives of other sentient beings, and because we all seek happiness and want to avoid suffering, non-harming is the best principle on which to base moral and behavioral standards.

The most common expression of vinaya is the Five Precepts. These amount to five fundamental aspects of non-harming that are the minimum required for healthy relationships in this world and to support any aspiration towards universal kindness and world peace. Further, the various monastic vinayas all derive from these and, ultimately, the single "precept" of non-harming. Understood in this light, vinaya and *sila* (ethics or morality), whatever the formulation, are expressions of the wisdom that sees the world as it is and the compassion that motivates us to live in it without causing suffering.

If we reflect on the examples of monks and nuns in the Buddha's time, we see that the original vinaya was unwritten and customary. It was based on the *samana* lifestyle that developed in the Ganges valley in the century or two before the Buddha's Great Awakening. When Prince Siddhartha left home and ordained himself by "going forth" as a *bhikkhu*, he joined this broad movement, in which a number of lifestyle customs and practices were developed to support the spiritual pursuits of the various groups of ascetics, wanderers, and monks. Further, it is crucial to note that these customs and practices made sense within and were therefore supported by the culture of the Ganges valley.

Vinaya is thus, in its essence, the lifestyle of a Buddhist: the way serious practitioners arrange, organize, and structure their lives in order to support Dhamma study, practice, service, and realization. This covers all physical and verbal actions. It involves all forms of relationships: interpersonal, social, economic, political, ecological, as well as with one's own body. It is "status neutral"; it applies equally to all mature students of Buddha Dhamma: to lays and monastics, men and women, and can even apply to children. This is crucial for those of us who seek a less hierarchical, more egalitarian understanding of Buddhist life and practice.

In order to fulfill the egalitarian vision that appeals to many modern Buddhists, all practitioners must adhere to an equally high standard. We don't want first- and second-class Buddhists; therefore, we can't have first- and second-class standards. If Dhamma-vinaya is an inseparable whole, access to higher teachings and practices previously limited to monastics requires parallel commitment to higher vinaya standards. Such standards need not mimic those of monastics in their details, but should uphold the same high standards. Otherwise, sloppiness around money, sex, and power, plus other areas delineated below, will corrupt those teachings and practices. Everyone involved will be harmed, not least those who are careless about this requirement. Higher practices such as *Vipassana, Dzogchen,* and Tantra will become hollow without the protection of suitable vinaya. This ancient principle still applies no matter how postmodern we become.

It is useful to look at vinaya as a partnership among all Buddhists that encompasses a diversity of lifestyles. We can learn from each other, especially in today's complex societies in which laypeople usually have much more hands-on experience with the economic, political, and technological systems. This also gives us a powerful tool of social critique. Rather than follow the mainstream of consumer self-indulgence, and the rat race toward a superficial Western version of success, Buddhist practitioners can more easily live out an alternative based on their aspiration for spiritual liberation and the "natural discipline" that this aspiration calls forth. Such a critique will be flexible rather than doctrinaire in order to serve the many living and working situations in which modern Buddhists find themselves. Yet, it can provide concrete standards with which to challenge society in order to flesh out the abstract virtues that Buddhism is pointing to.

There are various dimensions to the vinaya, and they overlap to some extent —just as the path is woven of many factors—but we can clearly distinguish some areas that have potentially important impact on our modern lives as consumers in a global marketplace. In what follows, I offer preliminary explorations of some that strike me as most crucial.

Whether or not we are in "positions of power" or have truly given up political, economic, sexual, and other forms of power as in the original bhikkhu ideal, we do not escape power and authority. Recognizing and respecting how these prop up the ego's illusions of security and strength in other ways, and again noting the violence that so often comes out of this posture, we should relinquish political and social control over others. Honestly observing that most institutions, including religious ones, create their own hierarchies of privilege and power, we ought to disavow such corruption and share whatever authority is given to us. Certain hierarchies may occur naturally and need not cause suffering. For example, our study and practice may give us a certain amount of authority among our co-practitioners and students, so we do what we can to exercise this authority honestly, openly, and Dhammically. The same applies to any moral authority that our lifestyle generates.

As a consumer, we can be seen as having a certain power over others who are engaged in the supply of materials and services to us. "Consumer," a term enshrined in law in many Western nations, denotes a person who, presumably, gets more than he gives. People acting in the role of consumers can become impatient and demanding. This deterioration of kindness and consideration is one of the most insidious blights on our karma—when our "rights" as consumers overshadow our responsibilities to each other as human beings and students of the Dhamma.

Recognizing that we all have basic material needs, we resolve to satisfy them without putting loathsome burdens on the planet or society. We are mindful of how our own accumulation can work to deprive others. We practice sharing the resources that come our way and cultivate a spirit of *dana* (generosity). Especially in societies that hold personal property to be sacred, we vow to acknowledge that we are merely stewards.

Monastics make themselves vulnerable by depending on alms, that is, the generosity of others. In return, they try to share as much of their material gains as they can realistically do, in addition to the fruits of their spiritual study and practice. The situation is not so different for laypeople as is generally assumed. Though food and other requisites may be purchased with cash or plastic, they were produced by farmers and workers, packaged and shipped by others, and retailed by shopkeepers and supermarket employees. Nothing comes to us without the benevolence of others. Dhamma students should regularly reflect on this and act accordingly.

In addition to basic human needs, we seek and acquire things in order to achieve and proclaim status, generate comfort and luxury, entertain and distract ourselves, cover up loneliness, and seek to gratify other emotions that have nothing to do with the material object involved. Nowadays, consumer capitalism—the engine of globalization—is based on these unhealthy non-necessities or false needs. They increasingly provide the meaning and purpose of our lives, thus determining "who" we are. It is very hard to live without lots of "stuff" if we live in the affluent segments of the world; we receive gifts with birthdays and other passages of life. Noting how much fighting goes on in the world, throughout human history, over limited material resources, we are wise to explore a life of simplicity wherein we are very careful about what we own and tend towards less rather than more. We might ask ourselves: How do we keep things from cluttering up our lives and minds? What purpose do they serve? How do we take responsibility for them without owning or being owned by them?

We recognize and respect how the accumulation of property, money, and wealth seems to provide the security the ego craves. We are mindful of how these bits of paper, metal, and plastic, as well as numbers on a screen, symbolize success, prestige, power, and all the other worldly values that ordinary folks aspire to. We even use it to measure the value of human beings. The illusory power of money easily cultivates the arrogance that overlooks how much we depend on the kindness of others. Given the power of this strange, symbolic—supposedly neutral—stuff, we will want to ask ourselves: How can it be handled mindfully? What is right investment? Which Dhamma related services can be charged for legitimately and which not? What is the real meaning of "dana"?

Tools are one of the things that make us human. We often measure our "development" in terms of the supposedly "can't turn back the clock" advance of technological wonders. We are awed by these gadgets and correspondingly honor the scientists, engineers, and other techno-priests that produce them. With the harnessing of coal and steam, petroleum fuels, nuclear power, and electronics, we have become mighty indeed. Consequently, other species and pristine ecosystems have vanished. Human life has been hugely transformed. Liberated from the natural rhythms of the seasons and the sun's daily cycle, we have increasingly less free time. Even if we don't have more stress than in the ancient past, we surely have new forms of stress that our biology was not evolved to handle. Increasingly, technology has become an interface between ourselves and others (e.g., telephone), and between our own bodies and minds (e.g., medical scanning equipment).

Computer technology, including email and the Internet, can be a useful tool for our Dhamma study and work, whether researching relevant topics, producing books and other teaching media, or communicating with mentors, peers, and students. At the same time, it provides access to vast and practically limitless worlds of data, entertainment, distraction, and delusion. Some of us may choose to do without such technology altogether, partly to show that happiness is still possible in this life without Internet access.

Most of this technology was developed originally for military applications, offensive as much as defensive. It then trickled down to other scientists and the business world. By the time it got to consumers, it was driven more by the profit motive than the fighting instinct. Nonetheless, both are highly aggressive. Do we know who or what controls these hugely complex systems? Can we know who or what is monitoring our use? Is it the fabled "marketplace," corporate boardrooms, or some cabal of military bureaucrats?

To what degree is it possible to use this technology in service of Dhamma? We can't just wave a few mantras like *"Om Mani Padme Hum"* over our keyboards to make the whole system clean. Those who choose to use such technology should reflect on what they might be giving up or missing by using this technology. Consumers of hi-tech tools might ask themselves: Is my physical health in any way harmed by use of this technology? Do the benefits accrued by using this technology justify the psychological, financial, and environmental costs?

Every time you boot up, think of the oil spills, salmon kills in hydroelectric dams, and other costs of all the electricity coursing through these global systems. Whenever the urge to upgrade strikes, remember the piles of junk plastic, silicon, chips, monitors, cords, and CDs that accumulate with each new upgrade.

Consuming technology comes into play with all the topics discussed here: power, wealth, communications, and even sex. How can we use these wonderful tools without being used by them? How do we insure that they serve spiritual needs, rather than merely economic or political ends?

A good laugh now and again, mirth, creativity, and the like can be used to support our practice and realization, or to hinder them. Most of society humors itself with meaningless entertainment. How do we behave as consumers or providers of entertainment? How much do we depend on technology for this? How much do we let the content of our entertainment shape our values and behaviors in conscious or unconscious ways? By seeking entertainment to "relax," do we become more tense by internalizing negative values and behaviors we observe in the entertainment? What really makes us relaxed? Do we neglect our families or the people we live with because we're too caught up in entertainment?

The rapid expansion of human populations has forced us to become aware of how we perturb other species and of the inability of technology to free us from dependence on the rest of the natural world. Slowly, we are relearning— after centuries of scientific hubris—how to fit in with other life forms within healthy ecosystems. Buddhists should not be surprised that the principle of non-harming applies directly here. Yet, the lifestyle choices implied by this awareness are profound. Only a true commitment to the welfare of all beings will empower us to make the necessary changes. If the Buddha were alive today, based on the complaints of concerned laypeople, he would set up monastic precepts regarding recycling, reducing consumption, car-pooling, taking public transport, etc. Many people may consider themselves ecologically concerned when it comes to the acts of multinational corporations, but hesitate when it comes to cutting back in their own lives.

It goes without saying that this approach of self-reflection in relation to the principles underlying the vinaya will only work with sincere, honest, committed students. We've already considered the drawbacks of rules. When there is no easy solution, we fall back on the only one that works—practice and skillful means. If somebody is visiting porn sites on the Internet or spending hours browsing inanely, something unhappy is at work in him or her. The solution isn't just to say, "Don't look at porn" or "Don't waste your time." The person must understand what's going on inside her or his mind.

Serious Dhamma students will need to observe and analyze the forces in their lives that can obstruct Dhamma practice. As things are so complex these days, everyone can benefit from the experiences, insights, and perspectives of other Dhamma students. As the obstacles become clearer, lifestyle choices can be found to neutralize each obstacle. Some lifestyle practices will help with more than one problem. This will involve experimentation which, again, is better done with the help of others. There will be ongoing monitoring and evaluation. Finally, group support will help us stick to the choices we have made, even in the face of the mainstream culture's materialism, individualism, and self-indulgence.

Dhamma-vinaya is always a dialogue between the texts that we cherish and our daily practice of what they teach, as well as between tradition and present reality. To support practical evaluation, here are some questions for reflection:

> What is the effect on one's own health?
> What is the effect on one's family and loved ones?
> What is the effect on one's work and workplace?
> What is the effect on one's community, neighborhood, and social groups?
> What is the effect on one's ecosystems — local, bioregional, national,
>   and global?
> What is the effect on one's Dhamma practice?

I hope that this essay contributes something to the necessary hard, creative work that lies before us and for many generations to come in the application of the vinaya to the vicissitudes of modern living.

Personal Planetary Practices

by Allan Hunt Badiner, John Seed, and Ruth Rosenhek

PERSONAL PLANETARY PRACTICES (PPP) are not rules, regulations, or commandments. Their purpose is to provoke thought, discussion, and change.

John Seed, Ruth Rosenhek, and Allan Hunt Badiner were sitting around in Andre Carother's Berkeley kitchen early in the summer of 1998. We noticed a paper sticker on the kitchen table that read: "every dollar is a vote. . . spend it wisely." This prompted a discussion about how one's personal awareness of the planetary crisis might most appropriately manifest in terms of being a consumer. What set of personal practices in the marketplace of modern life would, if widely adopted, further the goals of achieving ecological sustainability and social justice — not just by what we avoid, but also by what we choose to purchase?

We considered carefully which actions or agreements could make the most difference without being too personally sacrificial or impractical. PPP may represent a kind of consumer baseline for ecological activists and we offer them to you for discussion in the hope that you will share them with others for their consideration.

1) Aware of the unprecedented rates of destruction of our ancient forests, we are committed to avoid the purchase of any products that we suspect originate from old-growth forests anywhere in the world.

2) Aware of the damage to the natural systems of the Earth and the suffering inflicted on animal species from a meat-based diet, we are committed to avoid the purchase and consumption of animal products.

3) Aware of the pressures on living systems and indigenous communities created by mining the land for gold, we are committed to devalue gold and avoid the purchase of jewelry containing gold.

4) Aware of the benefits to the Earth and to the consumer of the use of clothing made from hemp or organic cotton, we are committed to avoid the purchase of clothing, paper, or personal accessories that do not contain natural or recycled fibers, hemp, organic cotton, or 100 percent post-consumer waste.

5) Aware of the peril to the Earth and all of its inhabitants from the use of toxic chemical fertilizers, pesticides, and herbicides, we are committed to avoid the purchase of food and beverage products that are not certified and labeled organic.

6) Aware of the growing threat to the vitality of the Earth from reliance on petrochemicals, petroleum products, nuclear power, and fossil fuels, we are committed to purchasing those products or systems that utilize sustainable or less polluting sources of energy such as solar, wind, biogas, water, hydrogen, or electricity.

7) Aware of the continuing destruction caused by capital that is trapped in unsustainable industries and economies, we are committed to make socially- and ecologically-screened investments.

8) Aware of the personal and social consequences of having a news and entertainment media saturated with images of violence and sexual oppression, we are committed to avoiding the consumption of cultural products containing violent and sexually exploitative materials.

Endnotes

1 See, for example, Paul Hawken, Amory Lovins, and Hunter Lovins, *Natural Capitalism* (New York: Little Brown, 1999).

2 See David Suzuki, "Technology & Globalization" (paper presented at the International Forum on Globalization, New York City, February 2001).

3 See Ignacio Ramonet, "The Control of Pleasure," *Le Monde Diplomatique,* May 2000.

4 See David Gilmore, *Manhood in the Making* (New Haven, CT: Yale University Press, 1990).

5 Ibid., p. 229.

6 Ibid., p. 110.

7 See Fritjof Capra, *The Turning Point* (New York: Simon & Schuster, 1982), p. 36ff.

8 See Fritjof Capra, *The Web of Life* (New York: Anchor/Doubleday, 1996), p. 3ff.

9 See Charlene Spretnak, ed., *The Politics of Women's Spirituality* (New York: Anchor/Doubleday, 1981).

10 See David Suzuki and Holly Dressel, *From Naked Ape to Superspecies* (Toronto: Stoddart, 1999), pp. 263–264.

11 Dalai Lama, keynote address (presented at Forum 2000, Prague, October 15–18, 2000).

12 Mary Ellen Cardella, "School to Work, A Corporate Raid on Public Education," *Z Magazine,* October 1996. The complete article is available at <http://www.zmag.org/ZMag/articles/oct96cardella.htm>

13 See David Edwards, *Free to Be Human: Intellectual Self-Defence in an Age of Illusions* (Totnes, U.K.: Green Books, 1995).

14 Ibid.

15 See Stephen Batchelor, *Buddhism Without Beliefs: A Contemporary Guide to Awakening* (New York: Riverhead Books, 1997), p. 112.

16 See Riane Eisler, *The Chalice and the Blade* (New York: Harper & Row, 1987) and Min Jiayin, ed., *The Chalice and the Blade in Chinese Culture* (Beijing: China Social Sciences Publishing House, 1995).

17 A brilliant video on this is "Advertising and the End of the World," available from the Media Education Foundation.

18 For a movie on the investigator who took on PG&E, see *Erin Brockovich,* starring Julia Roberts. For another expose on how giant oil companies kept denying their toxins-emitting storage plants were poisoning people living near them, see Jim Hightower, *There's Nothing in the Middle of the Road but Yellow Stripes and Dead Armadillos* (New York: Harper Collins, 1998), pp. 177–181.

19 Ven. S. Dhammika, comp. and trans., "Gemstones of the Good Dhamma (Saddhamma-maniratana): An Anthology of Verses from the Pali Scripture," *The Wheel* 342/344 (1987), saying #59.

20 Riane Eisler, David Loye, and Kari Norgaard, *Women, Men, and the Global Quality of Life* (Pacific Grove, CA: Center for Partnership Studies, 1995).

21 Pali Canon, M.I.10; Nd. 496.

22 Pali Canon, D.III.214; A.I.50; Dhs. 8, 234.

23 See *Economics '73–'74* (Guildford, CT: The Dushkin Publishing Group, 1973).

24 Pali Canon, A.I.30.

25 Pali Canon, Vin.I.9; S.V.421; Vbh.99.

26 See Stephen Batchelor, *Buddhism Without Beliefs,* p. 112.

27 Trevor Ling, *The Buddha: Buddhist Civilisation in India and Ceylon* (London: Wildwood House, 1973), p. 67.

28 Ibid., p. 68.

29 "Robin Cook's Speech on the Government's Ethical Foreign Policy," quoted in *The Guardian* (Manchester, U.K.), 12 May 1997.

30 Quoted ibid.

31 Michael E. Baroody, Executive Vice President, NAM, Letter to the President Concerning the Kyoto Protocol, May 16, 2001. The letter can be viewed at <http://www.nam.org>

32 *The Guardian,* 10 January 1997.

33 The Buddha. Quoted in Eknath Easwaran, trans., *The Dhammapada* (Berkeley, CA: Nilgiri Press, 1985), p. 167.

34 Aryasura, *The Marvellous Companion* (Berkeley, CA: Dharma Publishing, 1983), p. 99.

35 Ibid., p. 102.

36 Ibid., p. 103.

37 Ibid., p. 103.

38 Ibid., p. 103.

39 <http://www.adbusters.org>

40 See David Arnott, "Sri Lanka — Victim of a Deep Colonialism" (unpublished paper, 1984).

41 See Robert Chambers, *Whose Reality Counts?* (London: Intermediate Technology, 1997), pp. 178–179.

42 See Colin Stoneman, "The World Bank and the IMF in Zimbabwe," in Campbell and Loxley, eds., *Structural Adjustment in Africa* (New York: St. Martin's Press, 1989).

43 See Catherine Caufield, *Masters of Illusion: The World Bank and the Poverty of Nations* (London: Macmillan, 1996), p. 159.

44 Karl Polanyi, *The Great Transformation: The Political and Economic Origins of Our Time* (Boston: Beacon Press, 1957), pp. 46 and 57.

45 See David Little, "Ethical Analysis and Wealth in Theravada Buddhism," in *Ethics, Wealth, and Salvation: A Study in Buddhist Social Ethics* (Columbia, SC: University of South Carolina Press, 1993), pp. 77–86.

46 *Anguttara Nikaya* V, iv, 31.

47 See Frank Reynolds, "Ethics and Wealth in Theravada Buddhism: A Study in Comparative Religious Ethics," in *Ethics, Wealth, and Salvation.*

48 *Majjhima Nikaya*, Sutta No. 99.

49 See Frank Reynolds, "Ethics and Wealth in Theravada Buddhism: A Study in Comparative Religious Ethics."

50 See Winston L. King, *In the Hope of Nibbana* (LaSalle, IL: Open Court, 1964).

51 See Richard A. Gard, *Buddhism* (New York: George Braziller, 1962).

52 See N.A. Nikam and Richard McKeon, eds., *The Edicts of Asoka* (Chicago: University of Chicago Press, 1966).

53 Ibid.

54 Bhikkhu Buddhadasa, *Dhammic Socialism,* translated and edited by Donald K. Swearer (Bangkok: Thai Inter Religious Commission for Development, 1986).

55 See George Santayana, *Character and Opinion of the United States* (New Brunswick, NJ: Transaction Publications, 1920, 1999).

56 See "A Question of Skill: An Interview with Thanissaro Bhikkhu," *Insight Magazine Online,* <http://www.urbandharma.org/udharma3/interview1.html>

57 See Milan Kundera, *The Book of Laughter and Forgetting* (reprint, New York: Harper Perennial, 1999).

58 *Knight Ridder Washington Bureau,* 24 June 2001.

59 See Cheryl Stonehouse, "The Evil Slave Traders Who Deal in Misery so You Can Eat Chocolate," *Daily Express* (Malaysia),7 September 2000.

60 See Sumana Chatterjee, "Chocolate Industry Accepts Responsibility for Child Labor Practices," *San Jose Mercury News,* 1 October 2001.

61 See Bob Fernandez, "Hershey 'Shocked' by Possibility of Products Tainted by Slave Labor," *Philadelphia Inquirer,* 24 June 2001.

62 See <http://www.chocolatebar.com/aboutourchocolate/>

63 See <http://www.dagobachocolate.com/>

64 See <http://globalexchange.org/economy/coffee/>

65 See <http://www.freetheslaves.net/>

66 See Daniel R. Faber and Deborah McCarthy, *Green of Another Color* (Boston, MA: Northeastern University, 2001), p. 2.

67 Ibid.

68 See M.K. Gandhi, *Ashram Observances in Action* (Canton, ME: Greenleaf Books, 1983), p. 24.

69 See Sulak Sivaraksa, "Buddhists in a World of Change," in Fred Eppsteiner, ed., *The Path of Compassion: Writings on Socially Engaged Buddhism* (Berkeley, CA: Parallax Press, 1988), p. 17.

70 See Duane Elgin, *Voluntary Simplicity: Toward a Way of Life that Is Outwardly Simple, Inwardly Rich,* Revised Edition (New York: Quill/William Morrow & Co., 1993).

71 See Arnold J. Toynbee, *A Study of History* (London: Oxford University Press, 1948).

72 Ibid.

73 See Richard Gregg, *The Value of Voluntary Simplicity* (Wallingford, PA: Pendle Hill, 1936).

74 Henry David Thoreau, "Walden," in *Walden and Other Writings* (New York: Modern Library, 1937), p. 64.

75 See Richard Gregg, "Voluntary Simplicity," in V*isva-Bharati Quarterly,* August 1936.

76 See Simone de Beauvoir, *The Ethics of Ambiguity,* translated by Bernard Frechtman (New York: Citadel, 1992), p. 82.

77 See Michael F. Jacobson and Laurie Ann Mazur, *Marketing Madness: A Survival Guide for a Consumer Society* (Boulder, CO: Westview Press, 1995), p. 191, note 18.

78 See Arnold J. Toynbee, *A Study of History*.

79 See "Consumer Power: for Private Greed or Public Need?" *The New Internationalist* (145), 1985.

80 See John Vidal, *McLibel: Burger Culture on Trial* (New York: The New Press, 1998).

81 See Noam Chomsky, "Equality: Language Development, Human Intelligence, and Social Organization," in *The Chomsky Reader* (New York: Pantheon Books, 1987).

82 United States Department of Agriculture, Economics and Statistics System, *Livestock Slaughter, 2001 Annual Summary* <http://usda.mannlib.cornell.edu/ reports/nassr/livestock/pls-bban/lsano302.pdf>; *Poultry Slaughter, 2001 Annual Summary* <http://usda.mannlib.cornell.edu/ reports/nassr/poultry/ppy-bban/ pslaano2.pdf>

83 See Isaac Bashevis Singer, "The Letter Writer," *The Collected Stories of Isaac Bashevis Singer* (New York: Farrar, Straus, Giroux, 1981) p. 271.

84 See Thich Nhat Hanh, *The Present Moment: A Retreat on the Practice of Mindfulness* audiocassette series (Boulder, CO: Sounds True, 1994), cassette 3B.

85 The Fifth Mindfulness Training includes this sentence: "I am determined not to use alcohol or any other intoxicant or to ingest foods or other items that contain toxins, such as certain TV programs, magazines, books, films, and conversations." See Thich Nhat Hanh, *For a Future to Be Possible: Commentaries on the Five Mindfulness Trainings,* Revised Edition (Berkeley, CA: Parallax Press, 1998), p. 5.

86 See Thich Nhat Hanh, *The Heart of the Buddha's Teaching* (New York: Broadway Books, 1998), p. 97.

87 United States Department of Labor, Bureau of Labor Statistics, Industry Injury and Illness Data, *Table So1: Highest Incidence Rates of Total Nonfatal*

Occupational Injury and Illness Cases, Private Industry, 2000 <http://www.bls.gov/iif/oshwc/ osh/os/ostb0988.pdf>

88 Sir Paul McCartney, quoted by the International Vegetarian Union <http://www.ivu.org/people/music/macca.html>

89 See Dr. Tony Page, *Buddhism and Animals* (London: UKAVIS, 1999), p. 122–123.

90 See Roshi Philip Kapleau, *To Cherish All Life: A Buddhist View of Animal Slaughter and Meat Eating* (Rochester, NY: Zen Center, 1981), p. 31.

91 See Peter Singer, "A Vegetarian Philosophy," *Writings on an Ethical Life* (New York: Ecco Press, 2000), p. 68.

92 Charles Luk, trans., the *Surangama Sutra,* <http://home.wanadoo.nl/ekayana/5,1.html>

93 See Daisetz Teitaro Suzuki, *The Lankavatara Sutra: A Mahayana Text* (Boulder, CO: Prajna Press, 1978), pp. 213 and 219.

94 See Robert Thurman, *The Inner Revolution* (New York: Riverhead Books, 1998), p. 123.

95 Indian Vegetarian Congress, *The Vegetarian Way: Published on the Occasion of the XIX World Vegetarian Congress Held in India 1967* (Madras: Free India Press, 1967).

96 The Dalai Lama, *Live in a Better Way: Reflections on Truth, Love and Happiness* (New York: Viking Compass, 2001), p. 68.

97 See Thich Nhat Hanh, *Stepping into Freedom: An Introduction to Buddhist Monastic Training* (Berkeley, CA: Parallax Press, 1997), p. 34.

98 See Thich Nhat Hanh, "Cultivating Compassion, Responding to Violence," in the *Mindfulness Bell* (Winter 2001–2002): 11.

99 From talks given by Tai Situ Rinpoche at the Samye Ling Interfaith Symposium in Scotland in 1988 and 1989, available at <www.samyeling.org>

100 Ibid.

101 See E.F. Schumacher, *Small Is Beautiful.*

Contributors

Allan Hunt Badiner is a writer, ecological activist, a contributing editor at *Tricycle* magazine, and editor of *Dharma Gaia: A Harvest in Buddhism and Ecology*. He was a coeditor of *Zig Zag Zen: Buddhism and Psychedelics*.

Stephen Batchelor was a monk in both the Tibetan Geluk and Korean Zen traditions of Buddhism. He is the author and translator of several books, including *Buddhism Without Beliefs*. He teaches meditation retreats worldwide and lives in southwest France. <www.martinebatchelor.org>

Fritjof Capra, physicist and systems theorist, is the author of several international bestsellers, including *The Tao of Physics* and *The Web of Life*, and *The Hidden Connections: A Science for Sustainable Living*. <www.fritjofcapra.net>

Tyrone Cashman, philosopher of technology and religion, helped create the windpower revolution in the 1980s that continues to spread around the world. Philosophical questions about the place of humans in nature occupy his time these days.

His Holiness the Dalai Lama is the 14th Dalai Lama, Tenzin Gyatso, and is the head of state and spiritual leader of the Tibetan people. His Holiness was awarded the 1989 Nobel Peace Prize, and is the author of many books, including *Ancient Wisdom, Modern World — Ethics for a New Millennium, Freedom in Exile,* and *Kindness, Clarity and Insight*. <www.tibet.com>

David Edwards is the author of *Free to Be Human* (published as *Burning All Illusions* by South End Press in the U.S.) and *The Compassionate Revolution,* both published by Green Books. He is coeditor of *Media Lens* <www.medialens.org>. He can be contacted at david@awed.fsnet.co.uk

Riane Eisler, cultural historian, evolutionary theorist, and President of the Center for Partnership Studies is best known as the author of the international bestseller *The Chalice and the Blade.* Dr. Eisler's essay is based on her most recent book, *The Power of Partnership,* a handbook for personal and cultural transformation. <www.partnershipway.org>

Duane Elgin is the author of *Voluntary Simplicity: Toward a Way of Life that Is Outwardly Simple, Inwardly Rich,* and a speaker and media activist. <www.awakeningearth.org>

Joan Halifax Roshi is the head teacher and abbot of Upaya Zen Center, author, anthropologist, and social activist. <www.upaya.org>

Thich Nhat Hanh is a Buddhist monk, poet, peace activist, and the author of *Being Peace, The Miracle of Mindfulness,* and many other books. He lives in a monastic community in France called Plum Village, where he teaches, writes, gardens, and works to help refugees worldwide. <www.iamhome.org/tnh. htm>

Paul Hawken is the cofounder of several businesses, including Erehwon and Smith and Hawken, and is the author of *The Ecology of Commerce, Growing a Business* and, with Amory and Hunter Lovins, coauthor of *Natural Capitalism.*

Julia Butterfly Hill lived in the canopy of an ancient redwood tree called Luna for 738 days to help make the world aware of the plight of ancient forests. She is the founder of the Circle of Life Foundation, and author of *One Makes the Difference,* and *Legacy of Luna.* <www.circleoflifefoundation.org>

Shinichi Inoue was president of Miyazaki Bank in Tokyo, chairman of the Foundation for the Promotion of Buddhism, a member of the Buddhist Economics Research Institute of Komazawa University, and authored a series of books in Japanese on Buddhist business administration.

Rolf Jucker, German Studies scholar and political activist, is primarily interested in the various ways of bringing about a sustainable society. His essay is part of a wider project, just published in book form: *Our Common Illiteracy: Education as if the Earth and People Mattered.*

David Korten is the author of *The Post-Corporate World: Life After Capitalism* and the international bestseller *When Corporations Rule the World*, president of the People-Centered Development Forum and board chair of the Positive Futures Network, which publishes *YES! A Journal of Positive Futures.* <www.davidkorten.org>

Kate Lawrence is the assistant director of the Colorado Community for Mindful Living and has been educating the public about vegetarian issues for more than a dozen years. A past president of the Vegetarian Society of Colorado, she also plays banjo in a contradance band.

Renee Lertzman is a writer and consultant based in Brooklyn, New York. Her work focuses on the psychological and emotional dimensions of environmental degradation. She has a Master of Arts degree in Communication Studies and is pursuing a doctorate in Environmental Psychology at the City University of New York Graduate Center. Her work has appeared in the *Sun* magazine, *Orion* magazine, *Speak* magazine, *Parabola,* and *Terra Nova.*

David R. Loy is Professor in the Faculty of International Studies at Bunkyo University, Chigasaki, Japan. His work is in comparative philosophy and religion, particularly comparing Buddhist with modern Western thought. His books include *Nonduality: A Study in Comparative Philosophy* (1989), *Lack and Transcendence: The Problem of Death and Life in Psychotherapy, Existentialism and Buddhism* (1996), and *A Buddhist History of the West: Studies in Lack* (2002). He has practiced Zen Buddhism for many years. <www.innerexplorations.com/catew/d.htm>

Bo Lozoff is the author of several books, including the classic *We're All Doing Time*, now in its eleventh printing. He and his wife Sita are the directors of the Human Kindness Foundation and its well-known Prison-Ashram Project. <www.humankindness.org>

Joanna Macy, Ph.D., is an eco-philosopher grounded in Buddhism and general systems theory. Living and teaching in the San Francisco Bay Area, she is known worldwide for her workshops and trainings on the interface between social action and spiritual breakthrough. Her books include *Coming Back to Life: Practices to Reconnect Our Lives, Our World; World As Lover, World As Self; Rilke's*

Book of Hours; Mutual Causality in Buddhist Teachings and General Systems Theory; and her recent memoir, *Widening Circles.* <www.joannamacy.net>

Peter Montague, Ph.D., is the director and cofounder of Environmental Research Foundation, an organization that provides technical assistance to grassroots groups. He is writer and editor of *Rachel's Environment & Health News* and has written a number of books and journal articles on environmental problems. <www.rachel.org>

Colin Moore has received teachings in all the main traditions of Buddhism and teaches at Sharpham College for Buddhist Studies and Contemporary Enquiry and the Barn Rural Retreat Centre in Devon U.K. For more information see <www.clearlightassociates.co.uk>

L.D. Ness has chosen to be anonymous.

Helena Norberg-Hodge is the director of the International Society for Ecology and Culture (ISEC) and a leading analyst of the impact of the global economy on culture. She is author of several books and articles, including *Ancient Futures: Learning from Ladakh,* which has been translated into nearly forty languages, and is a recipient of the Right Livelihood Award (the Alternative Nobel Prize). <www.isec.org.uk>

Ven. P.A. Payutto is a Thai scholar monk and the author of more than 150 books in Thai and English, including the acclaimed *Buddhadhamma.* He addressed the 1993 Parliament of the World's Religions and was awarded the Mahidol Varanusorn Prize in 1989 and the Silver Conch Award in 1990. <www.geocities.com/Athens/Academy/9280/payutto.htm>

Stephen Prothero is an associate professor in the Department of Religion at Boston University, where he teaches courses on Asian religions in the United States. His most recent book is *Purified by Fire: A History of Cremation in America.* <www.bu.edu/religion/faculty/individualfaculty/prothero.htm>

Frederic L. Pryor, Ph.D., has written extensively in the field of comparative economic systems, including a series of essays exploring the views of various religious doctrines on the economy. He is an Emeritus Professor of

Economics at Swarthmore College. <www.swarthmore.edu/Home/News/Media/Sources/fpryor1.html>

Lewis Richmond, Buddhist teacher and software entrepreneur, is the author of the national bestseller *Work as a Spiritual Practice: A Practical Buddhist Approach to Inner Growth and Satisfaction on the Job,* as well as the recently published *Healing Lazarus: A Buddhist's Journey from Near Death to New Life.* <www.lewisrichmond.com>

John Robbins is one of the world's leading experts on the dietary link with the environment and health, and author of the international bestseller *Diet for a New America.* His latest book is *The Food Revolution: How Your Diet Can Help Save Your Life and Our World,* and he maintains a website at <www.foodrevolution.org>

Ruth Rosenhek is an environmental activist and organizational consultant who has worked with social change and environmental groups since 1982. <www.rainforestjukebox.org/deep-eco/rosenhek.htm>

Santikaro Bhikkhu is a Buddhist monk who trained under Buddhadasa Bhikkhu in Thailand and now lives outside St. Louis. He is involved in various aspects of socially engaged Buddhism and new experiments in Buddhist monasticism. He has translated and edited a number of his teacher's books, including *Mindfulness with Breathing* and *Heartwood of the Bodhi Tree.* <www.suanmokkh.org/skb2001.htm>

John Seed is founder and director of the Rainforest Information Centre in Australia, author of *Thinking Like a Mountain — Towards a Council of All Beings* (with Joanna Macy, Pat Fleming, and Arne Naess), and an accomplished bard and songwriter. <www.rainforestjukebox.org/deep-eco/johnseed.htm>

Judith Simmer-Brown is a Buddhist Studies professor at Naropa University, and has practiced Buddhism for thirty years. She authored *Dakini's Warm Breath: The Feminine Principle in Tibetan Buddhism,* and coauthored *Benedict's Dharma: Buddhists Comment on the Rule of St. Benedict.*

Sulak Sivaraksa of Bangkok, Thailand (Siam), is a prominent social critic and activist, and one of the major contemporary exponents of socially engaged Buddhism. Sulak was nominated for the Nobel Peace Prize in both 1993 and 1994 and received the Right Livelihood Award, also known as the Alternative Nobel Prize, in 1995. He is the author of several books, including *Seeds of Peace* and *Powers That Be: Pridi Banomyong and the Rise and Fall of Thai Democracy.* <www.sulak-sivaraksa.org>

Elizabeth Thoman is founder and president of the Center for Media Literacy, Los Angeles and a twenty-five-year pioneer in the U.S. media literacy movement.

Jonathan Watts coordinates the small socially engaged Buddhist think tank called Think Sangha <www.bpf.org/think.html> and edits *Think Sangha Journal* and other socially engaged Buddhist publications. He is a student of the late Buddhadasa Bhikkhu whose teachings he tries to further apply to social issues.

Duncan Williams is an Assistant Professor of East Asian Buddhism at University of California, Irvine. He is the translator of Shinichi Inoue's *Putting Buddhism to Work* and coeditor of *American Buddhism* and *Buddhism and Ecology.*

Ming Zhen Shakya is currently a disciple of Venerable Fo Yuen, Abbot of Yun Men (Ummon) Monastery in China. Originally, as Chuan Yuan Shakya, she was a disciple of the late Venerable Wei Yin, Abbot of Nan Hua Monastery, the monastery founded by Sixth Patriarch Hui Neng, and as such she was the first American to be fully ordained in the People's Republic of China in nearly half a century.

Credits

The Crisis of Consumerism by Judith Simmer-Brown was adapted from her keynote address given at the Buddhism in America Conference in San Diego in 1998, and from an article which first appeared in the *Shambhala Sun*.

Patriarchal Roots of Overconsumption by Fritjof Capra is based on his most recent book, *The Hidden Connections: A Science for Sustainable Living*.

Buddhism in the Global Economy by Helena Norberg-Hodge was first published in *Resurgence* (April 1997) and appears with the permission of the author.

Illuminating Darkness: Western Buddhism by L.D. Ness is taken from an essay that was offered by the author anonymously on the Internet at ZNet interactive.

A Systems View of Overconsumption by Riane Eisler is based on her book, *The Power of Partnership*, and previous works.

A New Economics to Save the Earth: A Buddhist Perspective by Shinichi Inoue appears here with the permission of the Japan Economic Foundation, and the family of the late author. The essay first appeared in the March/April 1999 issue of the *Journal of Japanese Trade and Industry*.

The Practice of Generosity by Stephen Batchelor was originally produced as a working document on Buddhist Economics for the New Economics Foundation in collaboration with the International Consultancy on Religion, Education, and Culture. It is the product of two meetings that took place under the auspices of the Sharpham Trust, Devon, England, in the early 1990s between the following people: Colin Ash, Sally Ash, Stephen Batchelor, Philip Eden, Dharmachari Kulananda, Jose Reissig, Sue Szabo, Andy Wistreich, and Simon Zadek. Additional material was contributed by Maurice Ash, Bhikkhu Bodhi, Ken Jones, Paul Willia, and notes provided by Wendy Ruthroff. Stephen Batchelor directed these meetings and drafted the text, the final version of which was published privately by the Sharpham Trust in 1993.

Looking Deeply at the Nutriments is based on Dharma talks by Thich Nhat Hanh.

Buddhist Perspectives on Economic Concepts by Ven. P.A. Payutto of Thailand (May, 1992) appears here with his permission.

The Religion of Consumption: A Buddhist Perspective by Jonathan Watts and David R. Loy is based on works appearing in *Think Sangha Journal* and other works by the authors. An earlier version of this article was published in the *Society for International Development* 41, no.1 (March 1998) in a special issue entitled "Consumption, Civil Action, and Sustainable Development."

How Not to Feast from the Poison Cake is based on previous works by Bo Lozoff and appears here with his permission.

What Then Must We Do? by David Edwards appears with the permission of the author.

Re-Imagining the American Dream by Elizabeth Thoman was previously published on the Center for Media Literacy website, and Issue #57, Winter 1992 of *Media&Values* magazine.

A Quick Q & A on Buddhism & Materialism by Joan Halifax Roshi is based on email conversations with the editor.

Ethical Economics by His Holiness the Dalai Lama was adapted with permission from a preface by the author for *Compassion or Competition: A Discussion on Human Values in Business and Economics* (Rotterdam, the Netherlands: Asoka Publishers, 2002).

Alternatives to Consumerism by Sulak Sivaraksa is taken from works by the author.

Buddhism and Poverty by David R. Loy was previously published in a longer version in the *Kyoto Journal,* Summer 1999, and *Contemporary Buddhism* 2, no. 1 (2001).

Buddhist Economic Systems, by Frederic L. Pryor, Ph.D. is a condensation of the second of two essays on the economics of Buddhism, and was previously published as: "A Buddhist Economic System— In Principle," *American Journal of Economics and Sociology* 49, no. 3 (July 1990): 339–51, and "A Buddhist Economic System—In Practice," *American Journal of Economics and Sociology* 50, no. 1 (January 1991): 17–33.

Boomer Buddhism by Stephen Prothero is based on a review by the author of a book by James William Coleman, *The New Buddhism: The Western Transformation of an Ancient Tradition,* published on <www.salon.com> on February 26, 2001.

Zen and Money by Ming Zhen Shakya comes from the Zen Buddhist Order of Hsu Yun's website of which she is the editor. <www.hsuyun.org>

A Meditation on Money by Lewis Richmond was excerpted from *Work as a Spiritual Practice.*

Down to Business: Paul Hawken on Reshaping the Economy is an interview by Renee Lertzman that previously appeared in the *Sun* magazine.

Is There Slavery in Your Chocolate? by John Robbins appears with permission of the author.

Sarvodaya by Joanna Macy appears with permission of the author.

Rebuilding the Movement to Win by Peter Montague, Ph.D., appears with permission of the author and *Rachel's Environment & Health News.*

Where Does It Come From? Where Does It Go? by Tyrone Cashman appears with permission of the Center for Media Literacy, and the author.

Right Livelihood, Spirituality, and Business by Duncan Williams appears with permission of the author.

Diet for a Mindful Society by Thich Nhat Hanh is based on Dharma talks, and works published in the *Mindfulness Bell* by the author, with the permission of Parallax Press.

Voluntary Simplicity by Duane Elgin is based on his book *Voluntary Simplicity: Toward a Way of Life that Is Outwardly Simple, Inwardly Rich.*

Toward Dematerialization by Rolf Jucker is taken from *Our Common Illiteracy: Education as if the Earth and People Mattered* by the author, and works published at *ON…* <http://www.onweb.org>

The New Storytellers by David Korten is taken from *The Post-Corporate World: Life after Capitalism* with the permission of the author, and the publisher, Berrett-Koehler.

Nourishing Ourselves, Nourishing Others: How Mindful Food Choices Reduce Suffering by Kate Lawrence appears with permission of the author.

Sustainable Living by Colin Moore appears with permission of the author.

Vinaya: A Modern Buddhist's Guide to Global Consumer Culture by Santikaro Bhikkhu appears with permission of the author.

Personal Planetary Practices by Allan Hunt Badiner, John Seed, and Ruth Rosenhek is a manifesto cowritten by the authors in Berkeley, California in the summer of 1998.